CASEBOOKS PUBLISHED

Austen: *Emma* DAVID LODGE
Austen: *'Northanger Abbey' & 'Persuasion'* B. C. SOUTHAM
Austen: *'Sense and Sensibility', 'Pride and Prejudice' & 'Mansfield Park'* B. C. SOUTHAM
Blake: *Songs of Innocence and Experience* MARGARET BOTTRALL
Charlotte Brontë: *'Jane Eyre' & 'Villette'* MIRIAM ALLOTT
Emily Brontë: *Wuthering Heights* MIRIAM ALLOTT
Browning: *'Men and Women' & Other Poems* J. R. WATSON
Bunyan: *Pilgrim's Progress* ROGER SHARROCK
Byron: *'Childe Harold's Pilgrimage' & 'Don Juan'* JOHN JUMP
Chaucer: *Canterbury Tales* J. J. ANDERSON
Coleridge: *'The Ancient Mariner' & Other Poems* ALUN R. JONES & WILLIAM TYDEMAN
Congreve: *Comedies* PATRICK LYONS
Conrad: *'Heart of Darkness', 'Nostromo' & 'Under Western Eyes'* C. B. COX
Conrad: *The Secret Agent* IAN WATT
Dickens: *Bleak House* A. E. DYSON
Dickens: *'Dombey and Son' & 'Little Dorrit'* ALAN SHELSTON
Dickens: *'Hard Times', 'Great Expectations' & 'Our Mutual Friend'* NORMAN PAGE
Donne: *Songs and Sonets* JULIAN LOVELOCK
George Eliot: *Middlemarch* PATRICK SWINDEN
George Eliot: *'The Mill on the Floss' & 'Silas Marner'* R. P. DRAPER
T. S. Eliot: *Four Quartets* BERNARD BERGONZI
T. S. Eliot: *'Prufrock', 'Gerontion', 'Ash Wednesday' & Other Shorter Poems* B. C. SOUTHAM
T. S. Eliot: *The Waste Land* C. B. COX & ARNOLD P. HINCHLIFFE
Farquhar: *'The Recruiting Officer' & 'The Beaux' Stratagem'* RAYMOND A. ANSELMENT
Fielding: *Tom Jones* NEIL COMPTON
Forster: *A Passage to India* MALCOLM BRADBURY
Hardy: *Poems* JAMES GIBSON & TREVOR JOHNSON
Hardy: *The Tragic Novels* R. P. DRAPER
Hopkins: *Poems* MARGARET BOTTRALL
James: *'Washington Square' & 'The Portrait of a Lady'* ALAN SHELSTON
Jonson: *'Every Man in his Humour' & 'The Alchemist'* R. V. HOLDSWORTH
Jonson: *Volpone* JONAS A. BARISH
Joyce: *'Dubliners' & 'The Portrait of the Artist as a Young Man'* MORRIS BEJA
Keats: *Narrative Poems* JOHN SPENCER HILL
Keats: *Odes* G. S. FRASER
D. H. Lawrence: *Sons and Lovers* GAMINI SALGADO
D. H. Lawrence: *'The Rainbow' & 'Women in Love'* COLIN CLARKE
Marlowe: *Doctor Faustus* JOHN JUMP
Marlowe: *'Tamburlaine the Great', 'Edward the Second' & 'The Jew of Malta'* JOHN RUSSELL
  BROWN
Marvell: *Poems* ARTHUR POLLARD
Milton: *'Comus' & 'Samson Agonistes'* JULIAN LOVELOCK
Milton: *Paradise Lost* A. E. DYSON & JULIAN LOVELOCK
O'Casey: *The Dublin Trilogy* RONALD AYLING
Osborne: *Look Back in Anger* JOHN RUSSELL TAYLOR
Peacock: *The Satirical Novels* LORNA SAGE
Pope: *The Rape of the Lock* JOHN DIXON HUNT
Shakespeare: *A Midsummer Night's Dream* ANTONY W. PRICE
Shakespeare: *Antony and Cleopatra* JOHN RUSSELL BROWN
Shakespeare: *Coriolanus* B. A. BROCKMAN
Shakespeare: *Hamlet* JOHN JUMP
Shakespeare: *Henry IV Parts 1 and 2* G. K. HUNTER
Shakespeare: *Henry V* MICHAEL QUINN
Shakespeare: *Julius Caesar* PETER URE

Shakespeare: *King Lear* FRANK KERMODE
Shakespeare: *Macbeth* JOHN WAIN
Shakespeare: *Measure for Measure* G. K. STEAD
Shakespeare: *The Merchant of Venice* JOHN WILDERS
Shakespeare: *'Much Ado About Nothing' & 'As You Like It'* JOHN RUSSELL BROWN
Shakespeare: *Othello* JOHN WAIN
Shakespeare: *Richard II* NICHOLAS BROOKE
Shakespeare: *The Sonnets* PETER JONES
Shakespeare: *The Tempest* D. J. PALMER
Shakespeare: *Troilus and Cressida* PRISCILLA MARTIN
Shakespeare: *Twelfth Night* D. J. PALMER
Shakespeare: *The Winter's Tale* KENNETH MUIR
Shelley: *Shorter Poems & Lyrics* PATRICK SWINDEN
Spenser: *The Faerie Queene* PETER BAYLEY
Swift: *Gulliver's Travels* RICHARD GRAVIL
Tennyson: *In Memoriam* JOHN DIXON HUNT
Thackeray: *Vanity Fair* ARTHUR POLLARD
Trollope: *The Barsetshire Novels* T. BAREHAM
Webster: *'The White Devil' & 'The Duchess of Malfi'* R. V. HOLDSWORTH
Wilde: *Comedies* WILLIAM TYDEMAN
Woolf: *To the Lighthouse* MORRIS BEJA
Wordsworth: *Lyrical Ballads* ALUN R. JONES & WILLIAM TYDEMAN
Wordsworth: *The Prelude* W. J. HARVEY & RICHARD GRAVIL
Yeats: *Poems, 1919–35* ELIZABETH CULLINGFORD
Yeats: *Last Poems* JON STALLWORTHY

Medieval English Drama PETER HAPPÉ
Elizabethan Poetry: Lyrical & Narrative GERALD HAMMOND
The Metaphysical Poets GERALD HAMMOND
Poetry of the First World War DOMINIC HIBBERD
Thirties Poets: 'The Auden Group' RONALD CARTER
Comedy: Developments in Criticism D. J. PALMER
Drama Criticism: Developments since Ibsen ARNOLD P. HINCHLIFFE
Tragedy: Developments in Criticism R. P. DRAPER
The English Novel: Developments in Criticism since Henry James STEPHEN HAZELL
The Language of Literature NORMAN PAGE
The Pastoral Mode BRYAN LOUGHREY
The Romantic Imagination JOHN SPENCER HILL

CASEBOOKS IN PREPARATION INCLUDE

Beckett: *'Waiting for Godot' & Other Plays* JOHN RUSSELL BROWN
Defoe: *'Robinson Crusoe' & 'Moll Flanders'* PATRICK LYONS
T. S. Eliot: *Plays* ARNOLD P. HINCHLIFFE
Pinter: *'The Caretaker' & Other Plays* MICHAEL SCOTT
Sheridan: *Comedies* PETER DAVISON

Poetry Criticism: Developments since the Symbolists A. E. DYSON
Post-Fifties Poets: Gunn, Hughes, Larkin & R. S. Thomas A. E. DYSON
Shakespeare: Approaches in Criticism JOHN RUSSELL BROWN
The Gothick Novel VICTOR SAGE

Charles Dickens

Dombey and Son
and
Little Dorrit

A CASEBOOK

EDITED BY

ALAN SHELSTON

MACMILLAN

First published 1985

Published by
Higher and Further Education Division
MACMILLAN PUBLISHERS LTD
Houndmills, Basingstoke, Hampshire RG21 2XS
and London
Companies and representatives
throughout the world

Typeset by
Wessex Typesetters Ltd
Frome, Somerset

Printed in Hong Kong

British Library Cataloguing in Publication Data
Dickens: Dombey and son, and Little Dorrit: a
selection of critical essays.— (Casebook series)
1. Dickens, Charles, *1812–1870*.   Dombey and son
2. Dickens, Charles, *1812–1870*.   Little Dorrit
I. Shelston, Alan   II. Series
823'.8   PR4559
ISBN 0–333–34641–6
ISBN 0–333–34642–4 Pbk

CONTENTS

GENERAL EDITOR'S PREFACE

The Casebook series, launched in 1968, has become a well-regarded library of critical studies. The central concern of the series remains the 'single-author' volume, but suggestions from the academic community have led to an extension of the original plan, to include occasional volumes on such general themes as literary 'schools' and genres.

Each volume in the central category deals either with one well-known and influential work by an individual author, or with closely related works by one writer. The main section consists of critical readings, mostly modern, collected from books and journals. A selection of reviews and comments by the author's contemporaries is also included, and sometimes comment from the author himself. The Editor's Introduction charts the reputation of the work or works from the first appearance to the present time.

Volumes in the 'general themes' category are variable in structure but follow the basic purpose of the series in presenting an integrated selection of readings, with an Introduction which explores the theme and discusses the literary and critical issues involved.

A single volume can represent no more than a small selection of critical opinions. Some critics are excluded for reasons of space, and it is hoped that readers will pursue the suggestions for further reading in the Select Bibliography. Other contributions are severed from their original context, to which some readers may wish to turn. Indeed, if they take a hint from the critics represented here, they certainly will.

A. E. DYSON

INTRODUCTION

Dombey and Son was published in twenty monthly parts from October 1846 to April 1848: *Little Dorrit* in identical form, from December 1855 to June 1857. In the intervening decade Dickens wrote *David Copperfield*, *Bleak House* and *Hard Times*, while at the same time editing and writing for his journal, *Household Words*. These were the middle years of his career, and they were marked by his commitment, both in his published work and his active life, to matters of social concern; they are the years of what critics have come to call the 'dark' novels. *Dombey and Son* opens with its image of a child born to be sacrificed to its father's commercial pride. *Little Dorrit* closes with a marriage through which hero and heroine are able to escape from the 'usual uproar' of the city streets.

Dickens, of course, did not discover his social conscience in October 1846, far less did he discover London. In the *Sketches by Boz* (1836), his first collection of published work, he explored the city streets, finding in them often the oppressive quality that he attributes to them in *Dombey and Son* and, with nightmarish effect, in *Little Dorrit*. In each of his early novels, from *Pickwick Papers* (1837) to *Martin Chuzzlewit* (1844), he expresses his anger at some form of social abuse. But invariably these concerns, large as they are, appear as individual instances – the workhouse in *Oliver Twist* (1838), the Yorkshire schools in *Nicholas Nickleby* (1839) – within the context of a more generally orientated narrative. In *Martin Chuzzlewit*, the novel which preceded *Dombey and Son*, one can certainly detect the sense of a comprehensive thematic intention that aims to absorb and co-relate its various expressions of topicality. It is based on a theme which Dickens himself defined as 'the number and variety of humours and vices that have their root in selfishness', and its intended relevance to contemporary society was indicated by the motto which Dickens proposed for it, but on the advice of Forster rejected: 'your homes the scene, yourselves the actors here'. But *Martin Chuzzlewit*, as Dickens himself acknowledged, was a novel in which his spontaneous creative impulse escaped the constraints which he wished to impose upon it, and in which overt topicality of reference is lost in a general Pickwickian boisterousness. In *Dombey and Son* Dickens located his action in the immediate contemporary world. By concentrating on his central idea, and above all on the central character in whom it is embodied, he was able to achieve a degree of fictional organisation that was new in his art.

The extent to which *Dombey and Son* represented a new departure for Dickens in terms of its formal coherence was first fully demonstrated by John Butt and Kathleen Tillotson in their seminal study of Dickens's working methods, *Dickens at Work*, published in 1957. Their chapter there on *Dombey and Son*, drawing as it does on such material as Dickens's long letter to John Forster outlining his plans for the novel (reprinted in the extract from Forster's *Life of Dickens* in Part One of this Casebook), his number-plans, and his involvement in the cover-design, shows how determinedly he stuck to his thematic priorities. (Given the nature of the evidence deployed by Butt and Tillotson in this study it has not proved practical to extract from it for this Casebook: instead I have reprinted Professor Tillotson's account of *Dombey and Son* in her *Novels of the Eighteen-Forties*.) The novelty of *Dombey and Son*'s content, with its concentration on a 'business' hero, its railway material and its 'London townscape' had always been acknowledged but was first fully illustrated by Humphry House in *The Dickens World* in 1941. As House remarks, 'in *Dombey and Son* the new style is so far developed as to be unmistakable. The people, places and things become "modern" '. (The paragraphs which immediately follow this observation are reprinted in Part One of our selection.)

Having adopted these priorities in *Dombey and Son*, Dickens was to sustain them in all his novels of the decade which followed it. *David Copperfield* (1850), it is true, is in some ways an exception, given its autobiographical theme; but that in itself provides for unity of a kind, a quality which is reinforced by its consistency of tone. Furthermore, what *David Copperfield* has to say about bourgeois society is perfectly consistent with the attitudes expressed in the explicitly social novels. *Hard Times* (1854) has a directness born of its briefer form and its specifically political intention. While the plots of *Bleak House* (1853) and *Little Dorrit* are deliberately designed to mystify the reader, in each of these novels Dickens deliberately devised formal structures – the dual narrative in *Bleak House*, the two-part division ('Poverty' and 'Riches') of *Little Dorrit* – that allowed him to organise his material in terms of an overall architectural conception. And in all of these novels he penetrated deeper into the heart of his own society. If it is still possible to argue, as Philip Collins has done, that in *Dombey and Son* 'Dickens is making a traditional moral point about pride and riches, not a specifically nineteenth-century one about a particular economic system'[1], that could scarcely be said about the manifestations of pride and riches that we see in *Little Dorrit*. The two positions, of course, are not mutually exclusive, but Dickens's return in *Little Dorrit* to the commercial world, or more specifically to the topic of money, and what it can, in the terms of Paul Dombey's question, 'do', allows us to see how, by the time he came to write the later novel, he had confirmed his commitment to the subject-matter provided by the world around him. Victorian society in the 1850s was increasingly conscious of its material success. *Dombey and Son* initiates Dickens's investigation of the implication of that materialism, while *Little Dorrit* – if it cannot be said to conclude it, for there were still *Great Expectations* and *Our Mutual Friend* to come – conducts that investigation at a level of penetration unique to itself.

The greater sense of purpose detectable in Dickens's middle and later fiction has led to a marked shift in critical opinion in this century. In 1865 the young Henry James began a review of *Our Mutual Friend* (1865) with the remark that '*Bleak House* was forced; *Little Dorrit* was laboured; the present work is dug out as with a spade and pickaxe'. Anticipating the question, 'who but Dickens would have written it?', James's reply is: 'Who, indeed?' A hundred years later such judgements would have seemed incomprehensible. Edmund Wilson's famous essay, 'Dickens: The Two Scrooges', which first appeared in book-form in *The Wound and the Bow* in 1941, posited a tortured and depressive Dickens, driven manically to the expression of his tormented personality in a series of increasingly pessimistic social fictions. 'Working always through the observed interrelation between highly individualised human beings rather than through political or economic analysis', says Wilson, Dickens 'sets out to trace an anatomy of . . . society.' *Dombey and Son* is 'the first attempt', while *Bleak House* 'is to realise this intention to perfection'. *Little Dorrit*, for its part, 'is full of the disillusion and discomfort' of a period of Dickens's life marked by an increasing sense of familial and social alienation.[2] (Wilson's discussion of *Little Dorrit* is reproduced in Part Two, below.)

Both Wilson's psychologising and his social analysis now seem heavy-handed, but his essay can fairly be said to have initiated a view of Dickens which, in contrast to traditionalist valuations, saw the expression of the personal and social pessimism of the post-*Dombey* novels as his significant achievement. The term 'dark novels' originates in the title of an essay by Lionel Stevenson ('Dickens's Dark Novels, 1851–7'), published in the *Sewanee Review* of Summer 1943, and thus only two years after *The Wound and the Bow*. Later landmarks in the movement might include Dorothy Van Ghent's famous essay, 'The Dickens World: A View from Todgers's' (*Sewanee Review*, 1950) and Lionel Trilling's 'Introduction' to *Little Dorrit* for the Oxford Illustrated Dickens (1953): an essay which is reprinted in full in this selection. When, in *Dickens the Novelist* (1970), F. R. Leavis entitled his opening chapter 'The First Major Novel: *Dombey and Son*', and devoted his other major contribution to that volume to *Little Dorrit*, he was only confirming what had become by then the generally accepted critical position.[3]

Dickens's contemporaries, however, were not so sure. If Henry James's comment, already quoted, is perhaps the gesture of a young cub towards an old lion, it is not an isolated instance of a more widespread dissatisfaction with the replacement of Dickens the social humourist by Dickens the social scourge. Where *Dombey and Son* was concerned commentators noticed and approved of its advances in technical accomplishment: it showed, noted the *Westminster Review*, 'the evidence of improved experience and pains-taking.' But while Mr Dombey was recognised as a hero for the times, Dickens's critical portrayal of him met with a mixed response. Thus *Blackwood's Magazine*, in 1848, found Dickens 'an uncomfortable writer' who was guilty of 'bringing into contempt, as unfeeling, the upper classes'. As the decade progressed and the image of the jovial Dickens receded, criticism was to become both sorrowful and angry. 'In the wilderness of *Little Dorrit* we sit down and weep when we remember thee, O Pickwick!' was E. B. Hamley's famous comment, again in a *Blackwood*'s review. (Extracts from this, and from the *Westminster Review* notice of *Dombey and Son*, are included in this Casebook.)

Undoubtedly much of the criticism of Dickens's later novels at the time when they appeared was motivated by animus against the attitudes that they expressed. It was also intensified, perhaps, by the writers' sense that they were swimming against the tide of popular opinion. Amy Cruse, in *The Victorians and their Books*, has given a graphic account of the enthusiasm with which *Dombey and Son* was received in the most respectable Victorian households,[4] and throughout these middle years Dickens was able to point to his sales figures in answer to his critics. He concludes the Preface to *Little Dorrit*, published with its final number, with the not altogether modest observation that 'In the Preface to *Bleak House* I remarked that I had never had so many readers. In the Preface to its next successor, *Little Dorrit*, I have still to repeat the same words.' But Dickens's popularity with his public is in itself somewhat surprising when we consider that his hostility to Victorian mores was developing in intensity during a decade when thinking Victorians could fairly claim that evidence of social improvement was plain to see. The 1850s was a period which saw the beginning of mid-Victorian prosperity; it was also a time of progressive institutional reform. Hence, one suspects, the note of exasperation in Sir James FitzJames Stephen's protest that Dickens seemed 'as a general rule, to get his first notions of an abuse from the discussions which accompany its removal'.[5] Given that it was in the nature of Dickens's position that it would offend progressive and conservative alike, attacks on him were likely to come from either front. Certainly he had his supporters, but it is perhaps telling that amongst them – judging from his reported comments – was Thomas Carlyle, another social visionary whose attitude to the world around him ran increasingly counter to the confidence of his contemporaries, whatever their political persuasion.

There is a further perspective against which to see the critical response to Dickens at this time. If the 1850s are important years in terms of Victorian material progress, the years between the publication of *Dombey and Son* and *Little Dorrit* are an important decade also in the history of the Victorian novel. In 1847, while *Dombey and Son* was appearing, Thackeray was publishing *Vanity Fair*. The same year saw the first edition of *Jane Eyre*. As George Ford has pointed out, before this date Dickens had scarcely a rival whose name has survived; from now on he was to be in competition not only, if most directly, with Thackeray, but with Charlotte Brontë and Elizabeth Gaskell as well.[6] George Eliot's first stories, moreover, were to appear at the same period in time as the monthly publication of *Little Dorrit*.

The point is not simply one of increased competition. What is significant is that, through the 1850s, a view of fiction developed which was to make the traditional Dickensian narrative mode – however modified – seem both unliterary and out of date. David Masson, writing in 1859 and comparing Dickens and Thackeray, noted in the case of Dickens 'a certain recoil from his later writings among the cultivated and the fastidious'.[7] (An extract from Masson's discussion of Dickens is reproduced in Part Two, below.) As George Ford remarks, the reviews of the 1850s and 1860s suggest that 'just as Dickens himself was becoming progressively conscious of the techniques of novel-writing, so were many of his critics'.[8] The problem where Dickens was concerned was that the criteria of the critics were becoming increasingly distanced from his own. Whereas Thackeray was able in his own way to satisfy 'the cultivated and the fastidious', Dickens could be attacked for his disregard of social proprieties. Where a critic like George Henry Lewes appealed to the standards of realism – and was shortly to have his views vindicated by the success of George Eliot – Dickens's characters could still be criticised as 'puppets, dummies and unnatural creations'.[9] Such attitudes are a compound of a genuine attempt on the part of the critics to grapple with the questions posed by a developing literary form, and simple cultural snobbery. And in this last respect, of course, Dickens's very popularity told against him: we are already on the way to Leslie Stephen's celebrated remark in his *Dictionary of National Biography* account of Dickens's life that 'if literary fame could be safely measured by popularity with the half-educated, Dickens must claim the highest position among English novelists.' In later years Virginia Woolf was to complete the Stephen family record of opposition to Dickens. He failed, she said, 'to think deeply, to describe beautifully' – even apparently in *David Copperfield*, a novel she professed to admire.[10] If modern academic criticism has its limitations – not least of them a humourlessness which inevitably inhibits its response to comic art – it is at least free of this kind of exclusiveness.

Dombey and Son

It is not modern criticism alone that has identified *Dombey and Son* explicitly as a point of new departure for Dickens. Certainly his contemporaries sensed it; and if, as I have suggested, the work of Butt and Tillotson gave the support of scholarship to a critical viewpoint which had established itself as an orthodoxy in the middle of this century, earlier writers like G. K. Chesterton and George Gissing were certainly aware of the novel's significance in terms of its author's development. In 1907 Chesterton began his Introduction to the Everyman's Library edition of *Dombey and Son* by insisting that it indicated a crucial break in the progress of Dickens's literary career. It marked, he said, 'his final resolution to be a novelist and nothing else, to be a serious constructor of fiction in the serious sense.' Gissing, for his part, writing in 1900, acknowledged the planning that had gone into the novel – although, like Leavis after him (who was to find its pretensions to unity 'specious'), he had serious reservations about 'the narrative of the later part'. (The essays by Chesterton and Gissing are substantially excerpted in Part One, below.)

The repeated emphasis from an early date on Dickens's sense of construction where *Dombey and Son* is concerned is hardly surprising. His letter to Forster outlining his plans for the novel is the most detailed statement of fictional intention on his part that we have – and one available since the publication of Forster's *Life of Dickens* in 1874. Forster himself, indeed, had written a review of *Dombey and Son* when it first appeared in which he drew on the information which was then only available to him privately but in which, by detailed quotation, he was able to illustrate 'the recurrence of particular thoughts and phrases . . . subtly connected with the emotion which it is the design of the book to create'. (See section 1 of Part One, below.) 'Re-iterative motif', in fact, although a mid-Victorian critic was hardly likely to call it that.

Dickens's contemporaries were also aware of *Dombey and Son*'s contemporary application, and of the consequences for his characters of his new-found sober-mindedness. 'The personages of this tale', said the review in the *Westminster*, 'are every-day men and women with their every-day faults and virtues'. Dombey himself, 'a character new to fiction . . . a counting house aristocrat',[11] was recognised by the French commentator, Hippolyte Taine, as 'the most complete and most English picture of the aristocratic spirit'. The irony for Taine, of course, is that the aristocratic spirit is likely to be found in England among the merchant class. (See his comments in section 1 of Part One, below.) As the letter cited by Forster indicates, *Dombey and Son* is essentially the story of Dombey's self-destructive pride: further comment by Forster indicates the extent to which Dickens was determined to avoid caricature in his presentation of his central character. The result is a figure who dominates the novel, providing both the focus of its theme and an opportunity for development in himself as does no other character of this kind in any other Dickens novel. The nearest equivalent, indeed, is William Dorrit, but the success of Dickens's characterisation there one feels to be a consequence of intuition as much as of design. Closely allied with the presentation of Dombey is that of his rejected daughter, Florence. The central irony of the merchant-father's position is indicated in the novel when, in the words of Miss Tox, 'Dombey and Son' becomes 'a daughter after all!' As A. W. Ward pointed out in 1882, 'upon the relations between this pair . . . the criticism to which the character of Mr Dombey has been so largely subjected must substantially turn'. (See the excerpt from Ward in section 2 of Part One, below.) For Gissing, and for Chesterton, Dickens's efforts in this respect had been largely in vain. Gissing finds Dickens 'lacking in the tragic gift' and 'not given to "analysis" ', while Chesterton – citing in particular the instance of Mr Dombey in a general discussion of Dickens's characterisation – was of the opinion that whenever Dickens 'tried to describe change in a character he made a mess of it.'[12] Having acknowledged then Dickens's shift in stance in *Dombey and Son*, these two critics turn their attention to the novel's wider cast of characters. Critics of recent times, however (see for example the essays of Tillotson, Milner and Auerbach in this volume), have reverted to Dickensian priorities in concentrating their attention on the central characters of the novel.

There is one feature of *Dombey and Son* which clearly relates it to the kind of novel which it is generally assumed to have superseded. The death of Paul Dombey at the end of the fifth number exacted the identical response from strong men as had done the death of Little Nell in *The Old Curiosity Shop* (1841). This was indeed Dickens's last sustained effort in pathos of this kind (the death of Jo in *Bleak House* is rather differently ordered) and, coming early in the novel rather than at its conclusion, it gave it a momentum that it was never going to be easy to sustain. Much of the recorded enthusiasm for *Dombey and Son*, in fact, was a direct reaction to those first five numbers. The story of Paul's career became one of Dickens's most celebrated public readings (a contemporary account of this reading is included in section 1 of Part One, below), but it is not for the death-scene alone that the story is memorable. Paul himself is one of the most subtly conceived of Dickens's child characters. His resourcefulness in the face of the Dombey 'world', as embodied in the questions he is always asking, is a beautifully contrived irony at the expense of its remorseless certainties. Paul dies, not because pathos demands it, but because there is no place for him in what Edgar Johnson calls 'the world of Dombeyism'; because, indeed, he represents a threat to its existence. (See section 3 of Part One, below.) The ultimate irony, then, is not that Dombey and Son is a daughter after all, but that in the story of Dombey and daughter the most sensitive study is that of the son.

In this short survey of existing criticism of *Dombey and Son* I have concentrated for the most part on material that it has been possible to include in this volume. Inevitably I have had to pass over important work: Peter Coveney's account of Paul, for example, in *The Image of Childhood*, and the studies by Steven Marcus and by John Lucas amongst others to be found in full-length critical studies of Dickens. (For full details of these and other sources see the Select Bibliography.) One further work from which it has not proved practical to select an extract for inclusion and which should be mentioned here is Susan Horton's *Interpreting Interpreting*, published in 1979. The diversity of Dickens's fictional modes has been a factor in his appeal to structuralist, post-structuralist and hermeneutical critics. Horton devotes her book in its entirety to *Dombey and Son* but with the object 'not so much to offer a new method for reading . . . *Dombey and Son* as . . . to offer a critique of *all* methods of reading Dombey, and also, by extention [sic], any and all texts'.[13] Whether she succeeds in all aspects of this ambitious intention is open to question, and many may feel that there are at least some paper tigers amongst the critics with whom she has engaged. But much of Horton's own commentary on the novel is instructive, and her conclusion that no one interpretation can be exclusive or final, if it elevates critical relativity to a dogma, is at the simplest level not out of place in the present context.

Little Dorrit

Whereas critical attitudes towards *Dombey and Son* have usually reflected a fair degree of critical consensus, *Little Dorrit* is the novel of Dickens which has most polarised opinion, amongst both his contemporaries and his modern critics.

In Dickens's own day the extreme comment that *Little Dorrit* attracted was provoked, at least in the first instance, by the very specific nature of its attack upon contemporary institutions. Whereas *Dombey and Son*, for all the modernity of its setting and its central character, conducts its social analysis in ultimately general terms, *Little Dorrit* aims at identifiable abuses and often only thinly disguised individuals: a fact that is hardly obscured by the setting of its action in the 1820s. The Marshalsea may not have been used as a prison after 1849, but the Circumlocution Office was very much an institution of the 1850s. H. P. Sucksmith, the editor of the Clarendon Edition of the novel, in an Introduction in which he examines its contemporary context, has fairly described *Little Dorrit* as 'the most topical of Dickens's novels'. It is also, as he says, 'the one in which he draws most widely upon the events of his life and times.'[14] Here again we have a contrast with *Dombey and Son*. The earlier novel is the novel by Dickens in which, for all its formal quality, there is least evidence of his own restless personality at work: it involved, as we know from his own comments, a self-imposed restraint upon his imagination. By contrast, *Little Dorrit* has always seemed, if in ways not easily definable, a particularly intense expression of its author's state of mind. This too, one suspects, has played a part in the diversity of response that it has provoked.

The most powerful onslaughts on *Little Dorrit* in its own time were those of Sir James Fitzjames Stephen in the pages of the *Saturday Review* and the *Edinburgh Review*. Stephen's father had been a distinguished civil servant and the son, then a young man, would seem to have seen the satirical presentation of Mr Tite Barnacle as a direct personal attack upon his parent. Stephen took every opportunity available to attack the novel, reviewing it anonymously both during the course of its publication and at its conclusion, and elsewhere writing articles alluding to the injustice of the Circumlocution Office scenes. (An extract from Stephen's final review, and Dickens's reply to it, are included in section 1 of Part Two, below.) If we can still hear in Stephen's utterance the authentic tones of English institutionalised pomposity, it has to be said that his position was not untenable. A believer in Victorian progress, he could justifiably argue that the Civil Service was at that very time in process of reform, and that Dickens's attack on it was blind to the necessarily complicated business of government in a rapidly changing society. At the same time the existence of the Administrative Reform Association, an organisation that Dickens joined in 1855, identified the urgency of the situation and, as other contemporary reactions show, he was not without his own supporters. (See, for example, the review by W. H. Dixon in the *Athenaeum* and the comment by David Masson in section 1 of Part Two.)

If *Little Dorrit* attracted criticism for its treatment of specific issues, it also tended to be seen more generally as evidence of declining powers on Dickens's part. The assumption, however, that it has only properly been appreciated in the twentieth century is less than accurate. For Gissing, for example – whose full-length study of Dickens published in 1898 remains one of the classics of Dickens criticism – it contained 'some of the best work Dickens ever did . . . especially in the matter of characterisation.' (Extracts from Gissing's *Charles Dickens: A Critical Study* are included in section 2 of Part Two, below.) He particularly drew attention to the 'delicacy of treatment' involved in Dickens's handling of William Dorrit, 'The father of the Marshalsea': a feature also admired by Swinburne and by modern critics such as Leavis and John Carey. Gissing was undoubtedly temperamentally attuned to the darker aspects of Dickens's fictional vision – as Chesterton was fond of pointing out[15] – but the intensity of *Little Dorrit*'s social criticism was a source of its attraction for a number of readers earlier in this century, notably of course George Bernard Shaw. (See in particular the extracts in section 2 of Part Two.) It is interesting, for example, to find the attitudes of critics like Trilling and Leavis anticipated by a writer like W. Walter Crotch who, as President of the Dickens Fellowship, one might have associated with a more festive tradition of Dickens commentary.[16]

It is in recent times, however, that *Little Dorrit* has come entirely into its own, most notably as a consequence of Trilling's essay of 1953, to which I have already referred. Philip Collins has argued that the emphasis on the prison symbolism in the novel, which is so central a feature in the modern orthodoxy, is a relatively recent development, as indeed is the general elevation of *Little Dorrit* to a position of pre-eminence.[17] Certainly that is a valuation offered by Trilling, by Hillis Miller and by Leavis amongst the critics whose work is represented in this Casebook. What they are united in finding in the novel is a complete co-ordination of social investigation and symbolic method. Leavis indeed sees Dickens's achievement in *Little Dorrit* as analagous to that of Blake. Such a view directly contradicts earlier suggestions that the novel fails to hold together. Dickens himself claimed in his Preface to the novel to have 'held its threads with a more continuous attention than anyone else could have given them', and John Holloway in his introduction to the Penguin edition has shown how the various characters and groups of characters come to be inter-related during the course of the story. Holloway goes on to argue that 'it is with [the] unrivalled vigour, detail and profusion of local life that a grasp of Dickens's work should . . . start'.[18] The claim is a familiar one, but it is not often made in respect of this novel.

Too strong a claim for the symbolic unity of *Little Dorrit*, however, perhaps plays down the stranger manifestations of Dickens's personality in the novel. More recently writers have been found to query whether it is quite the success in this respect that its admirers would claim. Collins, clearly, is less than convinced, while John Carey, in a study which emphasises the implications of Dickens's personality for his fiction, questions the validity of the prison symbolism itself.[19] (See the final extract in Part Two of this Casebook.) Carey's book is a direct challenge to that critical fashion which would deprive the text of its author: for him the author all too potently exists. What such reactions serve to remind us of is that even the most positive judgements can never be absolute, and that critical debate is never concluded. The point is one which perhaps now, more than ever, needs to be affirmed.

NOTES

1. Philip Collins, '*Dombey and Son* – Then and Now', *The Dickensian*, 63 (1967), p. 91. I must acknowledge at the outset my debt to Professor Collins's work throughout this Casebook: his *Dickens: The Critical Heritage* (London, 1971) and his various essays on aspects of Dickens's reputation have been invaluable sources of information. The other influence which it has been difficult to escape is that of George Ford, whose admirable *Dickens and His Readers* (Princeton, N.J., 1955) has inevitably prepared much of my ground for me.

2. Edmund Wilson, *The Wound and the Bow* (New York and London, 1941; paperback edition 1961), pp. 31, 46.

3. It should be noted that Leavis's chapter on *Dombey and Son* in *Dickens the Novelist* appeared in its first form in the *Sewanee Review*, 70 (1962), while his *Little Dorrit* chapter was a reworking of lectures given when he was Chichele Lecturer at Oxford in 1964.

4. Amy Cruse, *The Victorians and their Books* (London, 1935), pp. 157–8.

5. *The Edinburgh Review*, CVI (July 1857), p. 134.

6. Ford, op. cit. (paperback edition, 1965), p. 111.

7. David Masson, *British Novelists and their Styles* (Cambridge, 1859), p. 252.

8. Ford, op. cit., p. 127.

9. 'Remonstrance with Dickens', *Blackwood's Magazine*, LXXXI (April 1857), p.502.

10. Virginia Woolf, *'David Copperfield'*, reprinted in *Collected Essays*, vol 1 (London 1966), p. 193. It was in a letter following up this essay that Virginia Woolf made the observation that she 'would not cross the road to dine with Wordsworth, Byron or Dickens' (*Collected Essays*, vol. 1, p. 195).

11. *Sharpe's London Magazine*, VI (May 1848), p. 202. (See the extract from this review in Part One of this Casebook.)

12. G. K. Chesterton, *Charles Dickens* (London, 1906), p. 87.

13. Susan Horton, *Interpreting Interpreting* (Baltimore and London, 1979), p. *ix*.

14. H. P. Sucksmith (ed.), *Little Dorrit* – The 'Clarendon' Edition (Oxford, 1979), p. *xv*.

15. Cf., e.g., *Charles Dickens*, op. cit., p. 229; '*Little Dorrit* . . . is . . . so much more subtle and . . . so much more sad than the rest of his work that it bores Dickensians and especially pleases George Gissing. It is the only one of Dickens tales which could please Gissing, not only by its genius but also by its atmosphere.'

16. It is perhaps too readily assumed that the work of the enthusiastic Dickensians who formed themselves into societies and associations in the early part of this century is all of a piece in projecting the traditional idea of an optimistic and convivial Dickens. (Cf., e.g., Ford, op. cit. pp. 172–7.) In fact this is not always the case. Uncritical their work may be, by academic standards, but its enthusiasm can take surprising turns.

17. Philip Collins, '*Little Dorrit*: The Prison and the Critics', *Times Literary Supplement* (18 April 1980), pp. 445–6.

18. John Holloway (ed.), *Little Dorrit*, Penguin English Library edition (Harmondsworth, 1967), p. 23.

19. Elsewhere, Robert Garis, writing of *Little Dorrit*, has referred to 'the over-emphatic and misleading excitement about Dickens's symbolic structures' and to 'the essential failure of the novel as a whole' – *The Dickens Theatre* (Oxford, 1965), p. 187. Cf. also D. W. Jefferson, 'The Moral Centre of *Little Dorrit*', *Essays in Criticism* (October 1976), pp. 300–17); and R. F. Gill, 'How not to read a Novel', *Use of English* (May 1977), pp. 11–16.

PART ONE

Dombey and Son

Dombey and Son

Published in twenty monthly parts (at a shilling each) from October 1846 to April 1848; published in book form in 1848. In both the monthly-part and the book-form versions, the novel's original full title was *Dealings with the Firm of Dombey and Son, Wholesale, Retail, and for Exportation.*

1. ORIGINS AND RECEPTION

Dickens   (1858)

In Retrospect

I make so bold as to believe that the faculty (or the habit) of closely and carefully observing the characters of men is a rare one. I have not even found, within my experience, that the faculty (or the habit) of closely and carefully observing so much as the faces of men, is a general one by any means. The two commonest mistakes in judgment that I suppose to arise from the former default, are, the confounding of shyness with arrogance, and the not understanding that an obstinate nature exists in a perpetual struggle with itself.

Mr Dombey undergoes no violent internal change, either in this book, or in life. A sense of his injustice is within him all along. The more he represses it, the more unjust he necessarily is. Internal shame and external circumstances may bring the contest to the surface in a week, or a day; but it has been a contest for years, and is only fought out then, after a long balance of victory.

It is ten years since I dismissed Mr Dombey. I have not been impatient to offer this critical remark upon him, and I offer it with some confidence.

I began this book by the lake of Geneva, and went on with it for some months in France. The association between the writing and the place of writing is so curiously strong in my mind, that at this day, although I know every stair in the little Midshipman's house, and could swear to every pew in the church in which Florence was married, or to every young gentleman's bedstead in Doctor Blimber's establishment, I yet confusedly imagine Captain Cuttle as secluding himself from Mrs Mac Stinger among the mountains of Switzerland. Similarly, when I am reminded by any chance of what it was that the waves were always saying, I wander in my fancy for a whole winter night about the streets of Paris – as I really did, with a heavy heart, on the night when my little friend and I parted company for ever.

SOURCE: Preface to the Cheap Edition of *Dombey and Son* (London, 1858); usually reproduced in later editions and reprints of the novel.

Westminster Review   (1847)

... The happiest and most perfect of Dickens's sketches is that of 'Little Nell' in the story of 'Humphrey's Clock'. Her death is a tragedy of the true sort, that which softens, and yet strengthens and elevates; and we have its counterpart in the death of 'Little Dombey', in the new work of this gifted author now issuing in parts through the press.

We rejoice to observe, in 'Dombey and Son', the evidence of improved experience and pains-taking. If we may judge of the work as a whole from the early numbers, it is, to our thinking, the best of the productions of the same pen. The chief interest is tragic, but its material is not crime; and we notice this with satisfaction, as an illustration of our argument. The personages of the tale are every-day men and women, with their every-day faults and virtues. Among them, as yet, there is no great villain. Hobgoblins have been exorcised. The first part describes a dying mother – the fifth a dying child – subjects of the most commonplace obituaries, but both treated by a master. No other writer can approach Dickens in a perfect analysis of the mind of children; and in 'Dombey and Son' he has put forth the whole of his power. It was a novel but happy idea to sketch society, and human weaknesses, as seen through the eyes of infant philosophy. The satire is at once playful, delicate, and touching. We allude chiefly to the fourth number, where the reflections of little Dombey upon all that is passing about him at Dr Blimber's, is a study for moralists and metaphysicians. The number following concludes the biography of the sick child . . . we transfer to our pages the closing scene; – a long one, but its merit lies in the *minutiae* and truthfulness of its details, which will not bear abbreviation. [Quotes substantially from chapter 16, concluding with the final paragraphs, which are referred to below.]

A simple but effective narrative; and well told: – one in which every incident is true to nature, and given without any straining after effect. The only attempt at fine writing is in the last two passages, which are not very intelligible, and should have been omitted. Paul has been called 'old-fashioned', from the eccentricity of his manners, but the term is not appropriate to death and immortality: and we should never have guessed what came in with our first garments, without the author's explanation at the end of the sentence. This is but a trifling matter, and we are glad that beyond a little exaggeration in the portraiture of the fashionable physician, Sir Parker Peps, no graver defects appear. In the humorous parts of the narrative there is as usual a vein of caricature, but not too extravagant, nor more than is required to render the descriptions graphic.

The rising generation will have reason to be grateful to Mr Dickens, for his temperate but yet severe rebuke of all attempts to overtask a child's intellect. By his quiet satire of a fashionable classical institution, in the present work, not less than for his exposure of vulgar and brutal ignorance in another class of academies, described in 'Nicholas Nickleby', he deserves the thanks of all educational reformers. . . .[1]

SOURCE: extract from notice in the *Westminster Review* (April 1847): XLVII, pp. 6–11.

NOTE

1. [Ed.] This review is signed 'H'. Philip Collins suggests that the author may be William E. Hickson, editor of the *Westminster Review* from 1840 to 1832: cf. P. Collins (ed.), *Dickens: The Critical Heritage* (London, 1971), p. 225. The review is of the first five numbers of the part-publication of the novel – i.e., chapters 1 to 16.

Sharpe's London Magazine   (1848)

We have before us a new work from the pen of Mr Charles Dickens; and the promise which former excellence gave has been ably fulfilled. Scarcely any writer of the present day has so much power in his hands for good or evil as this gentleman: the extensive circulation of his works; their rapid succession; their peculiar appeal in language and subject to the middle classes – we had almost written, the masses of society, render him at all times an important and ever ready authority; whilst his high moral tone, and a certain internal evidence that he writes upon a conviction of the truths he is maintaining, place him in the first rank of the popular writers of the present day.

Perhaps few tastes have grown so rapidly of late years as the taste for works of fiction: and the increased demand has had a corresponding effect upon the supply; with this difference, that whilst education and other causes have combined to raise the standard of demand amongst the many, opportunities of profit and necessity for compliance of some sort have produced a proportionate deterioration of quality in the supply. It is of the greatest consequence in a country like this, where so many turn for relaxation from the stern realities of life (and the realities of our own times are very stern indeed), to the perusal of popular fictions, that those popular fictions should be of the highest possible class. Now we are anxious to assert our admiration of Mr Dickens; and we do so on the grounds above mentioned, viz. that he has always written, not only for the temporary amusement of his readers, but with a view to their general interests and improvement; and be his subject matter grave or ga$_j$, the broadest humour or the deepest pathos, he emits no opportunity of inculcating religious and philosophical truths in his homely characters, and surrounding the most ordinary objects with feelings and sentiments of virtuous interest. His faults – and he has them – are not those of every novelist, and his beauties are all his own.

We have for Mr Charles Dickens so profound a respect, that in censuring his writings we approach the task with the utmost diffidence; still we must confess that although the work before us is as full of beauties as any thing he has yet written, we believe it to be quite as full of faults.

There is a good broad road of probability, broad enough for anybody not utterly intoxicated with popularity, which might have answered the author's purpose, without travelling down the bye-lanes of possibility, and even losing his way in them in search of catastrophes. If Mr Dickens creates impossible characters, to be sure we have no right to quarrel with his pulling the strings his own way; but we protest as strongly against the falsities of fiction as we approve of its realities. Everybody likes to be able to sympathise with the characters portrayed; but when those characters are placed by the author in impossible or almost impossible positions, we lose that power: a virtuous interest is merged in an unhealthy curiosity or amazement; and the character ceases to be a beacon for our guidance, or a quicksand to avoid. Who ever dreamt of Edith Grainger, or rather Dombey, the proud, imperious, but generous Edith, running away with Carker, the managing clerk of her husband, known and despised by herself, only for the sake of humiliating the self-satisfied Dombey? Florence, too, the very gem of the book, kind, gentle, constant in her affection to her father, childlike as she is, might have spared herself the pain of kissing old Captain Cuttle, or asking the advice of his friend Bunsby on so delicate a subject as Walter's safety. When Mr Dickens began writing, the *semi-pathetic* was admirable, because original – it has ceased to be so; and we are more inclined to laugh at than with it. The book is moreover full to overflowing of waves whispering and wandering; of dark rivers rolling to the sea; of winds, and golden ripples, and such like matters, which are sometimes very pretty, generally very untrue, and have become, at all events, excessively stale.

But these are minor considerations – spots in the sun – as little affecting the real beauty of the work, or its intrinsic value as a moral lesson, as if they had never existed. Its excellences are of a high cast. Religious sentiments expressed in language whose simplicity enhances their innate beauty; a feeling for women, and a development of their best and loveliest natures, as in the simple Polly Toodle, and the despised Miss Tox; the accidental interpolation of good apart from the main story, so common in Mr Dickens's writings; and those admirably touching incidents, than which none are more exquisite or more exquisitely told than the reappearance of Susan Nipper before Florence in the old dress she used to serve her in; situations of the highest dramatic power as a whole, are rendered life-like by the wonderful talent for detail – a talent possessed by no writer of modern times in such perfection. We really feel inclined to doubt whether the scene between Mr and Mrs Dombey in the 40th chapter has, in its peculiar way, ever been surpassed; and though we think that Mr Dickens might sometimes avoid a difficulty by a little premeditation of his plan, we cannot but admire his consummate tact in releasing his creations from the awkward positions in which he places them. . .

Dombey is a character new to fiction, and uncommon in real life – a counting-house aristocrat. Not so rare in the higher classes of society, but then more dignified, with less cravat and more manner. Cold, selfish (though probably not in trifles), proud of his order, and of himself as one of its heads. To us there is something, we admit, rather respectable in this pride – something honourable in his vanity as 'a British merchant, and a devilish upright gentleman', as Cousin Feenix hath it. It is too much the fashion to turn up one's nose at the shop now-a-days. We are all West-end men: the son is all very well in the drawing-room near Portland Place, but we connect him not with our City greatness; we prefer St James's to St Olave's; and a cornetcy in the Blues, to a corner stool in the counting-house. Dombey was free from this vanity, at all events; and in his misfortunes proved it. He was selfish and proud, but he would be under dishonourable obligations to none; he exacted, and he paid, the uttermost farthing. Mr Morfin announces a great philosophical truth when he propounds to Miss Harriett, 'that it would do us no harm to remember oftener than we do, that vices are sometimes only virtues carried to excess!' We see but one contradiction throughout in the character of Dombey, and that is, his determination to make Carker his confidant in so private a matter as his wife's conduct to himself. We have read the work attentively, and though we think we see Mr Dickens's intention, we confess ourselves unable to go with him; we cannot reconcile it with Dombey's character, even on the score of his unbending tyranny.

It would not be fair to leave this portion of Mr Dickens's work without saying a few words on the excellent lesson to be learnt from his principal character. When a fashionable novelist introduces misfortune as attaching to his hero, it is usually in a manner *retributive:* the *corrective* has seldom any place in his mind. Misfortune, as the just penalty of folly or vice, is in his opinion a very handsome stretch of morality. Mr Dickens does more, for he applies to misfortune that which makes it truly valuable, its scriptural quality of correction: he makes it the dark cloud, and heavy storm, which precede the setting sun's beams of humility and resignation. . . .

SOURCE: extract from unsigned review in *Sharpe's London Magazine* (May 1848): VI, pp. 200–2.

John Forster   (1848)

. . . Mr Dickens . . . has given a direction to the popular tastes which before was not felt, and popular fiction shows everywhere the impression of his genius. . . .

The definition of a book which was given by a lively French writer, that it is a letter addressed to those unknown friends whom one possesses in the world, is particularly applicable to that remarkable series of books of which the last published is now before us. We doubt if any writer that ever lived has inspired such strong feelings of personal attachment, in his impersonal character of author. He counts his readers by tens of thousands, and all of them 'unknown friends' with perhaps few exceptions. The wonderful sense of the real thrown into his ideal creations may sufficiently account for this. There was probably not a family in this country where fictitious literature is read, that did not feel the death of Paul Dombey as something little short of a family sorrow. What was said of it by the author of the *Two Old Men's Tales*, that it flung a nation into mourning, was hardly an exaggeration;[1] and perhaps the extent and depth of the feeling was a surprise to even the author himself. Certainly it raised the interest in the story to a formidable height before the story was

well launched, and what was meant but as the key-note to a more
solemn after-strain had deepened into a pathos of its own too vivid to
play that secondary part. Thus the exclamation which breaks from
the weeping Miss Tox at the close of the celebrated chapter of Paul's
death (*Dear me, dear me! to think that Dombey and Son should be a Daughter
after all*), was felt as a jar at the time, and too light an intrusion on a
solemn catastrophe; though it now guides us to what the author's
intention really was, and enables us to judge of his design justly, as an
entire and proportioned one.

Turning to the completed book, and reading the chapter but one
following the death of Paul entitled 'Father and Daughter', we
perceive this strongly. The boy's death assumes its place in relation to
the character of Florence. It is as a fairy vision to a piece of actual
suffering; it is a piece of sorrow with heaven's hues upon it, to show the
contrast of a sorrow which has all the bitterness of earth. We think the
subsequent treatment of Florence worthy of this. In that child-like
heart there is always a brave, heroic struggle, a something which will
not be crushed, an endeavour and hope which does not sink or yield.
We have heard her compared to Little Nell, but rather in what
distinguishes the two characters do we seem to find the purpose the
author has chiefly in view. Little Nell amid her strange and violent
associates may symbolise the unconscious innocence of childhood,
pure and unsullied against shafts of worldly injury, and passing
unscathed as Una to her home beyond. Florence is this character in
action and resistance, and shows a strength in life's sorest trials
sufficient to work out their redemption even here.

Generally of the book before us, as of most part of the later
productions of Mr Dickens, we would say that with no abatement of
the life and energy which in his earlier works threw out such forcible
impressions of the actual, we have in a far higher degree the subtler
requisites which satisfy imagination and reflection. For there is
nature, in the common life of what she usually does; and there is
nature, in the higher sense of what in given circumstances she might
or would do; and from the latter the principal power of this novel is
derived. But we are not certain if the appeal thus made is not to deeper
sympathies than, in the swift and cursory reading which is one of the
effects of serial publication, are always at hand to respond to it. In one
of the later passages of eloquent reflection to be found in the book, the
author speaks of what is 'most unnatural, and yet most natural in
being so'; and this is probably what all his readers have not been able
to concede, in the instance of Mr Dombey and his wife. The past
antecedents of both make the truth of the existing picture. It is what a
tyrant passion in the one case, and a false education in the other, have

made of what nature had meant to make; nor can an artist take a
higher subject for his art than to show in this way how the courses of
life may run counter to the natural dispensations. There is great
boldness in making all Mrs Dombey's worst qualities but the
perversion of what ought to have been her best; and the picture of
herself and her mother by the side of a pair of beings as wretched in
the very lowest social grade, conveys a salutary warning of how
intimate are the vices that act and react in the opposite directions of
society.

When we turn to the more ordinary life of the tale, a crowd of most
pleasant figures greet us, endearing their author as they enrich his
book. Glorious Captain Cuttle, laying his head to the wind and
fighting through everything; his friend Bunsby, with a head too
ponderous to lay to, falling a victim to the inveterate MacStinger;
good-hearted modest considerate Toots, his brains rapidly going as
his whiskers show themselves coming, but getting back out of the
world in his shambling way some part of the sense that the forcing
Blimbers had pumped out of him; breathless Susan Nipper, beaming
Polly Toodle, the plaintive Wickam, and the awful Pipchin, each with
her duty in the starched Dombey household so nicely appointed as to
seem to have been born for only that; simple thoughtful old Gills, and
his hearty and honourable young nephew; Mr Toodle and his
children, with the charitable grinder's decline and fall; Miss Tox, an
obsequious flatterer from nothing but good-nature; the spectacled
and analytic, but not unkind Miss Blimber; and the droning dulness
of the good Doctor himself, withering even the fruits of his well-spread
dinner-table with his *It is remarkable, Mr Feeder, that the Romans —!* 'At
the mention of this terrible people', Mr Dickens proceeds, 'their
implacable enemies, every young gentleman fastened his gaze upon
the Doctor, with an assumption of the deepest interest.' The whole
forcing system and its fruits in education are hit off in that witty
sentence; and we may anticipate as much public benefit from the
good-natured exposure of the Blimber mistakes in *Dombey*, as from the
sterner revelation in *Nickleby* of the atrocities of Mr Squeers.

Criticism on a book so extensively known is necessarily at some
disadvantage. 'I do follow here in the chase', says *Roderigo*, 'not like a
hound that hunts, but one that fills up the cry.'[2] But in filling up the
cry, and recalling to the reader's recollection the leading features of
this remarkable book (which is all we profess to do), we have not
found any falling off in that handling of common life with clearness,
precision, and consistency of humorous delineation, which marked
Mr Dickens' outset in literature. The satire is not less wholesome, the
laugh not less hearty, the style not less natural, flexible, and manly.

What we occasionally find when we would rather have it absent, is, that what should be, and would formerly have been, a mere instinct shown in the silent action of a character, has here and there come to be too much of a conscious feeling, and receives a too elaborate expression. This occurs in the comic as well as tragic portions. But the fault springs from an abundance of resource, and is perhaps inseparable from a power which is even yet not fully developed in its higher and more ideal tendencies. Much that the ordinary reader may pass carelessly in the book, will seize upon the fancy alive to poetical expression, and accustomed to poetical art. The recurrence of particular thoughts and phrases is an instance of the kind, running like the leading colour through a picture, or the predominant phrase in a piece of music, because subtly connected with the emotion which it is the design of the story to create.

Thus, in the opening scene, where the death of Mr Dombey's first wife is described, the beautiful image with which it closes is found to present itself again and again. Florence, too young to be quite conscious of her impending loss, is locked in her dying mother's arms.

The two medical attendants exchanged a look across the bed; and the physician, stooping down, whispered in the child's ear. Not having understood the purport of his whisper, the little creature turned her perfectly colourless face and deep dark eyes towards him; but without loosening her hold in the least. The whisper was repeated. 'Mama!' said the child. The little voice, familiar and dearly loved, awakened some show of consciousness, even at that ebb. For a moment, the closed eye-lids trembled, and the nostril quivered, and the faintest shadow of a smile was seen. 'Mama!' cried the child, sobbing aloud. 'Oh dear Mama! Oh dear Mama!' The doctor gently brushed the scattered ringlets of the child, aside from the face and mouth of the mother. Alas, how calm they lay there; how little breath there was to stir them! Thus, clinging fast to that slight spar within her arms, the mother drifted out upon the dark and unknown sea that rolls round all the world.

The 'dark and unknown sea' – who has not felt its affinities with all that is most solemn in life, most mysterious and remote in death? . . .[3]

SOURCE: unsigned review in the *Examiner* (28 Oct. 1848), pp. 692–3.

NOTES

1. [Ed.] *Two Old Men's Tales: The Deformed*, and *The Admiral's Daughter* was the first publication of Mrs Anne Marsh, a prolific novelist of the 1840s and 50s.

2. [Ed.] The words quoted are from *Othello* II iii.

3. [Ed.] The evidence for assigning this anonymous review to John
Forster, friend and eventual biographer of Dickens, is given in Collins, *Critical
Heritage*, op. cit., p. 232.

Thomas Babington Macaulay   (1846)

X
... Have you seen the first number of Dombey ...? There is not
much in it: but there is one passage which made me cry as if my heart
would break. It is the description of a little girl who has lost an
affectionate mother, and is unkindly treated by every body. Images of
that sort always overpower me, even when the artist is less skilful than
Dickens. . . .

> SOURCE: extract from letter cited in G. O. Trevelyan, *Life and Letters
> of Lord Macaulay* (1876), II, p. 210.

Francis Jeffrey   (1846, 1847)

1846

X.. The Dombeys, my dear D! how can I thank you enough for them!
The truth, and the delicacy, and the softness and depth of the pathos
in that opening death-scene, could only come from one hand; and the
exquisite taste which spares all details, and breaks off just when the
effect is at its height, is wholly yours. But it is Florence on whom my
hopes chiefly repose; and in her I see the promise of another Nelly!
though reserved, I hope, for a happier fate, and destined to let us see
what a *grown-up* female angel is like. . . . Dombey is rather too hateful,
and strikes me as a mitigated Jonas, without his brutal coarseness and
ruffian ferocity. I am quite in the dark as to what you mean to make of
Paul, but shall watch his development with interest. . . . I love the
Captain . . . and his hook, as much as you can wish. . . .

> SOURCE: extract from letter to Dickens (on reading the first number
> of the novel), cited in John Forster, *Life of Dickens* (1874).

1847

... Oh, my dear dear Dickens! what a No.5 you have now given us![1] I have so cried and sobbed over it last night, and again this morning; and felt my heart purified by those tears, and blessed and loved you for making me shed them; and I never can bless and love you enough. Since that divine Nelly was found dead on her humble couch ... there has been nothing like the actual dying of that sweet Paul, in the summer sunshine of that lofty room. And the long vista that leads us so gently and sadly, and yet so gracefully and winningly, to that plain consummation! Every trait so true, and so touching – and yet lightened by that fearless innocence which goes *playfully* to the brink of the grave, and that pure affection which bears the unstained spirit, on its soft and lambent flash, at once to its source in eternity. In reading of these delightful children, how deeply do we feel that 'of such is the kingdom of Heaven'. . . .

... the scenes with *Florence* and *Edith*, are done with your finest and happiest hand; so soft and so graceful, and with such delicate touches of deep feeling, and passing intimations of coming griefs, and woman's loveliness, and loving nature, shown in such contrasted embodiments of gentle innocence and passionate pride; and yet all brought under the potent spell of one great master, and harmonized by the grace as well as the power of his genius, into a picture in which everyone must recognise, not only the truth of each individual figure, but the magic effect of their grouping. . . .

SOURCE: extracts from letters of 1847 to Dickens, cited in Lord Cockburn's *Life of Lord Jeffrey* (1852), II, pp. 406, 429.

NOTE

1. [Ed.] The fifth number, in the novel's publication in monthly parts, concludes with the death of Paul Dombey.

Edward FitzGerald   (1847)

✗ . . . Dickens's last *Dombey* has a very fine account of the overcramming Educator's system; well worth whole volumes of essays on the subject if History would believe that laughs may tell truth. The boy who talks Greek in his sleep seems as terrible as Macbeth. . . .

> SOURCE: extract from letter to Thackeray, cited in Gordon N. Ray (ed.), *The Letters and Private Papers of William Makepeace Thackeray* (London, 1945–46), II, pp. 266.

William Makepeace Thackeray   (1847)

. . . There's no writing against such powers as this – one has no chance! Read that stupendous chapter describing Paul's death: it is unsurpassed – it is stupendous!

> SOURCE: extract from letter of 1847, cited in Ray's edition of Thackeray's letters, op. cit., II, p. 267n.

Hippolyte Taine   (1859)

. . . the most complete and most English picture of the aristocratic spirit is the portrait of a London merchant, Mr Dombey.

In France people do not look for types among the merchants, but they are found among that class in England, as forcible as in the proudest châteaux. Mr Dombey loves his house as if he were a nobleman, as much as himself. If he neglects his daughter and longs for a son, it is to perpetuate the old name of his bank. He has his ancestors in commerce, and he would have his descendants. He maintains traditions, and continues a power. At this height of opulence, and with this scope of action, he is a prince, and with a prince's position he has his feelings. You see there a character which could only be produced in a country whose commerce embraces the globe, where merchants are potentates, where a company of merchants has speculated upon continents, maintained wars, destroyed kingdoms, founded an empire of a hundred million men. The pride of such a man is not petty, but terrible; it is so calm and high, that to find a parallel we must read again the *Mémoires* of Saint Simon. Mr Dombey has always commanded, and it does not enter his mind that he could yield to any one or anything. He receives flattery as a tribute to which he had a right, and sees men beneath him, at a vast distance, as beings made to beseech and obey him. His second wife, proud Edith Skewton, resists and scorns him; the pride of the merchant is pitted against the pride of the noble-born woman, and the restrained outbursts of this growing opposition reveal an intensity of passion, which souls thus born and bred alone could feel. Edith, to avenge herself, flees on the anniversary of her marriage, and gives herself the appearance of being an adulteress. It is then that the inflexible pride asserts itself in all its stiffness. He has driven out of the house his daughter, whom he believes the accomplice of his wife; he forbids the one or the other to be brought to his memory; he commands his sister and his friends to be silent; he receives guests with the same tone and the same coldness. Despairing in heart, eaten up by the insult, by the conscience of his failure, by the idea of public ridicule, he remains as firm, as haughty, as calm as ever. He launches out more recklessly in business, and is ruined; he is on the point of suicide. Hitherto all was well: the bronze column continued whole and unbroken; but the exigencies of public morality mar the idea of the book. His daughter arrives in the nick of time. She entreats him; he softens, she carries him away; he becomes the best of fathers, and spoils a fine novel. . . .

SOURCE: extract from Taine's *History of English Literature* – French original (1859, revised and enlarged, 1863–64), translated into English by H. van Laun (Edinburgh, 1871), II, pp. 362–3. (For Forster's comment on Taine's criticism, see the concluding excerpt in this section, below.)

Charles Kent   (1872)

Dickens's reading of the story of Paul Dombey

... The hushed silence with which the concluding passages of this
Reading were always listened to, spoke more eloquently than any
applause could possibly have done, of the sincerity of the emotions it
awakened. A cursory glance at the audience confirmed the impression
produced by that earlier evidence of their rapt and breathless
attention. It is the simplest truth to say that at those times many a face
illustrated involuntarily the loveliest line in the noblest ode in the
language, where Dryden has sung even of a warrior –

> And now and then a sigh he heaved,
> And tears began to flow.[1]

The subdued voice of the Reader, moreover, accorded tenderly with
one's remembrance of his own acknowledgment ten years after his
completion of the book from which this story was extracted, that with
a heavy heart he had walked the streets of Paris alone during the
whole of one winter's night, while he and his little friend parted
company for ever! ...

Hardly can it be matter for wonder ... that a mixed audience
showed traces of emotion when the profoundly sympathetic voice of
Dickens himself related this story of the Life and Death of Little
Dombey. Yet the pathetic beauty of the tale, for all that, was only
dimly hinted at throughout, – the real pathos of it, indeed, being only
fully indicated almost immediately before its conclusion. Earlier in
the Reading, in fact, the drollery of the comic characters introduced –
of themselves irresistible – would have been simply paramount, but
for the incidental mention of the mother's death, when clinging to that
frail spar within her arms, her little daughter, 'she drifted out upon
the dark and unknown sea that rolls round all the world'. Paul's little
wistful face looked out every now and then, it is true, from among the
fantastic forms and features grouped around him, with a growing
sense upon the hearer of what was really meant by the child being so
'old-fashioned'. But the ludicrous effect of those surrounding characters was nothing less than all-mastering in its predominance. ...

... At about the middle of the 47th page of the Reading copy of this
book about Little Dombey, the copy from which Dickens read, both
in England and America, there is, in his handwriting, the word –
'Pause'. It occurs just in between Little Dombey's confiding to his

sister, that if she were in India he should die of being so sorry and so lonely! and the incident of his suddenly waking up at another time from a long sleep in his little carriage on the shingles, to ask her, not only What the rolling waves are saying so constantly, but What place is over there? – far away! – looking eagerly, as he inquires, towards some invisible region beyond the horizon! That momentary pause will be very well remembered by everyone who attended this Reading. . . .

Wonderful fun used to be made by the Reader of the various incidents at the entertainment given upon the eve of the vacations by Doctor and Mrs Blimber to the Young Gentlemen and their Friends, when 'the hour was half-past seven o'clock, and the object was quadrilles'. . . . Thoroughly enjoyable though the whole scene was in its throng of ludicrous particulars, it merely led the way up appreciably and none the less tenderly, for all the innocent laughter, to the last and supremely pathetic incidents of the story as related thenceforth (save only for one startling instant) *sotto voce*, by the Reader.

The exceptional moment here alluded to, when his voice was suddenly raised, to be hushed again the instant afterwards, came at the very opening of the final scene by Little Dombey's death-bed, where the sunbeams, towards evening, struck through the rustling blinds and quivered on the opposite wall like golden water. Overwhelmed, as little Paul was occasionally, with 'his only trouble', a sense of the swift and rapid river, 'he felt forced', the Reader went on to say, 'to try and stop it – to stem it with his childish hands, or choke its way with sand – and when he saw it coming on, resistless, HE CRIED OUT!' Dropping his voice from that abrupt outcry instantly afterwards, to the gentlest tones, as he added, 'But a word from Florence, who was always at his side, restored him to himself' – the Reader continued in those subdued and tender accents to the end. . . .

Source: extracts from Charles Kent, *Dickens as a Reader* (London, 1872), pp. 176–85.

NOTE

1. [Ed.] These lines are misquoted from Dryden's ode, 'Alexander's Feast, or The Power of Music'. The first line should read 'And, now and then, a Sigh he stole'.

John Forster   (1874)

The writing of the novel

Though his proposed new 'book in shilling numbers' had been mentioned to me three months before he quitted England, he knew little himself at that time or when he left excepting the fact, then also named, that it was to do with Pride what its predecessor had done with Selfishness. But this limit he soon overpassed; and the succession of independent groups of character, surprising for the variety of their forms and handling, with which he enlarged and enriched his plan, went far beyond the range of the passion of Mr Dombey and Mr Dombey's second wife.

Obvious causes have led to grave under-estimates of this novel. Its first five numbers forced up interest and expectation so high that the rest of necessity fell short; but it is not therefore true of the general conception that thus the wine of it had been drawn, and only the lees left. In the treatment of acknowledged masterpieces in literature it not seldom occurs that the genius and the art of the master have not pulled together to the close; but if a work of imagination is to forfeit its higher need of praise because its pace at starting has not been uniformly kept, hard measure would have to be dealt to books of undeniable greatness. Among other critical severities it was said here, that Paul died at the beginning not for any need of the story, but only to interest its readers somewhat more; and that Mr Dombey relented at the end for just the same reason. What is now to be told will show how little ground existed for either imputation. The so-called 'violent change' in the hero has more lately been revived in the notices of Mr Taine, who says that '*it spoils a fine novel*'; but it will be seen that in the apparent alteration no unnaturalness of change was involved, and certainly the adoption of it was not a sacrifice to 'public morality'. While every other portion of the tale had to submit to such varieties in development as the characters themselves entailed, the design affecting Paul and his father had been planned from the opening, and was carried without real alteration to the close. Of the perfect honesty with which Dickens himself repelled such charges as those to which I have adverted, when he wrote the preface to his collected edition, remarkable proof appears in the letter to myself which accompanied the manuscript of his proposed first number. No other line of the tale had at this time been placed on paper.

When the first chapter only was done, and again when all was

finished but eight slips, he had sent me letters formerly quoted. What
follows came with the manuscript of the first four chapters on the 25th
of July. 'I will now go on to give you an outline of my immediate
intentions in reference to *Dombey*. I design to show Mr D. with that
one idea of the Son taking firmer and firmer possession of him, and
swelling and bloating his pride to a prodigious extent. As the boy
begins to grow up, I shall show him quite impatient for his getting on,
and urging his masters to set him great tasks, and the like. But the
natural affection of the boy will turn towards the despised sister; and I
purpose showing her learning all sorts of things, of her own
application and determination, to assist him in his lessons: and
helping him always. When the boy is about ten years old (in the fourth
number), he will be taken ill, and will die; and when he is ill, and when
he is dying, I mean to make him turn always for refuge to the sister
still, and keep the stern affection of the father at a distance. So Mr
Dombey – for all his greatness, and for all his devotion to the child –
will find himself at arms' length from him even then; and will see that
his love and confidence are all bestowed upon his sister, whom Mr
Dombey has used – and so has the boy himself too, for that matter – as
a mere convenience and handle to him. The death of the boy is a
death-blow, of course, to all the father's schemes and cherished hopes;
and "Dombey and Son", as Miss Tox will say at the end of the
number, "is a Daughter after all". . . . From that time, I purpose
changing his feeling of indifference and uneasiness towards his
daughter into a positive hatred. For he will always remember how the
boy had his arm round her neck when he was dying, and whispered to
her, and would take things only from her hand, and never thought of
him. . . . At the same time I shall change *her* feeling towards *him* for
one of a greater desire to love him, and to be loved by him; engendered
in her compassion for his loss, and her love for the dead boy whom, in
his way, he loved so well too. So I mean to carry the story on, through
all the branches and off-shoots and meanderings that come up; and
through the decay and downfall of the house, and the bankruptcy of
Dombey, and all the rest of it; when his only staff and treasure, and his
unknown Good Genius always, will be this rejected daughter, who
will come out better than any son at last, and whose love for him,
when discovered and understood, will be his bitterest reproach. For
the struggle with himself, which goes on in all such obstinate natures,
will have ended then; and the sense of his injustice, which you may be
sure has never quitted him, will have at last a gentler office than that
of only making him more harshly unjust. . . . I rely very much on
Susan Nipper grown up, and acting partly as Florence's maid, and
partly as a kind of companion to her, for a strong character

throughout the book. I also rely on the Toodles, and on Polly, who, like everybody else, will be found by Mr Dombey to have gone over to his daughter and become attached to her. This is what cooks call "the stock of the soup". All kinds of things will be added to it, of course.' Admirable is the illustration thus afforded of his way of working, and interesting the evidence it gives of the feeling for his art with which this book was begun.

The close of the letter put an important question affecting gravely a leading person in the tale. '. . . About the boy, who appears in the last chapter of the first number, I think it would be a good thing to disappoint all the expectations that chapter seems to raise of his happy connection with the story and the heroine, and to show him gradually and naturally trailing away, from that love of adventure and boyish light-heartedness, into negligence, idleness, dissipation, dishonesty, and ruin. To show, in short, that common, every-day, miserable declension of which we know so much in our ordinary life, to exhibit something of the philosophy of it, in great temptations and an easy nature; and to show how the good turns into bad, by degrees. If I kept some little notion of Florence always at the bottom of it, I think it might be made very powerful and very useful. What do you think? Do you think it may be done, without making people angry? I could bring out Solomon Gills and Captain Cuttle well, through such a history; and I descry, anyway, an opportunity for good scenes between Captain Cuttle and Miss Tox. This question of the boy is very important. . . . Let me hear all you think about it. Hear! I wish I could.'

For reasons that need not be dwelt upon here, but in which Dickens ultimately acquiesced, Walter was reserved for a happier future; and the idea thrown out took modified shape, amid circumstances better suited to its excellent capabilities, in the striking character of Richard Carstone in the tale of *Bleak House*. . . .

Several letters now expressed his anxiety about the illustrations. A nervous dread of caricature in the face of his merchant-hero, had led him to indicate by a living person the type of city-gentleman he would have had the artist select; and this is all he meant by his reiterated urgent request, 'I do wish he could get a glimpse of A, for he is the very Dombey'. . . .

. . . he left Lausanne for Paris, and my first letter to him there was to say that he had overwritten his number by three pages. 'I have taken out about two pages and a half', he wrote by return from the hotel Brighton, 'and the rest I must ask you to take out with the assurance that you will satisfy me in whatever you do. The sale, prodigious indeed! I am very thankful.' Next day he wrote as to Walter. 'I see it

will be best as you advise, to give that idea up; and indeed I don't feel
it would be reasonable to carry it out now. I am far from sure it could
be wholesomely done, after the interest he has acquired. But when I
have disposed of Paul (poor boy!) I will consider the subject farther.'
The subject was never resumed. He was at the opening of his
admirable fourth part, when, on the 6th of December, he wrote from
the Rue de Courcelles: 'Here am I, writing letters, and delivering
opinions, politico-economical and otherwise, as if there were no
undone number, . . . one must keep one's spirits up, if possible, even
under *Dombey* pressure. Paul, I shall slaughter at the end of number
five. His school ought to be pretty good, but I haven't been able to
dash at it freely, yet. However, I have avoided unnecessary dialogue
so far, to avoid overwriting; and all I *have* written is point.'

And so, in 'point', it went to the close; the rich humour of its picture
of Doctor Blimber and his pupils, alternating with the quaint pathos
of its picture of little Paul; the first a good-natured exposure of the
forcing-system and its fruits, as useful as the sterner revelation in
Nickleby of the atrocities of Mr Squeers, and the last even less
attractive for the sweet sadness of its foreshadowing of a child's death,
than for those images of a vague, strange thoughtfulness, of a shrewd
unconscious intellect, of mysterious small philosophies and question-
ings, by which the young old-fashioned little creature has a glamour
thrown over him as he is passing away. It was wonderfully original,
this treatment of the part that thus preceded the close of Paul's little
life; and of which the first conception, as I have shown, was an
after-thought. It took the death itself out of the region of pathetic
commonplaces, and gave it the proper relation to the sorrow of the
little sister that survives it. It is a fairy vision to a piece of actual
suffering; a sorrow with heaven's hues upon it, to a sorrow with all the
bitterness of earth. . . .

. . . The incident has been told which soon after closed his residence
abroad, and what remained of his story was written in England.

I shall not farther dwell upon it in any detail. It extended over the
whole of the year; and the interest and passion of it, when both
became centred in Florence and in Edith Dombey, took stronger hold
of him than any of his previous writings, excepting only the close of
the *Old Curiosity Shop*. Jeffrey compared Florence to Little Nell, but the
differences from the outset are very marked, and it is rather in what
disunites or separates them that we seem to find the purpose in each.
If the one, amid much strange and grotesque violence surrounding
her, expresses the innocent unconsciousness of childhood to such
rough ways of the world, passing unscathed as Una to her home
beyond it, the other is this character in action and resistance, a brave

young resolute heart that will *not* be crushed, and neither sinks nor
yields, but works out her own redemption from earth's roughest trials.
Of Edith from the first Jeffrey judged more rightly; and, when the
story was nearly half done, expressed his opinion about her, and
about the book itself, in language that pleased Dickens for the special
reason that at the time this part of the book had seemed to many to
have fallen greatly short of the splendour of its opening. Jeffrey said
however quite truly, claiming to be heard with authority as his
'Critic-laureate', that of all his writings it was perhaps the most
finished in diction, and that it equalled the best in the delicacy and
fineness of its touches, 'while it rises to higher and deeper passions,
not resting, like most of the former, in sweet thoughtfulness and
thrilling and attractive tenderness, but boldly wielding all the lofty
and terrible elements of tragedy, and bringing before us the appalling
struggles of a proud, scornful, and repentant spirit'. Not that she was
exactly this, Edith's worst qualities are but the perversion of what
should have been her best. A false education in her, and a tyrant
passion in her husband, make them other than nature meant; and
both show how life may run its evil course against the higher
dispensations.

   . . . The end came; and, at the last moment when correction was
possible, this note arrived. 'I suddenly remember that I have
forgotten Diogenes. Will you put him in the last little chapter? After
the word "favourite" in reference to Miss Tox, you can add, "except
with Diogenes, who is growing old and wilful". Or, on the last page of
all, after "and with them two children: boy and girl" (I quote from
memory), you might say "and an old dog is generally in their
company", or to that effect. Just what you think best.'

   That was on Saturday the 25th of March, 1848, and may be my last
reference to *Dombey* until the book, in its place with the rest, finds
critical allusion when I close. . . .

Source: extracts from Forster's *The Life of Charles Dickens*
(1872–74): ch. 2 of Book iv.

2. CRITICAL APPRAISALS, 1882–1933

A. W. Ward   (1882)

'One of its author's most ambitious endeavours'

. . . *Dombey and Son* has, perhaps, been more criticised than any other
among the stories of its author; and yet it certainly is not the one
which has been least admired, or least loved. Dickens himself, in the
brief preface which he afterwards prefixed to the story, assumed a
half-defiant air which sits ill upon the most successful author, but
which occasionally he was tempted to assume. Before condescending
to defend the character of Mr Dombey as in accordance with both
probability and experience, he 'made so bold as to believe that the
faculty (or the habit) of correctly observing the characters of men is a
rare one'. Yet, though the drawing of this character is only one of the
points which have been objected against the story, not only did the
book at the time of publication far surpass its predecessor in
popularity, but it has, I believe, always preserved to itself a special
congregation of enthusiastic admirers. Manifestly, this novel is one of
its author's most ambitious endeavours. In it, more distinctly even
than in *Chuzzlewit*, he has chosen for his theme one of the chief vices of
human nature, and has striven to show what pride cannot achieve,
what it cannot conquer, what it cannot withstand. This central idea
gives to the story, throughout a most varied succession of scenes, a
unity of action to be found in few of Dickens's earlier works. On the
other hand, *Dombey and Son* shares with these earlier productions, and
with its successor, *David Copperfield*, the freshness of invention and
spontaneous flow of both humour and pathos which at times are
wanting in the more powerfully conceived and more carefully
constructed romances of Dickens's later years. If there be any force at
all in the common remark, that the most interesting part of the book
ends together with the life of little Paul, the censure falls upon the
whole design of the author. Little Paul, in something besides the
ordinary meaning of the words, was born to die; and though, like the
writer, most readers may have dreaded the hour which was to put an
end to that frail life, yet in this case there could be no question – such

as was possible in the story of Little Nell – of any other issue. Indeed, deep as is the pathos of the closing scene, its beauty is even surpassed by those which precede it. In death itself there is release for a child as for a man, and for those sitting by the pillow of the patient; but it is the gradual approach of death which seems hardest of all for the watchers to bear; it is the sinking of hope which seems even sadder than its extinction. What old fashion could that be, Paul wondered with a palpitating heart, that was so visibly expressed in him, so plainly seen by so many people? Every heart is softened and every eye dimmed, as the innocent child passes on his way to his grave. The hand of God's angel is on him; he is no longer altogether of this world. The imagination which could picture and present this mysterious haze of feeling, through which the narrative moves, half like a reality, half like a dream, is that of a true poet, and of a great one.

What even the loss of his son could not effect in Mr Dombey is to be accomplished in the progress of the story by a yet stronger agency than sorrow. His pride is to be humbled to the dust, where he is to be sought and raised up by the love of his despised and ill-used daughter. Upon the relations between this pair, accordingly, it was necessary for the author to expend the greatest care, and upon the treatment of those relations the criticism to which the character of Mr Dombey has been so largely subjected must substantially turn. The unfavourable judgements passed upon it have, in my opinion, not been altogether unjust. The problem obviously was to show how the father's cold indifference towards the daughter gradually becomes jealousy, as he finds that upon her is concentrated, first, the love of his innocent little son, and then that of his haughty second wife; and how hereupon this jealousy deepens into hate. But, unless we are to suppose that Mr Dombey hated his daughter from the first, the disfavour shown by him on her account to young Walter Gay remains without adequate explanation. His dislike of Florence is not manifestly founded upon his jealousy of what Mrs Chick calls her brother's 'infatuation' for her; and the main motives at work in the unhappy man are either not very skilfully kept asunder, or not very intelligibly intermixed. Nor are the later stages of the relations between father and daughter altogether satisfactorily conceived. The momentary yielding of Mr Dombey, after his 'coming home' with his new wife, is natural and touching; but his threat to visit his daughter with the consequences of her stepmother's conduct is sheer brutality. The passage in which Mr Dombey's ultimatum to Mrs Dombey is conveyed by him in her presence through a third person, is so artifical as to fall not very far short of absurdity. The closing scene which leads to the flight of Florence is undeniably powerful; but it is the development of the relations between the pair, in which the art of the author is in my judgement occasionally at fault.

As to the general effect of the latter part of the story – or rather of its main plot – which again has been condemned as melodramatic and unnatural, a distinction should be drawn between its incidents and its characters. Neither Edith Dombey nor Mr Carker is a character of real life. The pride of the former comes very near to bad breeding, and her lapses into sentiment seem artificial lapses. How differently Thackeray would have managed the 'high words' between her and her frivolous mother; how differently, for that matter, he *has* managed a not altogether dissimilar scene in the *Newcomes* between Ethel Newcome and old Lady Kew! As for Mr Carker, with his white teeth and glistening gums, who calls his unhappy brother 'Spaniel', and contemplates a life of sensual ease in Sicily, he has the semi-reality of the stage. Possibly, the French stage had helped to suggest the *scène de la pièce* between the fugitives at Dijon – an effective situation, but one which many a novelist might have worked out not less skilfully than Dickens. His own master-hand, however, reasserts itself in the wondrously powerful narrative of Carker's flight and death. Here again, he excites terror – as in the same book he had evoked pity – by foreshadowing, without prematurely revealing, the end. We know what the morning is to bring which rises in awful tranquillity over the victim of his own sins; and, as in Turner's wild but powerful picture, the engine made by the hand of man for peaceful purposes seems a living agent of wrath.[1]

No other of Dickens's books is more abundantly stocked than this with genuinely comic characters; but nearly all of them, in accordance with the pathetic tone which is struck at the outset, and which never dies out till the story has run its course, are in a more subdued strain of humour. Lord Jeffrey was, I think, warranted in his astonishment that Dickens should devote so much pains to characters like Mrs Chick and Miss Tox; probably the habit remained with him from his earliest times of authorship, when he had not always distinguished very accurately between the humorous and the *bizarre*. But Polly and the Toodles household, Mrs Pipchin and her 'select infantine boarding-house', and the whole of Doctor Blimber's establishment, from the Doctor himself down to Mr Toots, and up again, in the scale of intellect, to Mr Feeder, B.A., are among the most admirable of all the great humourist's creations. Against this ample provision for her poor little brother's nursing and training Florence has to set but her one Susan Nipper; but she is a host in herself, an absolutely original character among the thousands of *soubrettes* that are known to comedy and fiction, and one of the best tonic mixtures ever composed out of much humour and not a few grains of pathos. Her tartness has a cooling flavour of its own; but it is the Mrs Pipchinses only upon whom she acts, as their type acted upon her, 'like early gooseberries'. Of course she has a favourite figure of speech belonging to herself, which rhetoricians would probably class among the figures 'working by surplusage':

'Your Toxes and your Chickses may draw out my two front double teeth, Mrs Richards, but that's no reason why I need offer 'em the whole set.'

Dickens was to fall very largely into this habit of 'labelling' his characters, as it has been called, by particular tricks or terms of speech; and there is a certain excess in this direction already in *Dombey and Son*, where not only Miss Nipper and Captain Cuttle and Mr Toots, but Major Bagstock too and Cousin Feenix, are thus furnished forth. But the invention is still so fresh and the play of humour so varied, that this mannerism cannot be said as yet seriously to disturb them. A romantic charm of a peculiar kind clings to honest Captain Cuttle and the quaint home over which he mounts guard during the absence of its owner. The nautical colouring and concomitant fun apart — for only Smollett could have drawn Jack Bunsby's fellow, though the character in his hands would have been differently accentuated — Dickens has never approached more nearly to the manner of Sir Walter Scott than in this singularly attractive part of his book. Elsewhere the story passes into that sphere of society in describing which Dickens was, as a novelist, rarely very successful. But though Edith is cold and unreal, there is, it cannot be denied, human nature in the pigments and figments of her hideous old mother; and, to outward appearance at all events, the counterparts of her apoplectic admirer, Major Bagstock, still pace those pavements and promenades which it suits them to frequent. Cousin Feenix is likewise very far from impossible, and is besides extremely delightful — and a good fellow too at bottom, so that the sting of the satire is here taken away. On the other hand, the meeting between the *sacs et parchemins*[2] at Mr Dombey's house is quite out of focus.

The book has other heights and depths, and pleasant and unpleasant parts and passages. But enough has been said to recall the exuberant creative force, and the marvellous strength of pathos and humour which *Dombey and Son* proves that Dickens, now near the very height of his powers as a writer of fiction, possessed. In one of his public readings many years afterwards, when he was reciting the adventures of Little Dombey, he narrates that 'a very good fellow', whom he noticed in the stalls, could not refrain from wiping the tears out of his eyes as often as he thought that Toots was coming on. And

just as Toots had become a reality to this good fellow, so Toots and
Toots's little friend, and divers other personages in this story, have
become realities to half the world that reads the English tongue, and
to many besides. What higher praise could be given to this wonderful
book? Of all the works of its author none has more powerfully and
more permanently taken hold of the imagination of its readers.
Though he conjured up only pictures familiar to us from the aspect of
our own streets and our own homes, he too wielded a wizard's wand.

SOURCE: extract from Ward's *Charles Dickens*, 'English Men of
Letters' series, (London, 1882), pp. 77–83.

NOTES

1. [Ed.] Ward points out in a note that Dickens 'had a strong sense of what
I may call the poetry of the railway train'. His reference to Turner is to the
painting 'Rain, Steam and Speed', exhibited at the Royal Academy in 1844 –
a little before the composition of *Dombey and Son*.

2. [Ed.] *sacs et parchemins*: the term may be glossed as 'moneyed people and
people of rank'. It appears as the title of a novel by Jules Sandeau (Paris,
1855), and would seem to have passed from that into more general currency.
(I am grateful for this information to Dr Tony James of the French
Department, University of Manchester.)

George Gissing   (1900)

'The "sacred simplicity" of Dickens'

I

'Dealings with the Firm of Dombey and Son, Wholesale, Retail, and
for Exportation' – thus was the book originally entitled – came out in
the familiar monthly parts, with illustrations by Hablot K. Browne,
from October 1846 to April 1848. Its success was immediate, and
great beyond expectation. Since the close of *Martin Chuzzlewit*
(commercially a disappointment) more than two years had elapsed,
Dickens's only publication meanwhile having been the *Christmas
Carol*; he had refreshed himself with a long sojourn in Italy (which,
oddly to our ears, he speaks of in a letter as likely to heighten his

prestige with the public) and turned once more to the composition of a long novel with that gusto which was an essential feature of his genius.

Dombey was begun at Lausanne, continued at Paris, completed in London, and at English seaside places; whilst the early parts were being written, a Christmas story, *The Battle of Life*, was also in hand, and Dickens found it troublesome to manage both together. That he overcame the difficulty – that, soon after, we find him travelling about England as member of an amateur dramatic company – that he undertook all sorts of public engagements and often devoted himself to private festivity – *Dombey* going on the while, from month to month – is matter enough for astonishment to those who know anything about artistic production. But such marvels become commonplaces in the life of Charles Dickens.

The moral theme of this book was Pride – pride of wealth, pride of place, personal arrogance. Dickens started with a clear conception of his central character and of the course of the story in so far as it depended upon that personage; he planned the action, the play of motive, with unusual definiteness, and adhered very closely in the working to this well-laid scheme; nevertheless, *Dombey and Son* is a novel which in its beginning promises more than its progress fulfils. Impossible to avoid the reflection that the death of Dombey's son and heir marks the end of a complete story, that we feel a gap between chapter 16 and what comes after (the author speaks of feeling it himself, of his striving to 'transfer the interest to Florence') and that the narrative of the later part is ill-constructed, often wearisome, sometimes incredible. We miss Paul, we miss Walter Gay (shadowy young hero though he be); Florence is too colourless for deep interest, and the second Mrs Dombey is rather forced upon us than accepted as a natural figure in the drama. Dickens's familiar shortcomings are abundantly exemplified. He is wholly incapable of devising a plausible intrigue, and shocks the reader with monstrous improbabilities such as all that portion of the dénouement in which old Mrs Brown and her daughter are concerned. A favourite device with him (often employed with picturesque effect) was to bring into contact persons representing widely severed social ranks; in this book the 'effect' depends too often on 'incidences of the boldest artificiality', as nearly always we end by neglecting the story as a story, and surrendering ourselves to the charm of certain parts, the fascination of certain characters.

It was unfortunate that Dickens planned his book to illustrate a passion – for the treatment of passion does not come within his scope. Compare his personages meant to be vehement with the like in Balzac; the difference is that between a drawing of Michael Angelo and one by Fuseli. Mr Dombey himself is consistently presented, but we regard him as an actor rather than a human being. Still more decidedly is this the case with Carker, whose deeds proclaim him an automaton, and with Edith, who has her place beside several other would-be haughty women in the other novels. In this parallel of aristocratic Mrs Skewton and her daughter with plebeian Mrs Brown and *her* daughter we note a happy conception, but neither of the younger women is convincingly drawn, and as for Alice Marwood, she is perhaps the most stagey figure in all Dickens; chapter 34, a scene between Alice and her mother, I take to be the worst he ever wrote.

Thus, as a satire on Pride, the book is not very effective. Contrast the life of Mr Dombey and his polite acquaintances with that which goes on below-stairs in Mr Dombey's house; in the one case we have conscientious labour, never quite successful in vitalising its subjects; in the other, the work of an artist with full command of his material. It is easy, and not much to the purpose, to disparage Dickens when he deals with the Dombey group by pointing to the masterpieces of Thackeray; these great writers differ widely in method and intention; each must be judged by the standard of achievement in his best work, and we need say no more than that Dickens is not seen at his happiest in certain parts of a novel which, for all that, remains a wonder and a delight. In one instance his reproofs and worldliness find adequate artistic expression; the death of Mrs Skewton is an excellent piece of grisly realism. Throughout, indeed, the picture of this decayed woman of fashion is more striking than that of her low-life parallel, Mrs Brown; and, after all objections, Mrs Skewton's daughter comes much nearer to the likeness of a real woman than the fierce castaway, Alice Marwood.

The fact of the matter is that Dickens fails in certain of his upper-class portraitures not, first and foremost, because that class is unfamiliar to his imagination, but rather because he had chosen types of character which his art finds uncongenial. He can fail just as decidedly in a picture from the humble world, when misled by the unfortunate hankering after lofty or violent passion. Dickens had not the tragic gift; with the possible exception of Sidney Carton, his novels present no figure which belongs in the true sense of the word to tragedy. What he can, and does often, excel in is the wildly or grimly picturesque – a totally different thing. Note how, in his efforts to give life to Mr and Mrs Dombey, where they are in fierce silent conflict, he falls into the rhetorical mood, and occasionally preaches at the reader for whole pages – a fault never so marked in his other novels. He is not given to 'analysis'; it is his merit that he makes us see and know his people directly, rarely endeavouring to dissect their minds for us. But turn to the opening pages of chapter 47, where one comes upon long paragraphs beginning with 'Alas!' and 'Oh!' and punctuated with notes of exclamation; it is Dickens woefully astray, so possessed with the need of emphasising what he has to show us (and ought to be content merely to show us) that his writing-desk becomes a pulpit, and is soundly thumped. As an example of how he progressed in his art, think of that lofty personage in a later novel, Sir Leicester Dedlock; from every point of view better work than Mr Dombey, and unspoilt by rhetorical excesses. Dickens was still engaged on refractory material, trying to attain what was beyond his limits; but we see clearly enough in Sir Leicester that it is character, not social position, which offers the stumbling-block.

II

It has become the fashion to sneer at Dickens's pathos, and the death of little Paul is commonly mentioned as an example of intolerable mawkishness. That the story is at this point too long drawn out everyone must admit; it was one of the unhappy results of a method of publication for which no good word can be said; but to some readers, not wholly uncritical, the child's deathbed is still genuinely pathetic, though they cannot speak of it in the terms of excited eulogy which flattered the author's ears. Paul Dombey is a picture of childhood such as only Dickens could draw; abounding in observation, enriched with imaginative sympathy; a thing very touching and tender. Remember, too, that, in the 'forties, such a picture as this was a national benefaction; England sadly needed awakening to her responsibilities in the matter of childhood, and who shall say how great an influence for good was exercised by Charles Dickens in his constant preoccupation with children, their sufferings, their education, their claims of every kind. Poor little Paul is crushed by a system of ignorant selfishness. Impossible to depict more skilfully the sorrows of an exceptionally gifted child ground in the mill of what was understood to be instruction; the appeal to our compassion, our indignation, is irresistible. As in writing of 'Little Nell', the writer somewhat lost control of himself; tears blurred his view of artistic proportion. So often has the effect been aimed at by subsequent novelists that it is grown a weariness, and is too often an obvious insincerity; we are apt to forget that Dickens imitated no one, that he spoke from his heart at the prompting of his genius. The thing has perhaps been more artistically done; never with truer emotion or gentler touch.

A review of all the scholastic persons in Dickens's novels would be very interesting and of historical value. Grant the 'exaggeration' which is inseparable from his methods (exaggeration is no vulgar sense, and far oftener an artistic merit than a defect), these masters and instructors represent very truly the state of middle-class education in early-Victorian days. That the author of *Nicholas Nickleby* must be credited with a share in the abolition of many a Dotheboys Hall has long been recognised, but his influence on public opinion as to the whole subject of teaching was probably much greater than is supposed. Dr Blimber's establishment is a well-chosen example of the private school for young gentlemen which survives in the memories of gentlemen at present neither young nor old; it has no connection whatever with Dotheboys; externally, it promises very well indeed, and only when we see its educational system at work do we become aware that nothing is taught here, nothing learnt. The education presumed to be given is 'classical'. Dickens himself, whose boyhood knew little or nothing of Greek and Latin, had a strong prejudice against the 'classics'; their true value he was not capable of appreciating, and his common sense told him that, as used in the average middle-class school, they were worse than valueless – the cover for every kind of inefficiency. Miss Blimber, a thoroughly conscientious person, was 'dry and sandy with working in the graves of deceased languages. None of your live languages for Miss Blimber. They must be dead – stone dead – and then Miss Blimber dug them up like a ghoul.' Mr Feeder, rejoicing in the degree of B.A., was 'a kind of human barrel-organ, with a little list of tunes at which he was continually working, over and over again, without any variation'. Contemporary readers made merry over the Blimber establishment; this was the veritable Dickens, greatest of sparkling jesters; but after merriment came reflection, and we may feel assured that many an English paterfamilias, who gave his opinion in favour of modern against ancient, and helped on the new spirit in matters educational, was more or less consciously influenced by the reading of *Dombey and Son*. Great is the achievement of a public man who supplies his audience with the picture that abides, the catch word unforgettable, and Dickens many a time did so. It is the picture and the catch-word, not reason or rhetoric, that effect reform.

III

Passing to the lighter features of the book, we see Dickens at his best in a large group of whimsical characters – figures not satirical (or not primarily so), but depicted for mere love of quaint humanity. And let

it be noted that not the least successful of these portraits is that of
Cousin Feenix, an aristocrat. Cousin Feenix is weak at the knees, and
anything but strong intellectually; doubtless he implies a good-
humoured joke at the expense of an 'effete' order; but, as we come to
know the man, we like and even respect him. Morally there is much to
be said for Cousin Feenix; he has fine sensibilities; his talk is always
entertaining, and often profitable. In the last chapter but one he plays
a delightful part; indeed, his appearance and behaviour make this
chapter one of the pleasantest of all. The absurd charge against
Dickens that he cannot represent a 'gentleman' is refuted by several
instances, and certainly Cousin Feenix must be numbered amongst
them.

Major Bagstock is, of course, not meant to be a gentleman; he
makes very good fun, however, and serves richly as a foil to 'our friend
Dombey'. Pungent is the irony in this juxtaposition of the overweening City merchant and the military vulgarian of social pretensions; as
we watch them go arm in arm, we feel Mr Dombey more living than
on most occasions. Miss Tox and Mrs Chick are well contrasted, a
contrast which helps us to sympathise with the angular maiden lady.
Better still are Mrs Pipchin and Miss Nipper. Were Florence Dombey
anything like so well depicted as her maid, the story, as a story, would
greatly profit by it; but Florence is merely a good girl of gentle
breeding, as difficult a subject as any novelist can undertake, and very
rarely (one thinks first of Mrs Gaskell) done with complete success;
whereas Susan Nipper is a young person after Dickens's heart, in her
habits of speech suggesting a shrill feminine echo of Sam Weller, and
morally a pattern of all virtues, all the proprieties. She does not belong
to the gallery of shrewish women; we feel her capable of outgrowing
her 'snappish' tendencies, and of becoming an excellent wife (guardian, one might say) to the egregious Mr Toots.

Toots himself is a figure of farce, and at moments we see just a little
too much of him. To be sure, the farce is good, so is that in which Jack
Bunsby plays his part; better was never written than the scene
exhibiting the matrimonial triumph of Mrs MacStinger. Dickens
throws himself into drollery such as this with extraordinary enjoyment. Read the passage (ch. 60) beginning 'While the Reverend
Melchisedech was offering up extemporary orisons', and when
laughter allows you to examine it critically, admire the dramatic
quality of that hurried dialogue between Jack and the Captain. Farce,
but of the finest, not a word too much, and every word telling of
hilarity. And if you would see how Dickens's broadest mirth can melt
into kindliest feeling, read on to the end of the chapter, through the
little scene between Mrs Toots and Florence, with the epilogue

spoken by Mrs Toots's husband; this was the kind of thing that made Dickens as much loved as admired; I cannot class myself with those who nowadays smile at it aloof.

Captain Cuttle has a larger humanity than his roaring friend, he is the creation of humour. That the Captain suffered dire things at the hands of Mrs MacStinger is as credible as it is amusing, but he stood in no danger of Bunsby's fate; at times he can play his part in a situation purely farcical, but the man himself moves on a higher level. He is one of the most familiar to us among Dickens's characters, an instance of the novelist's supreme power, which (I like to repeat) proves itself in the bodying forth of a human personality henceforth accepted by the world. His sentences have become proverbs; the mention of his name brings before the mind's eye an image of flesh and blood – rude, tending to the grotesque, but altogether lovable. Captain Cuttle belongs to the world of Uncle Toby,[1] with, to be sure, a subordinate position. Analyse him as you will, make the most of those extravagances which pedants of to-day cannot away with, and in the end you will still be face to face with something vital – explicable only as the product of genius.

Consider the Captain as he appears in chapter 49, one of the most delightful in English fiction. Florence Dombey, fleeing from her desecrated home, has taken refuge in the queer old house with the sign of the Midshipman, is living there under the guardianship of the tough and tender old seaman. With what infinite charm of fancy is this picture set before us! With what command of happy illusion are we reconciled to so many improbabilities! 'A wandering princess and a good monster in a story-book might have sat by the fireside and talked as Captain Cuttle and poor Florence talked.' Precisely, our novel is become a sort of fairy-tale; and for all that, we suffer no shock, no canon of arts is outraged. Dickens's art is consistent with itself. And arts mean illusion, in different degrees, of various kinds.

'In simple innocence of the world's ways and the world's perplex-ities and dangers, they were nearly on a level.' It is in this sacred simplicity that Dickens above all delights; this it is that makes him akin to Oliver Goldsmith and to the better part of Sterne. Florence and the Captain, as they sit together by the fireside, are enveloped in the atmosphere of homeliness, which, to our English thought, favours every form of moral good. Oddity and homeliness – these are the notes of Dickens at his best. For another instance of their combination, turn to the scene of Mr Toodle in the bosom of his family in chapter 38. Many such scenes of humble domesticity occur in Dickens, and once or twice it happens that his sympathy with the poor a little outweighs his judgement; but his Toodle household is safe from any such censure. One of its members, Rob the Grinder, is nothing more or less than a young scamp; probably born so, and with all his scampish propensities developed by a bringing up at the hands of the worst kind of 'charity'. Rob's backslidings and repentings, his periodical affection for the good mother who weeps over him, his proclivity to lying, his greediness and thievishness make, from one point of view, the most truthful picture of London boyhood to be found in Dickens's pages. One thinks of crossing-sweeper Jo and regrets that lost opportunity; but for the allurements of melodrama, Jo and Rob might have made such an admirable pair of young rascals, each after his kind.

IV

The 'realist' in fiction says to himself: Given such and such circumstances, what would be the probable issue? Dickens, on the other hand, was wont to ask: What would be the pleasant issue? Several times during the composition of this novel he consulted with Forster as to the feeling of his readers about some proposed incident or episode; not that he feared, in any ignoble sense, to offend his public, but because his view of art involved compliance with ideals of ordinary simple folk. He held that view as a matter of course. Quite recently it has been put forth with prophetic fervour by Tolstoy, who cites Dickens among the few novelists whose work will bear this test. An instinctive sympathy with the moral (and therefore the artistic) prejudices of the everyday man guided Dickens throughout his career, teaching him when, and how far, he might strike at things he thought evil, yet never defeat his prime purpose of sending forth fiction acceptable to the multitude. Himself, in all but his genius, a representative Englishman of the middle-class, he was able to achieve this task with unfailing zeal and with entire sincerity.

The aim of fiction, as Dickens saw it, was to amuse, to elevate, and finally to calm. When his evil-doers have been got rid of, he delights in apportioning quiet happiness to every character in the novel beloved by him and his readers. Forster tells a story about the close of *Dombey and Son*, which amusingly illustrates this desire to omit no sympathetic actor from the final benediction. 'I suddenly remember', wrote Dickens to his friend, who was correcting the proofs for him, 'that I have forgotten Diogenes. Will you put him in the last little chapter?' Diogenes was but a dog, yet Dickens could not bear to close the book without mention of him, and accordingly we read that when the white-haired Mr Dombey and his wedded daughter, with her children, walk on the sea beach, 'an old dog is generally in their company'. A light touch to the completed picture, but thoroughly characteristic of the artist's spirit and method.

SOURCE: 'Introduction' to the Rochester Edition of the novel (London, 1900); reprinted in George Gissing, *The Immortal Dickens*, (London, 1925), pp. 140–63.

NOTE

1. [Ed.] The 'Uncle Toby' of Sterne's *Tristram Shandy*.

G. K. Chesterton   (1907)

'An advance in art and unity'

In Dickens's literary life *Dombey and Son* represents a break so important as to necessitate our casting back to a summary and a generalisation. . . . [The] first of these breaks in Dickens may be placed at the point when he wrote *Nicholas Nickleby*. This was his first serious decision to be a novelist in any sense at all, to be anything except a maker of momentary farces. The second break, and that a far more important break, is in *Dombey and Son*. This marks his final resolution to be a novelist and nothing else, to be a serious constructor of fiction in the serious sense. Before *Dombey and Son* even his pathos had been really frivolous. After *Dombey and Son* even his absurdity was intentional and grave.

In case this transition is not understood, one or two tests may be taken at random. The episodes in *Dombey and Son*, the episodes in *David Copperfield*, which came after it, are no longer episodes merely stuck into the middle of the story without any connection with it, like most of the episodes in *Nicholas Nickleby*, or most of the episodes even in *Martin Chuzzlewit*. Take, for instance, by way of a mere coincidence, the fact that three schools for boys are described successively in *Nicholas Nickleby*, in *Dombey and Son* and in *David Copperfield*. But the difference is enormous. Dotheboys Hall does not exist to tell us anything about Nicholas Nickleby. Rather Nicholas Nickleby exists entirely in order to tell us about Dotheboys Hall. It does not in any way affect his history or psychology; he enters Mr Squeers's school

and leaves Mr Squeers's school with the same character, or rather
absence of character. It is a mere episode, existing for itself. But when
little Paul Dombey goes to an old-fashioned but kindly school, it is in a
very different sense and for a very different reason from that for which
Nicholas Nickleby goes to an old-fashioned and cruel school. The
sending of little Paul to Dr Blimber's is a real part of the history of
little Paul, such as it is. Dickens deliberately invents all that elderly
pedantry in order to show up Paul's childishness. Dickens deliberately invents all that rather heavy kindness in order to show up Paul's
predestination and tragedy. Dotheboys Hall is not meant to show up
anything except Dotheboys Hall. But although Dickens doubtless
enjoyed Dr Blimber quite as much as Mr Squeers, it remains true that
Dr Blimber is really a very good foil to Paul; whereas Squeers is not a
foil to Nicholas; Nicholas is merely a lame excuse for Squeers. The
change can be seen continued in the school, or rather the two schools,
to which David Copperfield goes. The whole idea of David Copperfield's life is that he had the dregs of life before the wine of it. He knew
the worst of the world before he knew the best of it. His childhood at
Dr Strong's is a second childhood. Now for this purpose the two
schools are perfectly well adapted. Mr Creakle's school is not only,
like Mr Squeers's school, a bad school, it is a bad influence upon
David Copperfield. Dr Strong's school is not only a good school, it is a
good influence upon David Copperfield. I have taken this case of the
schools as a case casual but concrete. The same, however, can be seen
in any of the groups or incidents of the novels on both sides of the
boundary. Mr Crummles's theatrical company is only a society that
Nicholas happens to fall into. America is only a place to which Martin
Chuzzlewit happens to go. These things are isolated sketches, and
nothing else. Even Todgers's boarding-house is only a place where
Mr Pecksniff can be delightfully hypocritical. It is not a place which
throws any new light on Mr Pecksniff's hypocrisy. But the case is
different with that more subtle hypocrite in *Dombey and Son* – I mean
Major Bagstock. Dickens does mean it as a deliberate light on Mr
Dombey's character that he basks with a fatuous calm in the blazing
sun of Major Bagstock's tropical and offensive flattery. Here, then, is
the essence of the change. He not only wishes to write a novel; this he
did as early as *Nicholas Nickleby*. He wishes to have as little as possible
in the novel that does not really assist it as a novel. Previously he had
asked with the assistance of what incidents could his hero wander
farther and farther from the pathway. Now he has really begun to ask
with the assistance of what incidents his hero can get nearer and
nearer to the goal.

The change made Dickens a greater novelist. I am not sure that it

made him a greater man. One good character by Dickens requires all
eternity to stretch its legs in; and the characters in his later books are
always being tripped up by some tiresome nonsense about the story.
For instance, in *Dombey and Son*, Mrs Skewton is really very funny. But
nobody with a love of the real smell of Dickens would compare her for
a moment, for instance, with Mrs Nickleby. And the reason of Mrs
Skewton's inferiority is simply this, that she has something to do in
the plot; she has to entrap or assist to entrap Mr Dombey into
marrying Edith. Mrs Nickleby, on the other hand, has nothing at all
to do in the story, except to get in everybody's way. The consequence
is that we complain not of her for getting in everyone's way, but of
everyone for getting in hers. What are suns and stars, what are times
and seasons, what is the mere universe, that it should presume to
interrupt Mrs Nickleby? Mrs Skewton (though supposed, of course,
to be a much viler sort of woman) has something of the same quality of
splendid and startling irrelevancy. In her also there is the same feeling
of wild threads hung from world to world like the webs of gigantic
spiders; of things connected that seem to have no connection save by
this one adventurous filament of frail and daring folly. Nothing could
be better than Mrs Skewton when she finds herself, after convolutions
of speech, somehow on the subject of Henry VIII., and pauses to
mention with approval 'his dear little peepy eyes and his benevolent
chin'. Nothing could be better than her attempt at Mahomedan
resignation when she feels almost inclined to say 'that there is no
What's-his-name but Thingummy, and What-you-may-call-it is his
prophet!' But she has not so much time as Mrs Nickleby to say these
good things; also she has not sufficient human virtue to say them
constantly. She is always intent upon her worldly plans, among other
things upon the worldly plan of assisting Charles Dickens to get a story
finished. She is always 'advancing her shrivelled ear' to listen to what
Dombey is saying to Edith. Worldliness is the most solemn thing in
the world; it is far more solemn than other-worldliness. Mrs Nickleby
can afford to ramble as a child does in a field, or as a child does to
laugh at nothing, for she is like a child, innocent. It is only the good
who can afford to be frivolous.

Broadly speaking, what is said here of Mrs Skewton applies to the
great part of *Dombey and Son*, even to the comic part of it. It shows an
advance in art and unity; it does not show an advance in genius and
creation. In some cases, in fact, I cannot help feeling that it shows a
falling off. It may be a personal idiosyncrasy, but there is only one
comic character really prominent in Dickens, upon whom Dickens
has really lavished the wealth of his invention, and who does not
amuse me at all, and that character is Captain Cuttle. But three great

exceptions must be made to any such disparagment of *Dombey and Son*.
They are all three of that royal order in Dickens's creation which can
no more be described or criticised than strong wine. The first is Major
Bagstock, the second is Cousin Feenix, the third is Toots. In Bagstock
Dickens has blasted for ever that type which pretends to be sincere by
the simple operation of being explosively obvious. He tells about a
quarter of the truth, and then poses as truthful because a quarter of
the truth is much simpler than the whole of it. He is the kind of man
who goes about with posers for Bishops or for Socialists, with plain
questions to which he wants a plain answer. His questions are plain
only in the same sense that he himself is plain – in the sense of being
uncommonly ugly. He is the man who always bursts with satisfaction
because he can call a spade a spade, as if there were any kind of logical
or philosophical use in merely saying the same word twice over. He is
the man who wants things down in black and white, as if black and
white were the only two colours; as if blue and green and red and gold
were not facts of the universe. He is too selfish to tell the truth and too
impatient even to hear it. He cannot endure the truth, because it is
subtle. This man is almost always like Bagstock – a sycophant and a
toad-eater. A man is not any the less a toad-eater because he eats his
toads with a huge appetite and gobbles them up, as Bagstock did his
breakfast, with the eyes starting out of his purple face. He flatters
brutally. He cringes with a swagger. And men of the world like
Dombey are always taken in by him, because men of the world are
probably the simplest of all the children of Adam.

Cousin Feenix again is an exquisite suggestion, with his rickety
chivalry and rambling compliments. It was about the period of
Dombey and Son that Dickens began to be taken up by good society.
(One can use only vulgar terms for an essentially vulgar process.)
And his sketches of the man of good family in the books of this period
show that he had had glimpses of what that singular world is like. The
aristocrats in his earliest books are simply dragons and griffins for his
heroes to fight with – monsters like Sir Mulberry Hawk or Lord
Verisopht. They are merely created upon the old principle, that your
scoundrel must be polite and powerful – a very sound principle. The
villain must be not only a villain, but a tyrant. The giant must be
larger than Jack. But in the books of the Dombey period we have
many shrewd glimpses of the queer realities of English aristocracy. Of
these Cousin Feenix is one of the best. Cousin Feenix is a much better
sketch of the essentially decent and chivalrous aristocrat than Sir
Leicester Dedlock. Both of the men are, if you will, fools, as both are
honourable gentlemen. But if one may attempt a classification among
fools, Sir Leicester Dedlock is a stupid fool, while Cousin Feenix is a

silly fool – which is much better. The difference is that the silly fool has a folly which is always on the borderland of wit, and even of wisdom; his wandering wits come often upon undiscovered truths. The stupid fool is as consistent and as homogeneous as wood; he is as invincible as the ancestral darkness. Cousin Feenix is a good sketch of the sort of well-bred old ass who is so fundamentally genuine that he is always saying very true things by accident. His whole tone also, though exaggerated like everything in Dickens, is very true to the bewildered good nature which marks English aristocratic life. The statement that Dickens could not describe a gentleman is, like most popular animadversions against Dickens, so very thin and one-sided a truth as to be for serious purposes a falsehood. When people say that Dickens could not describe a gentleman, what they mean is this, and so far what they mean is true. They mean that Dickens could not describe a gentleman as gentlemen feel a gentleman. They mean that he could not take that atmosphere easily, accept it as the normal atmosphere, or describe that world from the inside. This is true. . . . Dickens did not describe gentlemen in the way that gentlemen describe gentlemen. He described them in the way in which he described waiters, or railway guards, or men drawing with chalk on the pavement. He described them, in short (and this we may freely concede), from the outside, as he described any other oddity or special trade. But when it comes to saying that he did not describe them well, then that is quite another matter, and that I should emphatically deny. The things that are really odd about the English upper class he saw with startling promptitude and penetration, and if the English upper class does not see these odd things in itself, it is not because they are not there, but because we are all blind to our own oddities; . . . I have often heard a dear old English oligarch say that Dickens could not describe a gentleman, while every note of his own voice and turn of his own hand recalled Sir Leicester Dedlock. I have often been told by some old buck that Dickens could not describe a gentleman, and been told so in the shaky voice and with all the vague allusiveness of Cousin Feenix.

Cousin Feenix has really many of the main points of the class that governs England. Take, for an instance, his hazy notion that he is in a world where everybody knows everybody; whenever he mentions a man, it is a man 'with whom my friend Dombey is no doubt acquainted'. That pierces to the very helpless soul of aristocracy. Take again the stupendous gravity with which he leads up to a joke. That is the very soul of the House of Commons and the Cabinet, of the high-class English politics, where a joke is always enjoyed solemnly. Take his insistence upon the technique of Parliament, his regrets for the time when the rules of debate were perhaps better observed than

they are now. Take that wonderful mixture in him (which is the real
human virtue of our aristocracy) of a fair amount of personal modesty
with an innocent assumption of rank. Of a man who saw all these
genteel foibles so clearly it is absurd merely to say without further
explanation that he could not describe a gentleman. Let us confine
ourselves to saying that he did not describe a gentleman as gentlemen
like to be described.

Lastly, there is the admirable study of Toots, who may be
considered as being in some ways the masterpiece of Dickens.
Nowhere else did Dickens express with such astonishing insight and
truth his main contention, which is that to be good and idiotic is not a
poor fate, but, on the contrary, an experience of primeval innocence,
which wonders at all things. Dickens did not know, any more than
any great man ever knows, what was the particular thing that he had
to preach. He did not know it; he only preached it. But the particular
thing that he had to preach was this: That humility is the only
possible basis of enjoyment; that if one has no other way of being
humble except being poor, then it is better to be poor, and to enjoy;
that if one has no other way of being humble except being imbecile,
then it is better to be imbecile, and to enjoy. That is the deep
unconscious truth in the character of Toots – that all his externals are
flashy and false; all his internals unconscious, obscure, and true. He
wears loud clothes, and is silent inside them. His shirts and waistcoats
are covered with bright spots of pink and purple, while his soul is
always covered with the sacred shame. He always gets all the outside
things of life wrong, and all the inside things right. He always admires
the right Christian people, and gives them the wrong Christian
names. Dimly connecting Captain Cuttle with the shop of Mr
Solomon Gills, he always addresses the astonished mariner as
'Captain Gills'. He turns Mr Walter Gay, by a most improving
transformation, into 'Lieutenant Walters'. But he always knows
which people upon his own principles to admire. He forgets who they
are, but he remembers what they are. With the clear eyes of humility
he perceives the whole world as it is. He respects the Game Chicken
for being strong, as even the Game Chicken ought to be respected for
being strong. He respects Florence for being good, as even Florence
ought to be respected for being good. And he has no doubt about
which he admires most; he prefers goodness to strength, as do all
masculine men. It is through the eyes of such characters as Toots that
Dickens really sees the whole of his tales. For even if one calls him a
half-wit, it still makes a difference that he keeps the right half of his
wits. When we think of the unclean and craven spirit in which Toots
might be treated in a psychological novel of to-day; how he might

walk with a mooncalf face, and a brain of bestial darkness, the soul rises in real homage to Dickens for showing how much simple gratitude and happiness can remain in the lopped roots of the most simplified intelligence. If scientists must treat a man as a dog, it need not be always as a mad dog. They might grant him, like Toots, a little of the dog's loyalty and the dog's reward.

SOURCE: 'Introduction' to the Everyman Edition of the novel (London, 1907); reprinted in G. K. Chesterton, *Appreciations and Criticisms of Charles Dickens's Works* (London, 1911).

Stephen Leacock   (1933)

'The Death of Paul Dombey'

. . . the outstanding and remembered thing in *Dombey and Son* is the sweet and marvellous pictures of little Paul and the infinite pathos of his death. It is doubtful if we would write such things now, even if we could. The literature of every age and time has its peculiar conventions, its peculiar limitations. We do not, in our time, set down extended and harrowing pictures of physical torture; minute and accurate descriptions of the ravages of a loathsome disease. The fact that these things exist is no necessary justification for writing of them. And so it is doubtful at least whether a writer of to-day, even if he had the requisite literary power, would use it to call forth the agony of suffering involved in the last illness and the death scene of a little child. It is a cup that we would put from our lips.

But in the Victorian age it was different. The expression of sentiment over the common sorrows of life was still a new thing in literature; Shakespeare wrote of kings: Milton of hell: and Scott of the Middle Ages. It remained for the nineteenth century to break into a flood of tears over its own suffering. Scholars, who contradict everything, will deny this – their eyes can only peer at exceptions and never open to general truths. No wonder that in the exuberance of this new feeling, the current of this new stream, sentiment was washed into sentimentality. Again and again one feels that Dickens and his readers enjoy their tears. 'Come', said someone once in speaking to his disparagement, 'let us sit down and have a good cry.'

Over a lesser or a trivial object the tears become maudlin or even comic. To what extent are we to go when the occasion as depicted is real, is overwhelming. Take as the supreme example in literature the death of little Paul Dombey. Dickens spares us none of it, – the long-drawn illness of the little child, fading beside the sea: the waves that sing to the little mind already wandering away; the final illness; the sunlit room, the whispered murmur of farewell, and the unutterable end.

The public of the day read the book, shall we say enjoyed the book, in a flood of tears. 'I have cried and sobbed over it last night', wrote Lord Jeffrey, 'and again and again this morning; and felt my heart purified by those tears and blessed and loved you for making me shed them: and I never can bless and love you enough. Since the divine Nellie was found dead on her humble couch, beneath the snow and the ivy, there has been nothing like the actual dying of that sweet Paul in the summer sunshine of that lofty room.'

What are we to think of all this? Is this manly, or is it mawkish? Or what?

Dickens himself had written the chapter in a very agony of grief. Indeed he seems to have carried in his heart ever afterwards a sorrowing memory of little Paul. When he wrote some ten years later a preface for the first cheap edition of *Dombey and Son* he said, 'When I am reminded by any chance of what it is that the waves were always saying, I wander in my fancy for a whole night about the streets of Paris, – as I really did, with a heavy heart, the night when my little friend and I parted company forever.' An author may share the grief of his creations. But to what extent a reader may sit down to enjoy a good flood of tears and then jump up and play bridge, – that's another thing. Sorrow as a deliberate luxury is a doubtful pursuit, a dubious form of art.

On the other hand, it may be argued that Dickens knew perfectly well what he was doing. He may have felt that the reader could not sympathise with the main idea of his story unless he could feel to the full the poignant suffering brought by the death of the child and its effect on the character of Dombey and his future life. In *Dombey and Son* the main features of the story, contrary to the method of the earlier books, were firmly constructed in the writer's mind before the work began. The criticism was made at the time that the death of little Paul was needlessly inserted in the story to enhance a sentimental interest and that the change in the character of Dombey is violent and unnatural. Dickens resented this criticism, which is indeed groundless, and defends himself against it in his preface to the later edition.

Indeed, what he says in the preface is more than substantiated by what he wrote in a letter to John Forster while the story was still in the making. The death of little Paul, far from being incidentally introduced for sensation's sake, is the centre round which the narrative turns. The letter merits quotation. It marks as it were a landmark in Dickens's life. It shows the contrast with the unconscious and planless composition of *Pickwick*; it is leading on to the overplanned and underinspired work of much of the later books. [Leacock quotes the excerpt from the letter (beginning 'I will now go on to give you an outline') cited by Forster in his *Life*: see conclusion of section 1, above – Ed.] . . .

In the light of this view of the composition of the book, the harrowing description of little Paul's death becomes perhaps a literary necessity. . . .

SOURCE: extract from Leacock's *Charles Dickens: His Life and Work* (London, 1933) pp. 113–17.

3. CRITICAL STUDIES SINCE 1941

Humphry House   'Scenery and Mood'   (1941)

... The general chronology of *Dombey* works out quite well if we assume that the book's plot ended with the writing of it in 1848. Florence was then the mother of a son old enough to talk intelligently about his 'poor little uncle': supposing she was then twenty-one or two, Paul would have been born about 1833[1] and died 1840–1. This fits some of the main episodes that can be dated by historical events. The journey of Dombey and the Major to Leamington happened soon after Paul's death: the London and Birmingham Railway, by which they travelled, was fully opened in September 1838, and the Royal Hotel, Leamington, at which they stayed, was pulled down about 1841–2. In describing the Leamington scenes Dickens was obviously drawing on memories of a holiday he had there with Hablot Browne in the autumn of 1838; and Browne was their illustrator. Mr Carker's death at Paddock Wood station was only possible after 1844, when the branch line was opened from there to Maidstone. The book and the period thus hang together without any serious problems of anachronism. In it there is still a lot from the 1820s. Sol Gills with his decaying, out-of-date business, and even the Dombey firm itself, living on the worn maxim, ill-observed, of a pushing eighteenth-century merchant, are intended to appear as survivals from another age. As a whole the book shows an emotional as well as a practical 'consciousness of living in a world of change', an apprehension of what the changes meant in detail every day, the new quality of life they brought. *Dombey*, more than any of his major works, shows how quickly and surely Dickens could sense the mood of his time, and incorporate new sensations in imaginative literature.

The new mood and atmosphere are very largely caused by the railways: the publication of the book coincided with the railway mania of the middle forties.[2] It would be hard to exaggerate the effect of those years on English social life. Practically the whole country was money-mad; the public attitude to investment was quite altered, and it then first became clear that Joint Stock companies, however imperfectly managed, were certain to become a permanent and influential feature of finance. Railway works helped to absorb the unemployed and so to remove the fear of revolution. The growth of home consumption was enormously accelerated by improved transport: diet, furniture, fireplaces, and all the physical appurtenances of life changed character more rapidly; the very landscape was given a new aesthetic character – even perhaps a new standard – by embankments, cuttings and viaducts. But, above all, the scope and tempo of individual living were revolutionised, even for a workman and his family, on a Parliamentary train.

These vast and various changes were, of course, spread over a considerable period: but the years between 1844 and 1848 brought them dramatically into public notice, and saw the climax of a process begun in the later twenties. Dickens had been prompt to record in unobtrusive ways the earlier impact of railways on his world. One characteristic attitude found expression in Mr Weller's well-known outburst in *Master Humphrey's Clock* against the 'unconstitootional inwaser o' priwileges, . . . a nasty, wheezin', creakin', gaspin', puffin', bustin' monster, alvays out o' breath, vith a shiny green-and-gold back, like a unpleasant beetle in that 'ere gas magnifier'. Dickens also used the contrast between coach and train in the essay he wrote when giving up the editorship of *Bentley's Miscellany* in 1839, and was

led insensibly into an anticipation of those days to come when mail-coach guards shall no longer be judges of horse-flesh – when a mail-coach guard shall never even have seen a horse – when stations shall have superseded stables, and corn shall have given place to coke. 'In those dawning times', thought I, 'exhibition rooms shall teem with portraits of Her Majesty's favourite engine, with boilers after Nature by future Landseers. . . .'

It is interesting to find him so early (and in an essay mainly implying regret) taking it for granted even in a joke that railways would be everywhere victorious. Yet their comparatively small development combined with his own retrospective habit prevented mention of them in his major works. There is little railway in *Martin Chuzzlewit* (1843–5) – there is a lot of comic and melodramatic business with coaches and chaises in the Pickwick style – but *Dombey*, written in the mania years, is full of it. It is first the ambition and then the life of fireman Toodle; it is the Car of Juggernaut as seen by *Punch*, with red eyes, bleared and dim, in the daylight, which licked up Carker's 'stream of life with its fiery heat, and cast his mutilated fragments in the air'. 'Express comes through at four, sir. – It don't stop.'

The first railway journey fully described in Dickens is that of Dombey and the Major on their way to Leamington. They started from Euston, where Hardwick's gateway 'exhibiting the Grecian

Doric upon a scale hitherto unattempted in modern times', not yet
obscured by buildings round about it nor centralised by miles of solid
building to the North, seemed indeed a monumental boundary to the
town and an invitation to adventure beyond. To contemporaries the
station was a matter for pride and curiosity:

On passing within this gateway, we feel at once that as the mode of
conveyance is different, so is the place. We are not within the narrow
precincts of an inn-yard, jostled by porters and ostlers, and incommoded by
luggage; everything is on a large scale. Yet one's old associations are
disturbed by the sight of men in uniform keeping strict 'watch and ward', and
by the necessary yet rigid exactness of all the arrangements. . . . 'First' and
'second' class passengers have their different entrances, and their separate
booking desks; and on passing through the building have to produce their
tickets as passports into the covered yard where the trains lie.[3]

Dombey travelled, as was then common, in his own carriage fastened
to a flat truck. This comfortable independence of the gentry had its
dangers no less than the inconveniences which Bagstock found; but it
persisted for many years, and well on in the fifties Dr Dionysius
Lardner had to include among his rules for travellers: 'If you travel
with your private carriage, do not sit in it on the railway. Take your
place by preference in one of the regular railway carriages.'
    Dombey and Bagstock apparently went right through to Birming-
ham (instead of leaving the train, as they might have done, at Rugby
or Coventry), and drove down to Leamington from there. This made
it possible for Dickens to extend his description of the travelling itself;
and in doing so he established a standard, almost a formula, for such
writing, which he followed several times later. The amount of
observation he compresses into a few paragraphs is amazing. Some is
of what we have all wondered at from childhood – the 'objects close at
hand and almost in the grasp, ever flying from the traveller'
contrasted with the slow movement of 'the deceitful distance'; the
sensation of whirling backwards in a tunnel; the indifference of the
train to weather; the drippings from a hydrant spout. The rhythm of
the wheels he tries to catch in a rather blatant theme: 'Away, with a
shriek, and a roar, and a rattle', too often repeated; but in fact he
catches it far more subtly and with brilliant success in the lists of
things and scenes which the train passes; building on a fairly regular
anapaestic base, he manages by many variations to convey those
shifts and suspensions of beat caused in fact on a railway by passing
points and crossings, by shorter lengths of rail and by a slight
difference, perhaps, in the fixing of the chairs. The thing must be read
aloud. Some of the description belongs to an early astonishment

which we can never recapture; such, for instance, is the engineering-geological interest in cuttings – 'through the chalk, through the mould, through the clay, through the rock' – which has so large a place in the popular railway literature of the time,[4] and focused in particular upon the works at Tring and Blisworth on the Birmingham line.

The method of the description as a whole is to combine the more immediate effects of speed upon the sight and hearing – 'massive bridges crossing up above, fall like a beam of shadow an inch broad, upon the eye' – with a quick kaleidoscopic view of passing scenes,[5] which compel in their succession a number of social contrasts. Things seen from a carriage window enforced once more the gravity of the 'condition of England question'. The homes of the Two Nations might be seen as if from a single viewpoint, yet in their own settings. And on such a journey as this, which passed at least through the fringes of the Black Country, the southerner looked out with new surprise upon the industrial landscape. . . .

The scenery and mood of *Dombey* belong to the Railway Age and the London townscape, too, is transformed: it is in London that Dickens's pulse must be taken. The very office of 'The Firm of Dombey and Son, Wholesale, Retail, and for Exportation' has failed to keep his attention; many details in it are certainly described, but they are dead – hardly a reader would remember them. All his passionate interest in office furniture and routine, ledgers and rulers and ink, which leaves a trail of immortal offices through others of his books, has here declined into perfunctory humdrum. The focus of his attention has shifted from the well-known scenes of his youth to the new London of his manhood. The focus is on Stuccovia, the suburbs, and the terminus districts. The Dombey house 'between Portland Place and Bryanston Square' is the first of a series of dreary mansions continued in the houses of Merdle and Boffin. The relevant business-men no longer lived over their offices; and Dickens, moving west, through Regency Bloomsbury towards Belgravia, was moving in his art towards the problem of boredom. How was dullness to be enforced without being dull? One of his answers is the beginning of Book I, chapter 21 of *Little Dorrit.* . . .

Nor is regret the prominent tone of his many descriptions of changing London in *Dombey* and afterwards. The London of *Dombey* is being altered chiefly by the railways. It is the London of the forties, where Tennyson and Carlyle used to walk together at night, and Carlyle raved against the suburbs as a 'black jumble of black cottages where there used to be pleasant fields', and they would both agree that it was growing into 'a strange chaos of odds and ends, this

London'.[6] Dickens did not rave; he observed the chaos in ways that
implied his comment: here is his description of the ambiguous belt on
the northern side, where he put the house of John and Harriet Carker:

The second home is on the other side of London, near to where the busy
great north road of bygone days is silent and almost deserted, except by
wayfarers who toil along on foot. . . . The neighbourhood in which it stands
has as little of the country to recommend it, as it has of the town. It is neither
of the town nor country. The former, like the giant in his travelling boots, has
made a stride and passed it, and has set his brick-and-mortar heel a long way
in advance; but the intermediate space between the giant's feet, as yet, is only
blighted country, and not town; and, here, among a few tall chimneys
belching smoke all day and night, and among the brick-fields and the lanes
where turf is cut, and where the fences tumble down, and where the dusty
nettles grow, and where a scrap or two of hedge may yet be seen, and where
the bird-catcher still comes occasionally, though he swears every time to
come no more – this second home is to be found.   [ch. 33]

And he notes the jerrybuilders' work as 'a disorderly crop of
beginnings of mean houses, rising out of the rubbish, as if they had
been unskilfully sown there'. . . . The counterparts of this creeping
expansion across the fields are the sudden changes closer in, which
are directly the railway's doing: within the short life of little Paul the
whole Camden Town district was transformed:

There was no such place as Staggs's Gardens. It had vanished from the
earth. Where the old rotten summer-houses once had stood, palaces now
reared their heads, and granite columns of gigantic girth opened a vista to the
railway world beyond. The miserable waste ground, where the refuse matter
had been heaped of yore, was swallowed up and gone; and in its frowsy stead
were tiers of warehouses, crammed with rich goods and costly merchandise.
The old by-streets now swarmed with passengers and vehicles of every kind;
the new streets that had stopped disheartened in the mud and waggon-ruts,
formed towns within themselves, originating wholesome comforts and
conveniences belonging to themselves, and never tried nor thought of until
they sprung into existence. Bridges that had led to nothing, led to villas,
gardens, churches, healthy public walks. The carcasses of houses, and
beginnings of new thoroughfares, had started off upon the line at steam's own
speed, and shot away into the country in a monster train.   [ch. 15]

It is interesting to compare this reformer's admiration for what had
been done with the plain delight of the earlier description of Camden
Town in chapter 6; the district had then just been rent by the first
shock of the railway earthquake which produces 'a hundred
thousand shapes and substances of incompleteness, wildly mingled
out of their places'. The contrast is not between anything old and
interesting and beautiful with the prosaic new which has replaced it,

but between the process of change and the achievement. The process truly fascinated Dickens, the achievement merely wins sober moral approval; . . .

SOURCE: extracts from House's *The Dickens World* (London, 1941; paperback edn, 1960), pp. 136–42, 146–7, 148–50.

NOTES

[Reorganised and renumbered from the original – Ed.]

1. He was not weaned when work began at the London end of the Birmingham Railway – April 1834.
2. The peak year for the authorisation of new lines by Parliament was 1846, with 4538 miles; and for the opening of new lines for traffic, 1848, with 1,182 miles, of which 604 had been authorised in 1845 and 403 in 1846. These figures are for the whole of the United Kingdom. *Punch's Almanack* for 1846 is the only one based entirely on a railway motif.
3. *The Penny Magazine*, VII, p. 329.
4. E.g. Lardner's books, George Measom's illustrated Guides. Smiles's *Life of George Stephenson*, and *Our Iron Roads* by Frederick S. Williams.
5. This is the method used also in 'A Flight', *Household Words*, III (30 Aug. 1851) which describes a journey on the SER from London to Folkestone.
6. *Tennyson, A Memoir*, by Hallam, Lord Tennyson, I, p. 267.

Edgar Johnson   The World of Dombeyism
(1952)

. . . Dickens described the theme of *Dombey and Son* as pride, but Mr Dombey's pride, though a dark and omnipresent strand in the story, is not its dominant principle. That principle is the callous inhumanity of an economic doctrine that strips Mr Dombey's relations with everyone to an assertion of monetary power. He wants no ties of affection between his infant son and Polly Toodle, the wet nurse whom he engages for the child. 'When you go away from here, you will have concluded what is a mere matter of bargain and sale, hiring and letting: and will stay away' [ch. 2]. He is affronted to learn that Miss Tox, the poor toady on his grandeur, has dared to lift eyes of personal admiration to him and to dream that he might raise her to his side as his wife. It never enters his mind that he cannot hire the obedience of his subordinates to any of his commands, or that Mr Carker, his Manager, even while he does his great chief's bidding, can resent being employed in degrading and humiliating ways. He believes that he can buy the respect and obedience of an aristocratic wife whose pride and beauty are to reflect lustre on his greatness. Even his love for his son, though sincere and strong, is engendered in the doctrine that the wealth and pre-eminence of the House of Dombey and Son must go on forever.

The attitudes that Mr Dombey displays toward those with whom he comes into immediate contact are also his attitudes toward society as a whole, and toward the welfare of society. 'I am far from being friendly', he explains coldly, 'to what is called by persons of levelling sentiments, general education. But it is necessary that the inferior classes should continue to be taught to know their position, and to conduct themselves properly. So far I approve of schools' [ch. 5]. Fundamentally, however, Mr Dombey agrees with his companion Major Bagstock, who distrusts all education for the poor: 'Take advice from plain old Joe, and never educate that sort of people, Sir', says the Major. 'Damme, Sir, it never does! It always fails!' [ch. 20].

Mr Dombey is the living symbol of the nineteenth-century theory of business enterprise and its social philosophy. Not even the Lancashire industrialists who bitterly resisted the regulation of child labor and defied the law demanding the fencing-in of dangerous machinery exemplified a more relentless devotion to their own profits and power. Many factory owners, indeed, were decent enough men, devoted to their families, kind to those with whom they came in direct contact, and desirous of doing right by their workers. But they were helpless against ruthless competition and blinded by the belief that any protective interference with the operations of laissez-faire economics would be disastrous. Richard Oastler, the humane reformer who spent years trying to get the working man's day cut down to ten hours, explained the principles of competitive business to Dr Thomas Chalmers: 'Take advantage of another's poverty or ignorance, forcing or coaxing him to sell cheap; and when he is a buyer, using the same means to make him buy dear . . . get money any how, even at the cost of life and limb to those employed in his aggrandisement . . .' [1]

The entire complex development of *Dombey and Son* orchestrates these themes of callous indifference and social evil into a vast symphonic structure in which all the groups and individuals brought into contact with Mr Dombey and his affairs are organically related. The group at the Wooden Midshipman, old Sol Gills, his bright, high-spirited nephew Walter Gay, simple-minded Captain Cuttle, the wooden-headed Bunsby; Polly Toodle and her apple-cheeked

family; sharp-tongued Susan Nipper; poor, foolish, kind-hearted Mr
Toots; Cousin Feenix, with his wilful legs and wandering speech – all
display the warm humanity banished from the cold heart of Mr
Dombey. Even Miss Tox, toady though she is, reveals a disinterested
loyalty and devotion ignored and despised by the object of her
adulation. These characters surround with a glowing counterpoint
the icy dissonances of Mr Dombey's world.

The contrasts are developed with consummate artistry. Little Paul
Dombey's christening is rendered entirely in glacial imagery: the
freezing library with all the books in 'cold, hard, slippery uniforms',
Mr Dombey taking Mr Chick's hand 'as if it were a fish, or seaweed,
or some such clammy substance' [ch. 5], the chill and earthy church,
the cold collation afterwards, 'set forth in a cold pomp of glass and
silver', the champagne 'so bitter cold' as to force 'a little scream from
Miss Tox', the veal that strikes 'a sensation of cold lead to Mr Chick's
extremities', Mr Dombey as unmoved as if he were 'hung up for sale
at a Russian fair as a specimen of a frozen gentleman' [ch. 5].

From this silent, icy celebration the very next chapter plunges into
the warm clamor of Poly Toodle's visit to her family in Staggs's
Gardens with her 'honest apple face . . . the centre of a bunch of
smaller pippins, all laying their rosy cheeks close to it' [ch. 6], and all
growing noisy, vehement, dishevelled, and flushed with delight. Even
the calmer scenes of everyday domesticity in the Toodle household
are as different from those in the Dombey mansion as these two festive
occasions. Mr Toodle home from firing his locomotive engine
recharges himself with innumerable pint mugs of tea solidified with
great masses of bread and butter, with both of which he regales his
expectant circle of children in small spoonfuls and large bites: snacks
that 'had such a relish in the mouths of these young Toodles, that,
after partaking of the same, they performed private dances of ecstasy
among themselves, and stood on one leg a-piece, and hopped, and
indulged in other salutatory tokens of gladness' [ch. 38].

In the fierce sequence of climactic events centering around the
flight of Edith, Mr Dombey's second wife, with his treacherous
Manager, Mr Carker, Dickens designedly emphasises the same
contrasts. Again they occupy successive chapters, the heavy blow
with which the marble-hearted father almost fells his daughter to the
marble floor, her cry of desolation as she runs from that loveless and
pitiless house, understanding at last that she has 'no father upon
earth' [ch. 47]; and then Captain Cuttle, trembling and 'pale in the
very knobs of his face', soothing the weeping girl with murmured
endearments of 'Heart's Delight', and 'my pretty', as he tenderly
raises her from the ground [ch. 48]; the freezing rancor of Mr

Dombey's gloomy board, and the little dinner the Captain prepares at the parlor fire.

There is a wonderful radiance in the Captain bustling about this meal, his coat off and his glazed hat on his head, making the egg sauce, basting the fowl, heating the gravy, boiling some potatoes, keeping his eye on the sausages 'hissing and bubbling in a most musical manner', and at last removing his hat, putting on his coat, and wheeling up the table before Florence's sofa. 'My lady lass', he begs her, 'cheer up, and try to eat a deal. Stand by, my deary! Liver wing it is. Sarse it is. Sassage it is. And potato!' [ch. 49].

No less heart-warming is the Captain's endeavor to bestow on Florence the tin canister containing his savings of £14 2s. for any purchases she needs to make, his request to the shop girl to 'sing out' if any more is required, his casually 'consulting his big watch as a deep means of dazzling the establishment, and impressing it with a sense of property', and his disappointment when Florence does not use his money. 'It ain't o' no use to me', he says. 'I wonder I haven't chucked it away afore now' [ch. 49]. What an illustration of the ludicrous forms goodness of heart can take without ceasing to be real goodness! No speech was ever more absurd, and yet no gentleman ever said anything more truly imbued with delicacy and generosity.

Captain Cuttle, together with Mr Toots, is among the great portraits of the book, both irresistibly ridiculous and both at the same time possessed of a true dignity shining through all their absurdity. Poor Toots, with his 'It's of no consequence whatsoever', his vapid chuckle, the trousers and waistcoats that are masterpieces of Burgess and Company, and his hopeless devotion to Florence, rises to heights of noble selflessness. And even when Captain Cuttle is scrambling quotations like a parody on T. S. Eliot and rambling through chains of dim association suggestive of Joyce's Molly Bloom, there is a heart of tender sanity in his nonsense. 'If you're in arnest, you see, my lad', he comforts Toots, 'you're a object of clemency, and clemency is the brightest jewel in the crown of a Briton's head, for which you'll overhaul the constitution as laid down in Rule Britannia, and, when found, *that* is the charter as them garden angels was a singing of, so many times over. Stand by!' [ch. 39].

Seen with no such gentle satire as the Captain and Toots, certain other characters represent disguised forms of Mr Dombey's own cold egoism. Mrs Skewton, Edith Dombey's mother, with her specious cult of the 'heart', is a hypocritical parody of the sympathies that flow so sincerely in chuckle-headed Mr Toots and the acidulous Susan Nipper; underneath the languishing phrases she is completely selfish and venal. Major Bagstock, 'leering and choking, like an over-fed

Mephistopheles' [ch. 20], covers a toadying malignance in a bluster-ing pretense of blunt-spoken friendship.

The name of Dombey, the Major tells its owner, is one 'that a man is proud to recognise. There is nothing adulatory in Joseph Bagstock, Sir. His Royal Highness the Duke of York observed on more than one occasion, "there is no adulation in Joey. He is a plain old soldier is Joe. He is tough to a fault is Joseph"; but it's a great name, Sir. By the Lord, it's a great name!' [ch. 10]. And Mrs Skewton, reclining in her wheeled chair like Cleopatra in her gilded barge, wants to know what 'we live for *but* sympathy! What else is so extremely charming! Without that gleam of sunshine on our cold cold earth, how could we possibly bear it? . . .' I would have my world all heart; and Faith is so excessively charming that I won't allow you to disturb it . . .' [ch. 21].

As a part of her patter Cleopatra dotes upon the Middle Ages. 'Those darling bygone times, Mr Carker', she gushes, 'with their delicious fortresses, and their dear old dungeons, and their delightful places of torture . . . and everything that makes life truly charming! How dreadfully we have degenerated!' There is no such Faith today, she goes on, as there was in the days of Queen Bess, 'which were so extremely golden. Dear creature! She was all Heart!' And then there was her father, so bluff, so English, 'with his dear little peepy eyes, and his benevolent chin!' [ch. 27]. How appropriate that this creature of masks and attitudes should have detachable hair and a painted rosy complexion, and that when these are removed the little that is real of her should be put to bed 'like a horrible doll' [ch. 37].

Grim parallels to Cleopatra and Edith Dombey are two figures from that dark lower world on which Mr Dombey looked down from his railway carriage on the way to Leamington. But 'Good Mrs. Brown' and her daughter, Alice Marwood, are linked to Mrs Skewton and Edith by more than Dickens's desire for an artificial symmetry of plot. They symbolise the fatal mingling in society of those evils that creep from high to low like the greed-engendered cholera coiling from the slums into lordly homes. There is a deeper significance than mere accident in Alice Marwood's being the illegitimate daughter to an elder brother of Edith's father, and in her being seduced and abandoned by Carker, Mr Dombey's Manager, as Edith has been bought in matrimony by Mr Dombey himself. When the two mothers and their daughters meet by chance on the downs, Edith is fearfully struck by their dark resemblance to each other, and Mrs Skewton guiltily jabbers ber belief that Mrs Brown is a good mother, 'full of what's her name – and all that', 'all affection and et cetera' [ch. 40]. 'No great lady', Alice has previously said with bitter irony, ever thought of selling her daughter, 'and that shows that the only

instances of mothers bringing up their daughters wrong, and evil
coming of it, are among such miserable folks as us' [ch. 53] And
looking after Edith, she exclaims, 'You're a handsome woman; but
good looks won't save us. And you're a proud woman; but pride won't
save us' [ch. 40].

★

On every level in the world of *Dombey and Son*, although not in every
breast, the same forces are at work. From the stately mansions of the
aristocracy on Brook Street and the pineries of Mr Dombey's
banker-associates down to the rag-filled hovel of Good Mrs Brown,
competitive greed and indifference to the welfare of others create a
cynical economic system that spawns all the vices and cruelties of
society. And of that system – it might even be called Dombeyism – Mr
Dombey is the symbolic embodiment. He is not, of course, directly
and personally responsible for all the wrongs Dickens paints; and,
despite grave defects of character, he is not even inherently vicious.
He too has been shaped by the forces he now embodies. 'When I
thought so much of all the causes that had made me what I was',
Edith says of Mr Dombey, 'I needed to allow more for the causes that
had made him what he was' [ch. 61]. But Dickens has also come to
understand that, whatever the individual blame for the evils he is
fighting, a statistically large proportion of them must be laid at the
door of Dombeyism.

That is why even society's charities and generosities so often fail of
their stated objects. They are not really directed toward human
welfare, but are instruments of ostentation and keeping the poor in
their place. So of the Charitable Grinders' School, to which Mr
Dombey nominated Polly Toodle's son Rob. Beaten daily by his
master, 'a superannuated old Grinder of savage disposition, who had
been appointed schoolmaster because he didn't know anything, and
wasn't fit for anything' [ch. 6], what wonder that Rob turns out a liar
and a sneak? 'But they never taught honour at the Grinders' School,
where the system that prevailed was particularly strong in the
engendering of hypocrisy. Insomuch, that many of the friends and
masters of past Grinders said, if this were what came of education for
the common people, let us have none. Some more rational said, let us
have a better one. But the governing powers of the Grinders'
Company were always ready for *them*, by picking out a few boys who
had turned out well, in spite of the system, and roundly asserting that
they could only have turned out well because of it. Which settled the
business . . .' [ch. 38].

It is this emphasis on abstract forces that explains the diminished role of the villains in *Dombey and Son*. Though contemptible enough personally, they are not demonic creators of evil like Ralph Nickleby, Fagin, Quilp, Sir John Chester and Jonas Chuzzlewit. They batten, not on the weakness of innocent victims, but on the vices of the powerful. Major Bagstock, 'rough and tough old Joey', that hypocrite of truculence, exploits Mr Dombey's snobbery and pride; but Mr Dombey already had them, ripe for sycophancy. Mr Carker, with his feline smile and those glittering teeth whose symbolic falseness Dickens is constantly suggesting without ever stating directly, flatters the demand for absolute abasement that Mr Dombey was already making of all those about him. In a sense, Mr Dombey may be said to have tempted and corrupted Carker rather than the reverse. Both the Manager and the blue-faced Major merely smooth a way that everything in Mr Dombey's background and character predetermines he shall travel.

This way is hinted as early as the second page of the book and implicit in its very title. The three words 'Dombey and Son', we are told, 'convey the one idea of Mr Dombey's life. The earth was made for Dombey and Son to trade in, and the sun and moon were made to give them light. Rivers and seas were formed to float their ships; rainbows gave them promise of fair weather; winds blew for or against their enterprises; stars and planets circled in their orbits, to preserve inviolate a system of which they were the centre' [ch. 1]. His feeling about his first wife's death is hardly more than a sense of 'something gone from among his plate and furniture, and other household possessions, which was well worth the having, and could not be lost without sincere regret' [ch. 1]. He thinks of himself and his wealth as all-powerful. 'The kind of foreign help which people usually seek for their children, I can afford to despise; being above it, I hope' [ch. 5]. When his second wife asks if he believes he 'can degrade, or bend or break' *her* 'to submission and obedience', Mr Dombey smiles, as if he had been asked 'whether he thought he could raise ten thousand pounds' [ch. 40]. Such is the nature of the man whom Carker maliciously describes as 'the slave of his own greatness . . . yoked to his own triumphal car like a beast of burden' [ch. 45].

Given these elements in Mr Dombey, it is natural that he should regard his daughter with indifference and bring whatever affection is in his chill nature to the son who may carry on his name and business. 'He had never conceived an aversion to her: it had not been worth his while or in his humour' [ch. 3]. But when he sees her fear of him and feels his exclusion from the tenderness between her and her dying mother, he cannot avoid knowing that it is a reproach to him. Later still, as he realises that all the tenderness of his cherished son and heir is bestowed on his despised daughter, and observes in a moment of farewell the contrast between the limp and careless hand his boy gives him and the sorrowful face he turns to Florence, it is a bitter pang to the father's proud heart [ch. 11]. With what fateful steps it follows that as she reaps the love his riches cannot command his indifference should turn to jealous dislike! And that when Paul dies, he should see in her 'the successful rival of his son, in health and life' and find it 'gall to him to look upon her in her beauty and her promise' [ch. 18]?

In the course of the fierce duel between Mr Dombey and his obdurate second wife, his resentment of his daughter deepens. While his bourgeois pride dashes itself in vain against the barriers of her aristocratic pride, who is it that wins his wife as she had won his boy, 'whose least word did what his utmost means could not! Who was it who, unaided by his love, regard or notice, thrived and grew beautiful when those so aided died! Who could it be, but the same child at whom he had often glanced uneasily in her motherless infancy, with a kind of dread, lest he might come to hate her; and of whom his foreboding was fulfilled, for he DID hate her in his heart' [ch. 40].

All this is handled with enormous skill and power. That the cancerous growth of Mr Dombey's bitterness is delineated with absolute fidelity has never been denied. But there are readers who have not been convinced of his later change of heart. Their skepticism, however, ignores both the repeated psychological preparations Dickens makes for it in the book and the complex involutions of emotion in human beings. Is there anyone who has not often known, even as he sullenly persisted in a course of injustice, that his behavior was indefensible, and half longed to make the very change that he stubbornly resisted making? Does no one ever turn with unavailing remorse and belated affection to the memory of those he has wronged, and wish that he could make amends and win the love he has thrown away?

These emotions have struggled in Mr Dombey from the very beginning. He has never been utterly without tender emotion, even for his daughter. Seeing her clasped in her mother's arms, he has felt an uneasiness that troubled his peace. On a later night he looks from his door upon his two children going to bed, and in the time thereafter his memory is haunted by the image of her small figure toiling up the stairs, singing to the baby brother in her arms [ch. 8]. Leaving his boy at Brighton with Florence, and bending down to kiss him good-by, his sight dimmed 'by something that for a moment blurred the little face', he has a twinge of feeling about his injustice that makes his mental vision, 'for a short time', Dickens tells us, 'the clearer perhaps' [ch. 11].

Numerous impulses of contrition like these reach a culmination on the evening Mr Dombey returns from Paris with his bride and, pretending to sleep, secretly watches Florence bent over her work from which she occasionally raises to him pathetic speaking eyes. 'Some passing thought that he had had a happy home within his reach – had had a household spirit bending at his feet – had overlooked it in his stiff-necked arrogance, and wandered away and lost himself' [ch. 35], engenders a gentler feeling toward her. 'As he looked, she became blended with the child he had loved' and 'he saw her for an instant by a clearer and a brighter light, not bending over that child's pillow as his rival . . . but as the spirit of his home . . .' [ch. 35]. Almost about to call her to him, he hears Edith's footstep on the stairs, and the moment is lost. Florence becomes a weapon in his struggle with his wife, and his softening hardens once again to resentment.

But after the flight of Edith and Florence, the bankruptcy of his business, and the loss of his fortune, as he sits alone in his desolate house, there is not one of these things that does not return to his memory. Again he sees the small childish figure singing on the stair, again he hears her heartbroken cry at the blow he struck her, and knows that if he had not thrown it away he would always have had her love, even now, in his fall, and 'that of all around him, she alone had never changed. His boy had faded into dust, his proud wife had sunk into a polluted creature, his flatterer and friend been transformed into the worst of villains; his riches melted away', but 'she alone had turned the same gentle look upon him always. . . . She had never changed to him – nor had he ever changed to her – and she was lost.' In his anguish, 'Oh, how much better than this', he cries in his heart, 'that he had loved her as he had his boy, and lost her as he had his boy, and laid them in their early grave together!' [ch. 59].

Even in Mr Dombey's remorse, though, with a marvellous touch of psychological insight, Dickens shows him still his old self. If he had 'heard her voice in the adjoining room', Dickens writes, 'he would not have gone to her. If he could have seen her in the street, and she had done no more than look at him as she had been used to look, he would have passed on with his old cold unforgiving face, and not addressed her, or relaxed it, though his heart should have broken soon afterwards' [ch. 59]. In their superb penetration these few vivid words, for all their brevity, are equivalent to paragraphs of intricate psychological analysis.

His misery is resolved only by the unhoped-for return of Florence, imploring his forgiveness instead of proffering the forgiveness he could never have forced himself to beg. 'I was frightened when I went

away, and could not think' [ch. 59]. Although the mercy is undeserved, no reader who has understood the entire delineation of
Florence's character could doubt it any more than he could disbelieve
the behavior of Mr Dombey. What wonder that the broken man
exclaims, in a passion of grief, 'Oh my God, forgive me, for I need it
very much!' [ch. 59].

★

Throughout all this personal drama of pride, heartache and bankruptcy, Dickens has never lost sight nor allowed the reader to lose
sight of the social bearings of his theme. On the crash of Dombey and
Son, 'The world was very busy now, in sooth', he writes, 'and had a
deal to say. It was an innocently credulous and a much ill-used world.
It was a world in which there was no other sort of bankruptcy
whatever. There were no conspicuous people in it, trading far and
wide on rotten banks of religion, patriotism, virtue, honour. There
was no amount worth mentioning of mere paper in circulation, on
which anybody lived pretty handsomely, promising to pay great sums
of goodness with no effects. There were no shortcomings anywhere, in
anything but money. The world was very angry indeed; and the
people especially, who in a worse world, might have been supposed to
be bankrupt traders themselves in shows and pretences, were
observed to be mightily indignant' [ch. 58].

    Two-thirds of the way through the book, Dickens had sounded his
own deeper indignation in a powerful outburst. 'Hear the magistrate
or judge admonish the unnatural outcasts of society; unnatural in
brutish habits, unnatural in want of decency, unnatural in losing and
confounding all distinctions between good and evil', Dickens
exclaims; and then go 'down into their dens, lying within the echoes of
our carriage wheels', and look 'upon the world of odious sights', at
which 'dainty delicacy, living in the next street . . . lisps "I don't
believe it!" Breathe the polluted air', he bids us: 'And then, calling up
some ghastly child, with stunted form and wicked face, hold forth on
its unnatural sinfulness, and lament its being, so early, far away from
Heaven – but think a little of its having been conceived, and born and
bred, in Hell!'

    'Those who study the physical sciences', he goes on, '. . . tell us that
if the noxious particles that rise from vitiated air were palpable to the
sight, we should see them lowering in a dense black cloud above such
haunts, and rolling slowly on to corrupt the better portions of a town.
But if the moral pestilence that rises with them, and in the eternal
laws of outraged Nature, is inseparable from them, could be made
discernible too, how terrible the revelation! . . . Then should we stand

appalled to know, that where we generate disease to strike our children down and entail itself on unborn generations, there also we breed, by the same certain process, infancy that knows no innocence, youth without modesty or shame, maturity that is mature in nothing but in suffering and guilt, blasted old age that is a scandal on the form we bear. Unnatural humanity! When we shall gather grapes from thorns, and figs from thistles; when fields of grain shall spring up from the offal in the bye-ways of our wicked cities, and roses bloom in the fat churchyards that they cherish, then we may look for natural humanity and find it growing from such seed' [ch. 47].

In its faithfulness to the literal truths of human character and in its portrayal of their social consequences, *Dombey and Son* is a realistic development and elaboration of the themes fabulously set forth in *A Christmas Carol*. Like Scrooge, Mr Dombey is symbolic, but he is also the mercantile reality of which Scrooge is a pantomime caricature. The picturesque glimpses in the *Carol* of humble courage and generosity, of evil and suffering, like brightly lighted scenes in a fairy tale, give way to fully detailed pictures of life on a dozen levels, from Mrs Brown's slum to Portland Place, all suggested in their relation to each other. All the flashing intuitions of the *Carol* and *The Chimes* are richly worked out in the intellectual and emotional comprehension of *Dombey and Son*.

Though not, like them, an economic fantasy but a realistic study of contemporary society, it shares with them a curious strain of symbolism and symbolic imagery. To please his son and heir Mr Dombey relieves the distress of Walter Gay's uncle, but then gratifies his own dislike of the courageous, high-spirited Walter by sending him forth on the voyage of the ominously named *Son and Heir*. Walter Gay survives, but the ship is lost – almost at the same time as the child who was always wondering what the waves were saying and who was in a way its namesake. The cold depths of the mahogany board at which Mr Dombey sits just before his ill-fated marriage reflect vessels of dead-sea fruit riding there at anchor [ch. 30]. Beneath the picture that resembles Edith in Mr Carker's dining parlor, there swings a chafing and imprisoned bird in 'a pendant gilded hoop within the cage, like a great wedding-ring' ch. 33]. At Mr Dombey's table a 'long plateau of precious metal frosted . . . whereon frosted Cupids offered scentless flowers' [ch. 36] separates him from his second wife. Constantly Mr Dombey's house and the meals there are described in terms of cold 'and that unnecessary article in Mr Dombey's banquets – ice' [ch. 36]. And when his daughter takes her wounded heart to the Wooden Midshipman and its guardian, 'A wandering princess and a good monster in a story-book', Dickens writes, 'might have sat by the fireside and talked as Captain Cuttle and Florence thought – and not have looked very much unlike them' [ch. 49].

Such images – and there are many more of them – show that Dickens's creative powers were not working in naturalistic terms alone. With a surface observation almost as detailed as Balzac's and often far more brilliant, underneath there are always depths in which his vision pierces to something closely resembling myth and its mysterious power. These bold liberties with the canons of realism are no less exemplified by Dickens's melodrama at its best. It is as irrelevant to criticise some of the scenes between Edith Dombey and Carker by saying that people do not talk like that as to complain that Mirabell and Millamant converse in a shower of epigrams or that Iago distills his hate into a concentration of poisoned words. Drenched in theatricality, the interview in which Carker gives Edith Mr Dombey's ultimatum is also tightly knit, loaded in every word with bitter suggestion and emotional intensity, and dramatically effective throughout every coil of its intricate subtlety.

The total achievement of *Dombey and Son* makes it one of Dickens's great books. With a creative vitality hardly surpassed by any of the books between it and *Pickwick*, it leaves all its predecessors far behind in structural logic, intellectual power and social insight. His writing until now is the work of a brilliantly inspired youthful writer; *Dombey* is the first masterpiece of Dickens's maturity. Readers may prefer individual scenes in *Nickleby*, *Oliver*, or *Martin Chuzzlewit* to individual scenes in *Dombey* – although it is debatable that they contain anything really better than Captain Cuttle and Mr Toots – but no one could say critically that they are better books. The problem of building a unified plot around a central theme so imperfectly tackled in *Chuzzlewit* is triumphantly solved in *Dombey*. None of Dickens's later books exhibit the loose improvisation with which he had begun; their elaboration is not that of planlessness but of a vast cathedral. And with *Dombey*, above all, Dickens has achieved a form by means of which he can convey the more detailed and philosophic social criticism that was to animate his work in the future.

SOURCE: extract from Johnson's *Charles Dickens: His Tragedy and Triumph*, 2 vols (New York, 1952), II, pp. 630–43.

NOTE

1. Richard Oastler, quoted in Cecil Driver, *Tory Radical: The Life of Richard Oastler* (Oxford, 1946), p. 469.

Kathleen Tillotson ✓'Dombey and Daughter' (1954)

Dombey and Son stands out from among Dickens's novels as the earliest example of responsible and successful planning; it has unity not only of action, but of design and feeling. It is also the first in which a pervasive uneasiness about contemporary society takes the place of an intermittent concern with specific social wrongs. . . .

That the origin of the book lay in Mr Dombey is not indeed clearly attested by direct external evidence, as it is with Pickwick and Pecksniff; but everything even outside the novel itself points that way. Forster's report that as first conceived 'it was to do with Pride what its predecessor had done with Selfishness', Dickens's anxiety for secrecy – 'The very name getting out, would be ruinous', the 'outline of [his] immediate intentions' in the letter to Forster with the manuscript of Number 1, his 'nervous dread of caricature in the face of his merchant-hero' – all these agree in their emphasis. It is safe to assume that the originating idea took the form of a 'merchant-hero', in whom business and family pride are twisted into a single hard knot; the continued interplay between the affairs of the firm and the family is emphasised by the early chapter-titles and 'shadowed forth' in the semi-allegorical cover design; although in the working-out less is made of the firm than Dickens seems to have intended. The title is its epitome (there is no record of hesitation over this title as with most others); and is also deliberately misleading – serving to keep the secret of Paul's early death, and to point the irony of the book's true subject – which is, of course, Dombey and Daughter. The relation between Mr Dombey and Florence is the backbone of the whole book; structurally, the relation between him and Paul, and that between Florence and Paul, are only means of exposing and developing it.

From that time [Paul's death], I purpose changing his feelings of indifference and uneasiness towards his daughter into a positive hatred. . . . At the same time I shall change *her* feeling towards *him* for one of a greater desire to love him, and to be loved by him; engendered in her compassion for his loss, and her love for the dead boy whom, in his way, he loved so well too. So I mean to carry the story on, through all the branches and off-shoots and meanderings that come up; and through the decay and downfall of the house, and the bankruptcy of Dombey, and all the rest of it; when his only staff and treasure, and his unknown Good Genius always, will be this rejected daughter, who will come out better than any son at last, and whose love for him, when discovered and understood, will be his bitterest reproach.[1]

Through this changing relation works Mr Dombey's pride, the master-motive of the novel, the mainspring of all its events. Much then depends upon the adequacy of these two characters, Mr Dombey and Florence, to sustain this central interest, and especially upon Dickens's power – not hitherto manifested – to draw a character undergoing inner conflict.

This continued inner conflict was also a part of the original intention; the letter just quoted continues:

For the struggle with himself, which goes on in all such obstinate natures, will have ended then; and the sense of his injustice, which you may be sure has never quitted him, will have at last a gentler office than that of only making him more harshly unjust.

The last point alone shows Dickens's psychological insight; and it is repeated in the new Preface[2] added by the author twelve years later – apparently in reply to criticism of the supposed 'violent change' in the hero.

The two commonest mistakes in judgment . . . are the confounding of shyness with arrogance . . . and the not understanding that an obstinate nature exists in a perpetual struggle with itself.

Mr Dombey undergoes no violent change, either in this book, or in real life. A sense of his injustice is within him, all along. The more he represses it, the more unjust he necessarily is. Internal shame and external circumstances may bring the contest to a close in a week, or a day; but, it has been a contest for years, and is only fought out after a long balance of victory.

The moment in the novel when the contest is nearest to the surface is in chapter 35, where Mr Dombey watches Florence, who believes him asleep.

There are yielding moments in the lives of the sternest and harshest men, though such men often keep their secret well.

So begins the long paragraph in which his brief relenting is traced, and its hidden sources suggested. It ends with a dramatic turn; Edith enters, and, still unobserved, he witnesses her gentle and loving conversation with Florence – a double blow to his pride, and the stimulus to double revenge upon them.

'Such men often keep their secret well'; ' "Dombey", said the Major . . . "don't be thoughtful. . . . You are too great a man, Dombey, to be thoughtful" ' [ch. 20]. The difficulty, especially to a writer more practised in exhibition than analysis, is to suggest the secret self-doubting of 'stiff-necked sullen arrogance'. Such suggestion is conveyed sometimes by the use of carefully timed silent pauses in the narrative, moments sharply presented to the sight and impressing the imagination: as when Mr Dombey watches Florence carrying Paul up 'the great, wide, vacant staircase' in the moonlight, and singing to him [ch. 8]. Or by a revealing but unannotated gesture: as when Mrs Chick, promoting the Brighton scheme, hesitantly submits that Florence must accompany Paul:

'It's quite an infatuation with him. He's very young, you know, and has his fancies.'
Mr Dombey turned his head away, and going slowly to the bookcase, and unlocking it, brought back a book to read.   [ch. 8]

In Mr Dombey Dickens achieves the remarkable feat of making us aware of the hidden depths of a character, while keeping them largely hidden; his method respects Mr Dombey's own proud reserve. The only times his thoughts are unrolled at length before us it is through the phantasmagoria of the railway journey, where Dickens can 'analyse' as it were panoramically, with something of the picturesque freedoms of dream or allegory; and similarly again through the memories and visions called up when he roams through the silent house. Mr Dombey has 'lonely thoughts, bred late at night in the sullen despondency and gloom of his retirement' [ch. 20], but the reader is seldom admitted to them; yet he is often reminded, both by oblique reference and momentary pictures of that silent brooding presence, the shadow behind the figure which Mr Dombey presents to the world, 'self-important, unbending, formal, austere' [ch. 27]. What makes him interesting is the moral suspense: although Florence may serve partly as an externalised conscience, a troublesome and even hated reminder of the whole world of feeling that his pride has forsworn, she does so because something within him responds to her. Before Paul's birth, he had been merely indifferent; afterwards this indifference turns to uneasiness and resentment which increase after Paul's death. But in this resentment there is an unadmitted sense of guilt, and even the seeds of repentance. His love for his son, involved though it is in 'a partial scheme of parental interest and ambition', is yet also the rift in the ice. We are aware of it even in the cruellest moment in which he repulses Florence's affection, and even aware of it as his justification for doing so: he watches her, silently and hopelessly ascending the stairs.

The last time he had watched her, from the same place, winding up those stairs, she had had her brother in her arms. It did not move his heart towards her now, it steeled it: but he went into his room, and locked his door, and sat down in his chair, and cried for his lost boy.   [ch. 18]

In his momentary relenting towards her (so abruptly terminated by a new jealousy)

She became blended with the child he had loved, and he could hardly separate the two.   [ch. 35]

Such evidence keeps before us the 'contest [of] years, only fought out after a long balance of victory'; we can accept its bringing to a close, through 'internal shame and external circumstances', in a single chapter of the closing number [ch. 59]. We may feel that for 'internal shame' to reach the purpose of self-murder, and for 'external circumstances' to bring Florence home in the nick of time, savours overmuch of the theatre; we may feel that the year's lapse between the last two numbers has cheated us, or spared us, too much of the slow undermining of Mr Dombey's obstinate pride. But in the account of his days and nights of restless wandering through the desolate house, Dickens prevents us from feeling that the reconciliation is cheaply purchased. In a passage of no more than four pages he condenses Mr Dombey's history and his present state. And he does it, as always, by a combination of picture and analysis. The deserted rooms, the staircase (that recurring symbol) with its remembered footsteps, carry us backward in time. In Mr Dombey's thoughts, the whole of the original design of the novel is retraced. It is not a static view; the contest still continues. He has passed beyond Paul's death, the wreck of his marriage, his fallen fortunes:

That which was his own work, that which he could so easily have wrought into a blessing, and had set himself so steadily for years to form into a curse: that was the sharp grief of his soul. . . .
And yet – so proud he was in his ruin . . . that if he could have heard her voice in an adjoining room, he would not have gone to her. . . . He chiefly thought of what might have been, and what was not. What was, was all summed up in this: that she was lost, and he bowed down with sorrow and remorse.   [ch. 59]

Inevitably, the passage is introduced by a reiteration of the earlier prophecy: 'Let him remember it in that room, years to come' [chs 18, 59]. But the heavily emphasised pattern of sin, curse, retribution is not the 'figure in the carpet' of *Dombey and Son*. Dickens's impulse towards the cruder simplifications should not obscure from us that his hero is a character of tragic stature. Not seldom, towards the close of the novel, we think of another unbending but vulnerable man of affairs, who wished to stand 'as if a man were author of himself'; or of another proud father and banished daughter, Lear and Cordelia. And no more than there is forgiveness a sentimental concession; the famous criticism that Mr Dombey 'becomes the best of fathers, and

spoils a fine novel' is wide of the mark. It might have been ill judged if
he were fully shown as 'the best of fathers'; but after this climax we see
him only in the moral convalescence of physical illness, and in the
afterglow of the epilogue.

The contest for Mr Dombey's soul requires no more of Florence than
a perfect goodness and persistent affection; in the words of a
chapter-heading, 'The Study of a Loving Heart'. But the balance of
the novel requires her to be prominent, and she is not completely
absent from the scene for more than a single number. A character
conceived in terms of pure feeling, passive, innocent to the point
of being almost 'incapable of her own distress', can hardly sustain this
prominence. The dilemma, though it is doubtful if Dickens saw it as
such, is clear. Conflict within her, introspection, or initiative, would
mitigate the pathos of her situation; unmitigated, the pathos risks
monotony, if not self-defeat. (It may even raise the more serious
criticism that if her state of mind is not morbid, it is improbable; and it
is not within Dickens's range in *this* novel to regard it as morbid.)[4]

She has to be entirely lovable, in order to leave us in no doubt of the
guilt of Mr Dombey (and his own sense of it); for the same reason, she
has to be, with that noticeable exception, universally loved. The love
according to their lights of almost all the other characters carries
conviction, and at times Florence gains some reflected vitality from
Susan Nipper, Mr Toots and Captain Cuttle; even Mrs Chick was on
one occasion struck into silence and 'lost . . . her presence of mind' at
the sight of Florence grieving for Paul. But on the whole the effect is
still of a space where Florence's character ought to be, with our
attention drawn from the vacuum by the ring of admirers. Dickens's
difficulties are not peculiar to him, or to this novel; besides the
timeless problem of making perfect virtue, and especially the passive
virtues, attractive, he has his age's problem of vitalising a heroine in a
period of limiting ideals for girlhood. Yet let the Victorian novel itself
dictate our standards, and we see what is lacking in Florence as a
heroine attracting the reader; that endearing solidity, even of
appearance, that touch of individualising charm, which Trollope was
able to give to all the fifty or so of his young heroines; and which
Dickens was to find for his less perfect ones – Dora, Pet, Bella and
Rosa.

This is not to say that Florence fails; only that one must approach
her differently from Mr Dombey, and see her as a character drawn
wholly within the bounds of her situation; to an extent that she, and
the pathos of that situation, are one and the same. Two approaches
have at least the merit of being included in Dickens's own. First, by

beginning with Florence as a child of six years old, he is able to sustain our pity and tenderness for her as a child, even after she grows to be seventeen. Because we have seen her 'pressing her small hands hard together' [ch. 3] as she timidly enters her father's room, or ragged and lost in the City streets, or clinging crying to Polly's skirts; because we have seen her through Paul's eyes, and Walter Gay's, we continue to think of her, when she is thirteen, fifteen, seventeen, as a child still. Her fear of Carker is of the same colouring as her fear of Good Mrs Brown; Walter is her 'brother'; flying from her home, she is once again the lost child. Not with the Esthers and Agneses or the child-wives, but with the children of Dickens's novels – Nell and Oliver – should Florence be classed. There is one qualification. Though her feeling for Edith may begin as childish – the 'new mama' – it becomes more mature. When Florence, now sixteen, is drawn into the orbit of the unhappy domestic situation, Dickens does not leave her wholly innocent and bewildered. He attempts to suggest a transition from childhood; which is indeed necessary if he is to lead up to her flight from home – the sole occasion on which she is to act as well as suffer. But in the Dombey–Carker–Edith situation she is chiefly a pawn in the game; and the idiom in which it is conducted makes her less and not more alive.

The other approach is by way of the mysterious simplicities of fairy-tale, never far away in Dickens's work. Walter Gay, before ever he has seen Florence, is compared by his romantic uncle to Dick Whittington, who married his master's daughter; when he finds her as a lost child in the City streets, he feels like Cinderella's prince, and also 'not to say like Richard Whittington – that is a tame comparison – but like Saint George of England, with the dragon lying dead before him' [ch. 6].

The 'great dreary house' where Florence lives alone is like a 'magic dwelling-place in magic story, shut up in the heart of a thick wood', with the ironwork of the doorway instead of 'two dragon sentries'; but she 'bloomed there, like the king's fair daughter in the story' [ch. 23]. When she has taken refuge with Captain Cuttle, they are compared to 'a wandering princess and a good monster in a story-book' [ch. 49]. With these as pointers,[5] we can discern other, unstated, analogues; the recurring witch-figure (Good Mrs Brown, and Mrs Pipchin, who has a black cat), the helpful animal (Diogenes attacking Carker), and the comic knight and squire of the anti-masque (Toots and the Game Chicken). The 'adult' characters, Mr Dombey, Edith and Carker, are clear of this tincture of romance, but the children (and the fools) not wholly so. It affects us more than we are aware; and it relates *Dombey* to the world of the earlier novels – *Oliver Twist, Nicholas Nickleby* and

The Old Curiosity Shop. If we can see Florence as the princess under a spell, or the unrecognised child of royal birth from whom a strange light shines, or even as Spenser's Una, we may come nearer Dickens's own intention. The presence of different modes in a narrative is something we must accept in his novels, as in poetic drama.

SOURCE: extracts from K. Tillotson's *Novels of the 1840s* (Oxford, 1954; paperback edn, 1961), pp. 157, 163–75.

NOTES

[Reorganised and renumbered from the original – Ed.]

1. [Ed.] For Forster's account, and his quotation of Dickens's letter referred to here, see the conclusion of section 1, above.

2. [Ed.] This Preface of 1858, reprinted in full, opens section 1, above.

3. [Ed.] The criticism was made by Hippolyte Taine: see section 1, above.

4. Not that the emotional stress of adolescent girlhood lay altogether outside Dickens's range; witness Tattycoram (in *Little Dorrit*), also hungry for affection.

5. And others; Paul is compared to a changeling, Mrs Pipchin's establishment to an ogress's castle.

Ian Milner   The Dickens Drama: Mr Dombey
(1971)

There are various ways of looking at Mr Dombey. He is Pride going before a fall on a Jonsonian stage. He is mercantile man, rich, self-sufficient, domineering, in a trading empire on which the sun never sets. He is alienated man, shut within himself by nature and the illusory power of wealth, robbed of his only son, self-isolated from his daughter. He is man redeemed when in the end, pride broken and fortune gone, Florence brings him by love and tears into 'the community of feeling'. He has been seen as suffering and remorseful man, 'a character of tragic stature'.[1] He is also, for a time, domestic man: husband of a woman whose will he cannot subdue and whose strong sensual presence fascinates and baffles him.

In the 'outline' of his 'immediate intentions' Dickens makes it plain that 'Dombey and Son' is merely the necessary prelude to the central theme of 'Dombey and Daughter': 'I purpose changing his feeling of indifference and uneasiness towards his daughter into a positive hatred. . . . At the same time I shall change *her* feeling towards *him* for one of a greater desire to love him, and to be loved by him. . . .'[2] We are to witness the fall of worldly Pride in Dombey's ruin. But the dramatic potential is located in his inner conflict, to be resolved by the final reconciliation: 'For the struggle with himself, which goes on in all such obstinate natures, will have ended then; and the sense of his injustice, which you may be sure has never quitted him, will have at last a gentler office than that of only making him more harshly unjust.' Dickens's primary interest in the inner moral drama is evident from his 'apologia' in the preface to the 1858 edition of the novel: 'Mr Dombey undergoes no violent change, either in this book, or in real life. A sense of his injustice is within him, all along. The more he represses it, the more unjust he necessarily is. Internal shame and external circumstances may bring the contest to a close in a week, or a day; but, it has been a contest for years, and is only fought out after a long balance of victory.' The extended treatment given to the complicating triangle of emotional forces arising from Dombey's second marriage, and the entry of Carker into that field of tension, indicates how far Dickens became absorbed, as the novel progressed, in the personal theme.

The role of Mr Dombey is therefore something of a test case for Dickens's art. Henry James, reviewing *Our Mutual Friend* [in 1865], found that Dickens was incapable of effectively treating the inner life: 'it is one of the chief conditions of his genius not to see beneath the surface of things. . . . He has created nothing but figures. He has added nothing to our understanding of human character.'[3] Recently the thesis has been elaborated that Dickens's peculiar gift, and limitation, was for 'theatrical art' in which 'the primary object of our attention is the artist himself, on the stage of his own theatre, performing his brilliant routines. The characters he "creates" on this stage will come to us, and be consistently known to us, as the embodiments of his brilliant gift for *mimicry*.'[4] Dickens is accordingly disqualified as a practitioner of what is called 'serious art': 'he did not ever learn to practise the mode of moral drama which is the norm for serious art, that mode which consists of the dramatisation of moral choice in the inner life of the individual human consciousness'.[5]

Concerning the presentation of the inner life, if Dickens is judged by Jamesian criteria he is naturally found wanting. He does not deal in the 'finer consciousness' and its nuances nor is he concerned with intellectual inquiry, self-analysis, and debate. G. H. Lewes complained, with some reason considering his own phrenological bumps, that 'Dickens sees and feels, but the logic of feeling seems the only logic he can manage. Thought is strangely absent from his works.'[6] *Thought* is a tricky word. We know Mr Casaubon's thoughts; we know Strether's.[7] Mr Dombey also has his thoughts, simpler and at an appropriately conventional level. But what Dickens is concerned with are the dominant elements in Dombey's motivation: the nature of his inner conflict and its development: the 'passions' that 'spin the plot'.

As to method we are not usually shown Dombey reflecting about himself. Nor does Dickens much analyse his state of mind, although both authorial comment and *.iyle indirect libre*[8] are used as supplementary means with fine effect. Dickens's primary mode is to show us Dombey, and Edith, at a series of nodal points in the action. These points have been selected so as to provide the dramatic intensity and vividness of focus needed for the most effective illumination of personality. What Dombey says or does at such a point offers a sudden and peculiarly revealing vision of his inner self and its motivations. Character is shown in action; the mode is kinetic. And it is impressionistic. Character, and inner growth, is evoked and suggested by the discontinuous, selective 'picturing' of high points of experience. There is not the linear sense of character development depending on the knowledge and insights derived from continuous authorial or other mediation. Rather an intermittent series of dramatic illuminations imply and suggest instead of interpreting and defining. But the impressionism is cumulative in its effect. We come to know, or sense, a great deal about Dombey's inner life and the less conscious and submerged impulses involved in its primary conflict as we pass from one nodal point to another.

We meet Mr Dombey, and son, in the opening chapter. Curiously little is said, descriptively, about him: 'Dombey was about eight-and-forty years of age . . . , rather bald, rather red, and though a handsome well-made man, too stern and pompous in appearance, to be prepossessing.' What he does suggests the kind of person he is: 'Dombey, exulting in the long-looked-for event, jingled and jingled the heavy gold watch-chain that depended from below his trim blue coat, whereof the buttons sparkled phosphorescently in the feeble rays of the distant fire.' The jingling of the watch chain, heavy gold, is no mere externalised mannerism like the pantings and chokings that always signalise Major Bagstock. It has here a metonymic quality; it fixes on our senses the potentate presence of its wearer and his euphoric pride. And what is then *said* rounds out the picture, deftly and economically suggesting the kind of husband the watch chain jingler is: ' "The house will once again, Mrs Dombey", said Mr Dombey, "be not only in name but in fact Dombey and Son; Dom-bey and Son!" The words had such a softening influence, that he appended a term of endearment to Mrs Dombey's name (though not without some hesitation, as being a man but little used to that form of address): and said, "Mrs Dombey, my-my dear".'

The rhetoric of the first chapter is exuberant, the irony heavily marked. But the mind of Mr Dombey is not a finer consciousness. And it is his mind that we here see ticking as clearly as we hear his 'very loud ticking watch'. Very little has been authorially said about him. But his personality has been exposed to the reader as sharply focused as it appeared, through a chil. 's eyes, to Florence: 'the blue coat and stiff white cravat, which, with a pair of creaking boots and a very loud ticking watch, embodied her idea of a father'. The initial picture may be that appropriate to a comedy of humors. But it is extremely alive, economical and objective. There is no Manager of the Performance getting in between us and Mr Dombey. Dombey himself is out at the center of the stage from the start. With a minimum of stage directions (such as the familiar irony of 'the earth was made for Dombey and Son to trade in, and the sun and moon were made to give them light') his actions and his words, heightened by the precise dramatic context, show us the man.

The death of Paul sets the stage for the central drama of Dombey and Florence. A key chapter in this development is 18, entitled 'Father and Daughter', an admirable instance of Dickens's skill in dramatic composition, particularly of his ability to use scene to suggest inner qualities. There are six interlinked scenes arranged in tonal contrast. First the funeral procession and church service. Nothing is authorially said about Dombey's thoughts, scarcely anything of his looks. There is only the little incident, presented in dialogue, in which his inscription for the grave ('beloved and only child') has to be corrected. Suddenly we see the vein of pathos in Dombey's obsessive pride in his son and heir. Without a word of analysis, commentary, or *erlebte Rede*, Dickens 'shows' Dombey in a new light.

There follows the conversation between Mrs Chick, Miss Tox and Florence about his desire to be left to himself and his decision to go away to the country. Florence's lonely sad reverie then leads into the contrasting 'fairy-tale' mode of 'the rosy children' playing with their father in the house opposite. Then the brief intermezzo in sombre tones of Florence's nightly visits to her father's always closed door, anticipating the tragic encounter at the close. Comic relief intervenes in the shape of Mr Toots and Diogenes, the dog who serves as a 'sort of keepsake' for Paul, followed by another brief intermezzo in which Susan Nipper informs Florence that her father is to leave the next morning (she has not even seen him since the funeral). Again making

her nightly visit Florence finds the door slightly open. There is a
special significance in this chance detail. Florence is the estranged
child of humanity crying to be let into the house of love and
community; but 'the door was ever closed, and he shut up within'.[9]
Seeing him now in his 'utter loneliness', she speaks to him:

> He started at her voice, and leaped up from his seat. She was close before
> him, with extended arms, but he fell back. 'What is the matter?' he said,
> sternly. 'Why do you come here? What has frightened you?'
> If anything had frightened her, it was the face he turned upon her. The
> glowing love within the breast of his young daughter froze before it, and she
> stood and looked at him as if stricken into stone.
> There was not one touch of tenderness or pity in it. There was not one
> gleam of interest, parental recognition, or relenting in it. There was a change
> in it, but not of that kind. The old indifference and cold restraint had given
> place to something: what, she never thought and did not dare to think, and yet
> she felt it in its force, and knew it well without a name: that as it looked upon
> her, seemed to cast a shadow on her head.   [ch. 18]

It is characteristic of Dickens that he does not offer at this dramatic
point any analysis or interpretation of that 'something' in her father's
face. There is the string of accompanying questions, on a 'Jamesian'
reading crudely intrusive rhetorical questions suggesting possible
motives: Florence as his 'successful rival' in Paul's affection, a kind of
'mad jealousy', the 'gall' of seeing her 'in her beauty and her promise'
while his son is dead. The questions are Dickens's way of indicating
that Dombey is himself not yet conscious of the motives for and extent
of his new darker feelings toward his daughter. What the reader is
given is the intuitive shock of recognition of that change on Florence's
part, and, with the insight and command of great art, the conflicting
impulses and genuine suffering of Mr Dombey. Even at this point he
is, in his way, compassionate, taking her by the arm (though his hand
is 'cold, and loose') and saying she must be tired: 'I will remain here to
light you up the stairs. The whole house is yours above there', says the
father slowly. 'You are its mistress now. Good night!' The chilling
irony of this property grant ('Dombey and son had often dealt in
hides, but never in hearts') is lost on the father. Then with a natural
simplicity of means Dickens reveals another side to Dombey's cold
indifference:

> The last time he had watched her, from the same place, winding up those
> stairs, she had had her brother in her arms. It did not move his heart towards
> her now, it steeled it: but he went into his room, and locked his door, and sat
> down in his chair, and cried for his lost boy.   [ch. 18]

The cadence and finely achieved tragic insight of this final sentence
prove Dickens in command of resources that might easily in such a

context have slipped into facile pathos. The chapter as a whole shows the hand not of any 'theatrical' manipulator of externalised characters but that of the born dramatist who matches control of stage and scene with searching insight into basic human motivations.

The drama of father-daughter tension is now both diversified and intensified by the 'external circumstances' of Dombey's second marriage. Dickens offers a preview of the direction the tension will take. Carker comes to Leamington to consult Dombey and mentions casually, immediately after being told about Edith, that he has 'seen Miss Dombey'. The father has no comment nor apparent interest, but 'there was a sudden rush of blood to Mr Dombey's face'. It is a small touch but deliberate and expressive. The earlier cold hostility toward his daughter has given way to something so blood-suffusing as to suggest hate. During the train journey from London he had formed the homicidal thought that he could have lost Florence 'without a pang' if only Paul had been spared. And in the 'rush of blood' there is also implied an element of sexual frustration and resentment. While informing Carker much later on [ch. 42] of Edith's insubordination (and remembering the encounter in her apartment where her sexual allure was most evident), Dombey feels 'the blood rush to his own face'. In regard to Florence, the deepening of his resentment into hate is overtly linked with her transition from girl to young woman. He suddenly becomes possessive. The night he returns home from his 'honeymoon' in Paris, he sits alone with Florence secretly watching her 'in her beauty, almost changed into a woman without his knowledge'. For a moment he relents and is on the point of calling her to him when Edith enters. He observes without illusion the affection that exists between them and from then on his attitude to Florence is overlaid by sexual jealousy fed by his own inability to subdue Edith's will.

Dombey's motivation in regard to wife and daughter is partly expressed scenically. The dramatic mode works to a climax with Edith's elopement. As he rushes from her dressing-room where he found 'in a costly mass upon the ground' every ornament and dress Edith had possessed, Dombey has the 'frantic idea of finding her yet . . . and beating all trace of beauty out of the triumphant face with his bare hand' [ch. 47]. When a little later Florence approaches him to offer her sympathy, he tells her what Edith was, and bids 'her follow her, since they had always been in league' and strikes her so heavily on the breast (it remained not merely figuratively 'bruised') that she falls to the marble floor. She sees him 'murdering that fond idea' of gaining his affection; she sees his 'cruelty, neglect, and hatred dominant above it, and stamping it down' [ch. 47]. The suddenly unleashed violence and savage energy of act and mood, and the particular direction his impulses take in each instance, make this a revealing dramatisation of Dombey's interlocked sexual frustration, jealousy and rage.

Dickens does not rely on the dramatic mode alone. In chapter 40, titled with cool irony 'Domestic Relations', Dombey's ambivalent attitude toward Florence, linked with that toward his wife, is indicated in a blend of authorial interpretation and *style indirect libre*:

> In his sullen and unwholesome brooding, the unhappy man, with a dull perception of his alienation from all hearts, and a vague yearning for what he had all his life repelled, made a distorted picture of his rights and wrongs, and justified himself with it against her [Florence]. The worthier she promised to be of him, the greater claim he was disposed to ante-date upon her duty and submission. When had she ever shown him duty and submission? Did she grace his life – or Edith's? Had her attractions been manifested first to him – or Edith? Why, he and she had never been, from her birth, like father and child! They had always been estranged. She had crossed him every way and everywhere. She was leagued against him now. Her very beauty softened natures that were obdurate to him, and insulted him with an unnatural triumph.   [ch. 40]

Such a passage (by no means the only one of its kind in this novel) indicates how effectively Dickens uses on occasion a mode so characteristic of George Eliot when treating the inner life of her characters. The sudden, natural shift away from the authorial stance ('When had she ever shown him duty and submission?') brings all the advantages of dramatic immediacy and authentic expression of Dombey's tortured rationalising. The 'insulted him with an *unnatural* triumph' suggests the sexual element in his frustration which is made over in the immediately following scene with Edith.

The distinctive use of scene to suggest phases of character and motivation is well displayed when Dombey confronts his wife, late at night in her own apartment, with his 'ultimatum' that she show him more obedience. Edith is of course 'melodramatic'; she makes her way in the novel accompanied by a mounting array of rhetorical cliché (flashing eye, haughty brow, scornfully curled lip). But her melodramatic aspect is insisted upon much more heavily after her flight with Carker. As she defies her husband in this scene in her 'brilliant dress', her 'white arms' folded 'upon her swelling breast', there is a good deal more than the simplified motivations of melodrama in the rendering:

> If she had been less handsome, and less stately in her cold composure, she might not have had the power of impressing him with the sense of disadvantage that penetrated through his utmost pride. But she had the

power, and he felt it keenly. He glanced round the room: saw how the splendid means of personal adornment, and the luxuries of dress, were scattered here and there, and disregarded; not in mere caprice and carelessness (or so he thought), but in a steadfast haughty disregard of costly things: and felt it more and more. . . . The very diamonds – a marriage gift – that rose and fell impatiently upon her bosom, seemed to pant to break the chain that clasped them round her neck, and roll down on the floor where she might tread upon them.

He felt his disadvantage, and he showed it. Solemn and strange among his wealth of colour and voluptuous glitter, strange and constrained towards its haughty mistress, whose repellent beauty it repeated, and presented all around him, as in so many fragments of a mirror, he was conscious of embarrassment and awkwardness.   [ch. 40]

The atmospheric and suggestive power of the narration here enables Dickens to present the conflict between husband and wife as more complex than the clash of strong wills or the resentment of a 'purchased' wife against husbandly domination. We are made aware of the sexual undercurrent on both sides. Dombey is embarrassed and constrained face to face with Edith's beauty and the 'voluptuous glitter' in which she moves. In the same chapter she reveals in high rhetorical color the passionate potential under her officially 'cold' self. At Dombey's mention of Carker who, she knows, is well aware of her real nature, her face and bosom glow 'as if the red light of an angry sunset had been flung upon them'. Characteristically Dickens uses a visual detail, in this instance a compulsive mannerism, to complement and vivify the narrative. As the tension mounts between them she sits – 'still looking at him fixedly – turning a bracelet round and round upon her arm; not winding it about with a light, womanly touch, but pressing and dragging it over the smooth skin, until the white limb showed a bar of red'. The image here is at the level of poetic metaphor. In that 'bar of red' on the smooth skin we see, in a flash of rare insight that fuses the personal and the social elements, Edith Dombey's divided and tortured nature: her need, and capacity, for love, her scorn, and the passionate self-contempt she had herself voiced in an earlier conversation with her mother: 'There is no slave in a market; there is no horse in a fair; so shown and offered and examined and paraded, mother, as I have been, for ten shameful years' [ch. 27].

Dickens has been criticised for contriving his dénouement too summarily: 'The year was out, and the great House was down' [ch. 58]. Ironically for those who see him as a writer of 'external' life, he here skimps the treatment of his social framework in order to concentrate on the inner life. His finale is centered on the last agonised stage of Dombey's self-conflict and its resolution. Those who find the redemption a purely stage-managed surrender to Florence's all-too-consistent Angel of Mercy mission should in all fairness not ignore the registration of Dombey's preceding mood. Bankrupt and 'shut up' (again this image of alienation) in the rooms of his house now given over to creditors, disgraced by his wife and abandoned by his daughter, he turns his back, still proud, on the world. The savage contest between 'pride' (and all that emotionally repressive mechanism that we have seen at work in his relations with daughter and wife) and remorse drive him – we are made to feel it – to the verge of madness and suicide.

The means used to represent the intensity of his suffering are varied. If there is for many readers the melodramatic dross of the invocation, reiterated from chapter 18, 'Let him remember it in that room, years to come!', there is dramatic gold as well. Alone at night he thinks of the spoliation of his house, and life, in terms of the innumerable footsteps of the funiture removers and creditors' agents:

Of all the footmarks there, making them as common as the common street, there was not one, he thought, but had seemed at the time to set itself upon his brain while he had kept close, listening. . . . He began to fear that all this intricacy in his brain would drive him mad; and that his thoughts already lost coherence as the footprints did, and were pieced on to one another, with the same trackless involutions, and varieties of indistinct shapes.   [ch. 59]

If it is 'theatre', then it is effective theatre when in the end he watches, doppelgänger fashion, his image in the mirror, a separated and impersonal thing: 'Now it rose and walked about; now passed into the next room, and came back with something from the dressing-table in its breast.'

The highly wrought tension here may seem suspect in view of the miraculously timed coup de théatre of Florence's kneeling before the would-be suicide and praying for forgiveness. But the overriding impression, created by the finely controlled blend of scenic presentation, authorial interpretation, and *erlebte Rede*, is of the father's suffering – and of the slow changes forced on him by experience: the death of Paul, remarriage, the relations of Edith and Florence, Edith's willfulness and adultery (in spirit; Dombey thinks of her as 'sunk into a polluted creature'), Carker's treachery, Florence's flight and marriage, his own disgrace and financial ruin. The nerve-shattered aging man whom Florence rescues has come a long way from the 'handsome well-made' Dombey who jingled his heavy gold watch chain in pride at his son's birth. And Dickens has so vividly caught the 'felt life' of that human journey that the reader accepts at the end the

portrayal of the breaking of Dombey's pride not as theatrical
manipulation but as the objective revelation of great art.

SOURCE: Milner's essay, 'The Dickens Drama: Mr Dombey', in
Ada Nisbet and Blake Nevius (eds), *Dickens Centennial Essays*
(Berkeley, Cal. and London, 1971), pp. 155–65.

NOTES

[Reorganised and renumbered from the original – Ed.]

1. Kathleen Tillotson, *Novels of the 1840s* (Oxford, 1954), p. 170.
2. John Forster, *The Life of Charles Dickens* (1874), Book VI, ch. 2. [The
excerpt is reproduced in the concluding item of section 1, above – Ed.]
3. See James's review in *The House of Fiction: Essays on the Novel*, ed. Leon
Edel (New York and London, 1957), pp. 256–7. [It is also reproduced in the
Casebook on *'Hard Times'*, *'Great Expectations'* and *'Our Mutual Friend'*, ed.
Norman Page (1979) – Ed.]
4. Robert Garis, *The Dickens Theatre: A Reassessment of the Novels* (Oxford,
1965), p. 54 – emphasis as in the original.
5. Ibid., pp. 253–4.
6. G. H. Lewes, 'Dickens in Relation to Criticism', *Fortnightly Review* (Feb.
1872); reproduced in George H. Ford and Lauriat Lane, Jnr (eds), *The
Dickens Critics* (New York, 1961), p. 69.
7. [Ed.] Mr Casaubon is a character in George Eliot's *Middlemarch*;
Strether is the central character in Henry James's *The Ambassadors*.
8. [Ed.] *Style indirecte libre* and *erlebte Rede* – Milner uses both the French and
the German expression in this essay – are terms which indicate a prose
technique by means of which the author expresses, apparently directly and
without authorial intrusion, the flow of his character's thoughts while
retaining the third-person form of indirect speech. There is no generally
accepted English term to describe this feature, although the phrase 'free
indirect speech' has sometimes been used.
9. Images of immurement recur throughout the novel: Dombey is 'shut up
within himself' [ch. 20]; he would (with Paul) 'shut out all the world as with a
double door of gold' [ch. 20]; he is 'shut up in his supremacy' [ch. 51]; he lives
'encased' in 'the cold hard armour of pride' [ch. 40]; Florence is 'shut out' and
'lost' [ch. 18]; she 'stand(s) without, with a bar across the door' [ch. 24]; she is
'shut up' in the lonely house [chs 23 and 28].

Nina Auerbach   Dickens and Dombey: A Daughter After All   (1976)

Dickens's daughter's indictment – 'my father did not understand women'[1] – continues to gain momentum, until for some readers, it has threatened to obliterate his entire achievement. His heroines are regularly dismissed as 'so many pale-pink blancmanges, in the same dutiful mould';[2] he is placed historically as 'not so much the recorder of Victorian womanhood as the dupe or the exploiter of its ideal'.[3]

But if Dickens dreamed the Victorian dream of 'wooman, lovely wooman' diffusing rarified conjugal salvation to man in his besotted worldliness, his life and his novels quietly dramatise its component human loss. The 'two nations' into which his England was divided defined the worlds of the sexes as well as those of Disraeli's rich and poor. Men and women were allotted different boundaries, different dreams, different vices and virtues; the ideal woman revolved alone in her unique 'sphere', suggesting a cosmic dimension to the home she created and purified as an intermittent refuge for men from the machinery of their lives. Despite the wedding bells that clang manically through Dickens's novels, there is a note of sexual sadness and loss at the heart of all his work that suggests the isolation inherent in this sexual division, looking forward to such formulated feminist complaints as that of Elizabeth Wolstenholme: 'Of the saddest results of the separate education and life of the sexes, it is impossible here to speak; as a slighter, but still mischievous result, it is sufficient to notice the profound ignorance of each other's real nature and ways of thinking common to both men and women. . . . Many a life has been wrecked upon mistakes arising out of this ignorance.'[4]

As *Great Expectations* is Dickens's most definitive indictment of his own earlier dream of miraculous metamorphosis from waif into gentleman, so *Dombey and Son* seems to me his most thorough exploration of his own and his contemporaries' doctrine of the 'two spheres', with each sex moving in a solitary orbit inaccessible to the other one. The distance between the icy merchant, Paul Dombey Snr, and his boundlessly loving daughter, Florence, and the incessant need of each for the other, disclose more intimately one reality behind Victorian sexual relationships than does the transfiguration of Dickens's forgettable lovers when the plot forces them together. Unable to sit easily together in the same room, father and daughter illuminate a cultural abyss which is reflected in the stereotyped gestures toward bliss of Dickens's husbands and wives.

Throughout his novels, Dickens's dream of love is inseparable from his dream of kinship. Even Pip's obsession with Estella, which is usually considered the most sustained and adult passion in the canon, is revealed at the end to be effectively the love of brother for sister. After his own separation from his wife, Dickens tried to stave off rumors about his affair with Ellen Ternan in conventional language with ambiguous overtones: 'I know her to be innocent and pure, and as good as my own dear daughers.'[5] As in Freud's Victorian paradigm of emotional development, the language of love is at one with the language of family. But among the novels, *Dombey and Son* alone stays within the family walls and reveals the emotional waste beneath its institutional pieties. In most of Dickens's novels, 'home' is 'an intimate and emotion-laden word', a vague haven of love and light waiting to embrace the wandering protagonists. But in *Dombey*, Dickens writes: 'Oh for a good spirit who would take the house-tops off, with a more potent and benignant hand than the lame demon in the tale, and show a Christian people what dark shapes issue from amidst their homes, to swell the retinue of the Destroying Angel as he moves forth among them!' [ch. 47]. The novel's narrator, who is himself the 'good spirit' hovering over the action and exposing it, reveals the pestilence hidden in 'home', rather than reassuring us at the end with its glow.

The rift of home in *Dombey and Son* is defined by the rift between Mr Dombey and Florence, who spend much of the novel haunting their solitary rooms in the great dark house and brooding about each other. They are the polar deities of this polarised novel, and the tension between them generates the tension of the book. They exist as absolutes, memorable less for their individual psychologies than for their magnitude as embodiments of masculinity and femininity as these were conventionally perceived. According to Sylvia Manning: 'In his work Dickens reveals a certain consciousness, though never articulated, of a polarity between the male and female that is both physiological and psychological and of this duality of the sexes as a reflection of metaphysical realities.'[6] Dombey and his daughter are scarcely plausible as physiological and psychological beings alone; in the novel's scheme, they seem less to reflect than to embody the 'metaphysical realities' Manning defines, as the iron force of Dombey's masculine will gives way before Florence's quietly irresistible magnetic field. In Victorian terminology, the power of the man who controls the world gives way before the influence of the woman who controls the mind. A popular conduct book of the day demarcates the spheres in which power and influence, respectively, exert their sway:

[Man's] power is principally exerted in the shape of authority, and is limited in its sphere of action. [Woman's] influence has its source in human sympathies, and is as boundless in its operation. . . . We see that power, while it regulates men's actions, cannot reach their opinions. It cannot modify dispositions nor implant sentiments, nor alter character. All these things are the work of influence. Men frequently resist power, while they yield to influence an unconscious acquiescence.[7]

Men and women possess the world and the self, respectively, and their holdings do not touch. Seen in the light of these radically separate spheres, *Dombey and Son* tells the story of male and female principles who can neither evade nor understand each other, whose tragedy and whose force come from their mutual exclusiveness.

In the first chapter of the novel, the postures and the rhythms of the central characters introduce us to the warring worlds they embody. Stiff and erect as always, Dombey jingles his 'heavy gold watch-chain' over his newborn son and heir. Meanwhile Florence clings to her dying mother, her hair spreading over the pillow as Mrs Dombey's consciousness ebbs away on 'the dark and unknown sea that rolls round all the world' [ch. 1]. The ticking of Dombey's watch fights the silence of birth and death, seeming to speed up incessantly in a senseless race with that of Dr Peps, until, in Florence's embrace, his wife cuts herself loose from time.

The loud watch which is so inseparable a part of Dombey is the voice of the civilisation which gives him his power. The implacable, arbitrary dominance of clock-time counterpoints his wife's equally implacable diffusion into death and space; time here is masculine; space, feminine. The tendency of his watch to accelerate is an emblem of his own attempt to force natural processes to march to the imperious rhythm of his manufactured ticking: 'Therefore he was impatient to advance into the future, and to hurry over the intervening passages of [Paul's] history' [ch. 8]. 'Dear me, six will be changed to sixteen, before we have time to look about us' [ch. 11], he insists as he sends Paul to Dr Blimber's 'great hothouse' in which 'all the boys blew before their time' and 'Nature was of no consequence at all' [ch. 11]. Captain Cuttle, who lives near the sea's cycle, has a ritual formula to prevent his own treasured silver watch from outrunning nature – 'Put it back half an hour every morning, and about another quarter towards the arternoon, and it's a watch that'll do you credit' [ch. 20] – but Dombey, with his network of power, seems to have no reason to check the time he carries with him in his pocket.

The new reliance on watches, with their arbitrary and manufactured measurement of arbitrary and manufactured time-units, was
a reality in the 1840s and 1850s: England was in the process of
attuning itself to the railroad and its schedule. Later in the novel, the
loud ticking of Mr Dombey's watch will swell into the railroad's
prefabricated roar, in a manner which is anticipated beforehand:

Wonderful Members of Parliament, who, little more than twenty years
before, had made themselves merry with the wild railroad theories of
engineers, and given them the liveliest rubs in cross-examination, *went down
into the north with their watches in their hands*, and sent on messages before by the
electric telegraph, to say that they were coming. Night and day the
conquering engines rumbled at their distant work, or, advancing smoothly to
their journey's end, and gliding like tame dragons into the allotted corners
grooved out to the inch for their reception, stood bubbling and trembling
there, making the walls quake, as if they were dilating with the secret
knowledge of great powers yet unsuspected in them, and strong purposes not
yet achieved.   [ch. 15: my italics]

As the railroad and the watch came to demarcate the day, the
agricultural calendar, with its seasons and ceremonies of growth and
harvest, receded into a picturesque anachronism: natural rural time
was out of joint with most men's lives. But its organic and cyclical
rhythms are still a powerful reality in *Dombey and Son*: in the sea that
'rolls round all the world' which Dombey tries to wind up like his
watch; in the 'odd weedy little flowers' in the bonnets and caps of Miss
Tox, and the 'strange grasses' that are 'sometimes perceived in her
hair'; and in the agricultural immortality with which Polly Toodle
comforts Florence for the loss of her mother:

'Died, never to be seen again by any one on earth, and was buried in the
ground where the trees grow.'
'The cold ground?' said the child, shuddering again.
'No! The warm ground . . . where the ugly little seeds turn into beautiful
flowers, and into grass, and corn, and I don't know what all besides. Where
good people turn into bright angels and fly away to Heaven!'   [ch. 3]

To Dombey, who lives by progression, events are completed by the
ceremonies which define them: funerals, christenings and weddings.
At the same time, the females are the custodians of the natural cycle of
eternal return, guarding its unwilled comings and goings with their
somewhat ominous ability to wait.

To Dombey, this other, revolving world is invisible: he 'intimated
his opinion that Nature was, no doubt, a very respectable institution'
[ch. 21]. He is as single-minded an artifact of civilisation as his watch
is. Early in the novel, we see him 'turning round in his easy chair, as

one piece, and not as a man with limbs and joints' [ch. 2]. His identification of himself with the machinery of his civilisation is at one with his emphatic masculinity. Throughout the book, he is referred to in terms of his stiffness, rigidity, unbendingness, which at times seem to make him less a phallic symbol than the thing itself: 'The stiff and stark fire-irons appeared to claim a nearer relationship than anything else there to Mr Dombey, with his buttoned coat, his white cravat, his heavy gold watch-chain, and his creaking boots' [ch. 5]. 'He is not "brought down", these observers think, by sorrow and distress of mind. His walk is as erect, his bearing as stiff as ever it has been' [ch. 18]. Toward the end of the novel, Mrs Brown reduces his perpetual erectness to one unconquerable attribute: 'Oh, hard, hard, hard!' [ch. 52]. This almost incantatory insistence upon a single set of traits makes Mr Dombey seem the appropriate male divinity of an iron world.

His ethos is at one with his inveterate phallicism. Though he is supposed to be the Victorian businessman par excellence, reducing everything to financial terms, his outlook is more fundamentally sexual than it is monetary; he is more aware of his firm's thorough-going maleness than of its profits. His vision is cosmic and complete. He will not bring the flowing Polly Toodle into contact with his son until he has masculinised her by forcing on her the name of 'Richards'. His firm is the masculine axis at the turning of the world: 'The earth was made for Dombey and Son to trade in, and the sun and moon were made to give them light. Rivers and seas were formed to float their ships; rainbows gave them promise of fair weather; winds blew for or against their enterprises; stars and planets circled in their orbits, to preserve inviolate a system of which they were the centre. Common abbreviations took new meanings in his eyes, and had sole reference to them. A.D. had no concern with anno Domini, but stood for anno Dombei – and Son' [ch. 1]. Unlike other overweening institutions in Dickens's novels – Chancery in *Bleak House*, or the Circumlocution Office in *Little Dorrit* – Dombey and Son is defined in terms that are sexual and metaphysical rather than social. It exists as a gigantic end, the source and destination of all motion, all order, the center not so much of its society as of its universe.

Implicit in this religion is its sense of the female as defective because she is out of tune with the basic masculine rhythm of the cosmos. 'But what was a girl to Dombey and Son! In the capital of the House's name and dignity, such a child was merely a piece of base coin that couldn't be invested – a bad Boy – nothing more' [ch. 1]. Dombey's devaluation of the lovely Florence is the first hint of his lack of business skill, his obsession with gender rather than profits, for in fact a girl is an excellent investment if she is equipped to marry well: Mrs Skewton knows this as she hawks her accomplished and exquisitely-groomed Edith, Mrs Brown as she sells her Alice. Dombey's inability to see beyond his inviolate masculine 'system' into the female business of love is the flaw that will bring down his House. His vision of a girl as nothing more than 'a bad Boy' recalls the sick spleen of Tennyson's narrator in *Locksley Hall*, published four years before *Dombey*:

> Weakness to be wroth with weakness! woman's pleasure, woman's pain—
> Nature made them blinder motions bounded in a shallower brain:
>
> Woman is the lesser man, and all thy passions, matched with mine,
> Are as moonlight unto sunlight, and as water unto wine—
> [lines 149–52]

Like Dombey, Tennyson's speaker judges woman by himself, refusing to recognise her as unique and discrete. The lesson of *The Princess* will correct him: 'For woman is not undevelopt man, But diverse' [VII, lines 259–60]. From the recognition of incompatibility comes conversion into love. This vision of love predicated on divergence is inherent in the titles of the two lectures that form John Ruskin's *Sesame and Lilies*, 'Of Kings' Treasuries' and 'Of Queens' Gardens'. His strictures in the latter admonish many Dombeys: 'We are foolish, and without excuse foolish, in speaking of the "superiority" of one sex to the other, as if they could be compared in similar things. Each has what the other has not: each completes the other, and is completed by the other: they are in nothing alike [.]' But this sweet ideal of mutual completion scarcely takes place in the torn *Dombey* world. As Dombey becomes increasingly aware of Florence as something more potent than 'a bad Boy', he is also increasingly – and, it seems, justly – aware of her as his antagonist, exposing rather than completing him by her unlikeness: 'Who was it whose least word did what his utmost means could not! . . . She was leagued against him now. Her very beauty softened natures that were obdurate to him, and insulted him with an unnatural triumph' [ch. 40]. As Sarah Lewis writes in her conduct book: 'Men frequently resist power, while they yield to influence an unconscious acquiescence.'

Dombey himself, who is all power, seems at first impervious to any influence whatever: 'it seemed as if its icy current, instead of being released by this influence [of his schemes for his son], and running clear and free, had thawed for but an instant to admit its burden, and then frozen with it into one unyielding block' [ch. 5]. But the influence equipped to thaw this unyielding block of power is expressed prophetically in Polly Toodle's first words about Florence: 'I never saw such a melting thing in all my life!' [ch. 3]. Florence herself is literally melting in that she weeps incessantly, but she is most important as an almost disembodied influence that causes the melting of others around her. Unlike her father's power, her influence is unwilled: she will never 'make an effort', as her aunt Louisa bemoans. Its operation is unconscious, almost psychic: '[Mr. Dombey] almost felt as if she watched and distrusted him. As if she held the clue to something secret in his breast, of the nature of which he was hardly informed himself. As if she had an innate knowledge of one jarring and discordant string within him, and her very breath could sound it' [ch. 3]. In contrast to her father's rigidity, Florence is, like George Eliot's Dorothea Brooke, 'incalculably diffusive', almost shapeless, seeming to seep into the recesses of the mind. Her genius for presiding over sickbeds has seemed ghoulish to some readers;[8] the avidity with which she nurses her dying brother, and seems almost to leap at her father whenever he is sleeping, injured, or ill, reminds us that to many Victorians, woman's true sphere was neither the kitchen nor the bedroom, but the sickroom. Yet a sickroom needs a patient, and Florence's melting influence needs her father supine; she can touch him only at the end, when she can nurse him. As Moynahan puts it, 'Florence wants to get Dombey's head down on the pillow where she can drown him in a dissolving love'.[9] Her 'woman's mission' is to make the stiff and erect spreading and diffuse in a manner ungraspable by definition: women's influences 'act by a sort of moral contagion, and are imbibed by the receiver as they flow from their source, without consciousness on either side'.[10] If Dombey is so rigid that he seems to lack joints, Florence, the novel's undiluted woman, seems to have liquidity as her essence: she, too, is less a body with limbs and joints than purely a 'melting thing'.

The kinship between Dombey and Florence lies in the single-minded obsessiveness of their approaches to life. If 'the one idea of Mr Dombey's life' is the House, an inviolate masculine system of regulated enterprise, 'nothing wandered in [Florence's] thoughts but love – a wandering love, indeed, and cast away – but turning always to her father. There was nothing . . . that shook this one thought, or diminished its interest' [ch. 18]. As these absolute ideas cannot coexist in a single universe, father and daughter can only try to obliterate each other. After his son's death, Dombey hands to the statuary his inscription for the monument:

'Will you be so good as read it over again? I think there's a mistake.'
'Where?'

The statuary gives him back the paper, and points out, with his pocket rule, the words, 'beloved and only child'.
'It should be "son", I think, Sir?'
'You are right. Of course. Make the correction.'   [ch. 18]

And when Florence is struck by her father: 'She only knew that she had no Father upon earth, and she said so, many times, with her suppliant head hidden from all, but her Father who was in Heaven' [ch. 49]. This radical denial is in part a result of the distance between 'Kings' Treasuries' and 'Queens' Gardens' – that 'profound ignorance of each other's real nature and ways of thinking' that Elizabeth Wolstenholme was to see as one of the tragedies of the age, and which in *Dombey and Son* is the blight of the family.

For despite their distance from each other, Dombey's power and Florence's influence are alike in their potentially murderous seeds: '[Mr Dombey] stood in his library to receive the company, as hard and cold as the weather; and when he looked out through the glass room, at the trees in the little garden, their brown and yellow leaves came fluttering down, as if he blighted them' [ch. 5]. Florence seems at times an equally blighting force: 'As the image of her father whom she loved had insensibly become a mere abstraction, so Edith, following the fate of all the rest about whom her affections had entwined themselves, was fleeting, fading, growing paler in the distance, every day' [ch. 47]. The language of this passage implies that, like that of the vampire, Florence's love drains its objects into ghosts. In this she resembles the child described by Paul's lugubrious nurse, Mrs Wickham: 'She took fancies to people; whimsical fancies, some of them; others, affections that one might expect to see – only stronger than common. They all died' [ch. 8]. Florence's love seems as secretly lethal as Dombey's ambition is overtly life-withering. Their very isolation in their own absoluteness, whereby they contain nothing of each other, is the only bond between father and daughter, and, it seems, between the sexes in general. In part, they kill because 'they are in nothing alike'.

This schism between masculine and feminine spheres seems more fundamental to the novel's world than the usual division critics make between the 'money world' of the firm and the 'water world' of the Wooden Midshipman group. Gender links these inviolate male systems together against the depredations of the Mrs MacStingers of the earth. In *Dombey and Son* and throughout Dickens's other novels, money is ultimately fluid and plentiful, and class lines are illusory and easily crossed. The real, and absolute, barrier is sexual, and it separates not merely individuals, but the landscape of the novel itself.

The two main symbols that dominate *Dombey and Son* can be divided equally into male and female poles which exclude each other. We have seen the link between Dombey's accelerating watch and the new rhythms of the railroad, between the incessant flow of Florence's tears and that of the sea. Each can generate life, but, untempered by the other, each becomes the reaper of its own kind of death.

Like Mr Dombey, the railroad is an artifact of civilisation, the sphere of the mechanical and masculine rather than the organic and feminine. It too is part of a closed and regulated system, without flowing and diffusing beyond one. Like Dombey on a grand scale, the railroad embodies phallic force; and like clock-time's, its progress is implacably linear. Dombey is always wishing for time to end in the apocalypse of Paul's development from self into Son: a boy has 'a destiny' as the train has a preordained destination, to which terminus its violent movement is directed. The train, like the man again, has no private language; its voice is deafeningly public; its speech is 'a shriek, and a roar, and a rattle', 'a shrill yell of exultation'. Dombey's careful periodic eloquence is meant only to be heard by all ears. In chapter 1, he can scarcely lower his voice to say 'my dear', and later he forces Carker to intervene between himself and Edith, so repugnant is private conversation to him. The railroad pulls together all the values of his masculine sphere. Its shrieking linear progress makes us turn with relief to the secret, private sphere of feminine dissolution.

Florence's realm, the sea, exists independent of the mechanised products of civilisation. It is natural and eternal: Paul's dying vision relates it both to Brighton and to the River of Life, flowing through Paradise. Like the ebb and flow of the female cycle, its cyclical ebbs and flows bear no relation to the human will; its rhythms are involuntary and unconscious, related to the flow of emotion and dream; lacking a destination to shape its movements, it has all the interminable attraction of a world without end. Unlike the railroad's shriek, its voice is quiet and its language is private: only Paul can hear 'what the waves are always saying', and that only when he is on the edge of death. The mindlessness of its repeated motions reminds us of Florence's incessant returns to the unyielding breast of her father until it melts for her. Her persistence seems more plausible in geological than in psychological terms: throughout most of the novel, her movements are as involuntary and unwilled as the sea's are. Her kinship with the sea is appropriate to her role as vessel of woman's influence, which is 'imbibed by the receiver as [it] flows from [its] source, without consciousness on either side'.

Opposed as they are in every way, the railroad and the sea have similar effects: both are simultaneously fertile and murderous. Our first awareness is of the lively, generative power of the railroad: it brings prosperity to the good and prolific Toodles, and gives birth to the bursting community of Stagg's Gardens. But on Dombey's long journey to Leamington, it snakes into an engine of death, plowing through a wasteland, its iron will the final blind extension of the Dombey creed of 'making an effort': 'The power that forced itself upon its iron way – its own – defiant of all paths and roads, piercing through the heart of every obstacle, and dragging living creatures of all classes, ages, and degrees behind it, was a type of the triumphant monster, Death' [ch. 20]. The waste and sterility with which its power is finally associated erupt symbolically in Carker's 'mutilated fragments'; retributive though his death is, the explosion of his body and Dombey's swoon suggest the train's unnatural, annihilating arrival at its final destination. The last words in the chapter describe 'some dogs' '[sniffing] upon the road, and [men soaking] his blood up, with a train of ashes' [ch. 55]. The 'conquering engines' have become 'a train of ashes', whose accelerating progress, like Dombey's, destroys more life than it conceives.

The sea, too, seems full of vitality at first. Its power underlies the thriving firm of Dombey and Son itself, as well as its raucous and kindly analogue, the Wooden Midshipman's, with its chanteys and sea-tales and toasts. Yet Mrs Dombey and Paul ebb away on the sea, which, like the railroad, becomes a type of 'the old, old fashion – Death!' Florence's loving influence is itself a sweet drowning and dissolution. In its boundless sweep toward eternity, the sea carries the danger of loss of contour, of sanity, of life itself, until the living and the dead reach to interpenetrate:

'As I hear the sea', says Florence, 'and sit watching it, it brings so many days into my mind. It makes me think so much—'
'Of Paul, my love. I know it does.'
Of Paul and Walter. And the voices in the waves are always whispering to Florence, in their ceaseless murmuring, of love – of love, eternal and illimitable, not bounded by the confines of this world, or by the end of time, but ranging still, beyond the sea, beyond the sky, to the invisible country far away!   [ch. 57]

As Florence seems to preside over the sea, traditional mysticism comes together with a ravenous hunger for death. This sense of life 'not bounded by the confines of this world', but spilling over to touch death, gives the tone to Dombey's cathartic rebirth at the end of the novel, as Florence succeeds at last in encircling his prone head in her oceanic arms. Moynahan is right to see a loss of will, of contour, of intelligence and strength, in Dombey's final conversion into a weeping old man dripping love at the seashore: 'Ambitious projects trouble him no more. His only pride is in his daughter and her husband' [ch. 62]. Carker's iron death was an abrupt explosion into an ending; Dombey's baptismal death is more of an interminable ebb. But the shrieking 'train of ashes' and the 'ceaseless murmuring' of the waves both produce the vitality of loss, not of growth. The masculine and the feminine, the mechanical and the vital, the temporal and the spatial, untempered by each other's qualities, become destroyers. The separation between railroad and sea metaphysically extends the separation between Mr Dombey and Florence at the heart of the novel's split world. . . .

SOURCE: extract from Auerbach's essay, 'Dickens and Dombey: A Daughter After All', in Robert B. Partlow (ed.), *Dickens Studies Annual*, 5 (Carbondale, Ill., 1976), pp. 95–105.

NOTES

[Reorganised and renumbered from the original – Ed.]

1. Quoted in Gladys Storey, *Dickens and Daughter* (London, 1939), p. 100.
2. Patricia Thomson, *The Victorian Heroine: A Changing Ideal, 1837–73* (London, 1956), p. 93.
3. Andrew Sinclair, *The Better Half: The Emancipation of the American Woman* (New York, 1965), p. 164.
4. Elizabeth C. Wolstenholme, 'The Education of Girls, its Present and its Future', in Josephine Butler (ed.), *Woman's Work and Woman's Culture* (London, 1869), pp. 290–330.
5. Dickens's 'Violated Letter', published in the *New York Tribune* (16 Aug. 1858) and reproduced by Ada Nisbet, *Dickens and Ellen Ternan* (Berkeley and Los Angeles, Cal., 1952), p. 67.
6. Sylvia Manning, *Dickens as Satirist* (New Haven, Conn., 1971), pp. 46–7.
7. Sarah Lewis, *Woman's Mission* (Boston, Mass., 1840), p. 13.
8. See Julian Moynahan, 'Dealings with the Firm of Dombey and Son: Firmness *versus* Wetness', in John Gross and Gabriel Pearson (eds), *Dickens and the Twentieth Century* (London, 1962), pp. 121–31.
9. Moynahan, loc. cit., p. 126.
10. Sarah Lewis, loc. cit., p. 95.

PART TWO

Little Dorrit

Little Dorrit

Published in twenty monthly parts from December 1855 to June 1857, and in book form in 1857.

1. ORIGINS AND RECEPTION

Dickens   (1855)

. . . As to the suffrage, I have lost hope even in the ballot. We appear to me to have proved the failure of representative institutions without an educated and advanced people to support them. What with teaching people to 'keep in their station', what with bringing up the soul and body of the land to be a good child, or to go to the beershop, to go a-poaching and go to the devil; what with having no such thing as a middle class (for though we are perpetually bragging of it as our safety, it is nothing but a poor fringe on the mantle of the upper); what with flunkeyism, toadyism, letting the most contemptible lords come in for all manner of places, reading *The Court Circular* for the New Testament, I do reluctantly believe that the English people are habitually consenting parties to the miserable imbecility into which we have fallen, *and never will help themselves out of it*. Who is to do it, if anybody is, God knows. But at present we are on the down-hill road to being conquered, and the people WILL be content to bear it, sing 'Rule Britannia', and WILL NOT be saved.

In No. 3 of my new book[1] I have been blowing off a little of indignant steam which would otherwise blow me up, and with God's leave I shall walk in the same all the days of my life; but I have no present political faith or hope – not a grain. . . .

SOURCE: extract from letter to W. C. Macready, the actor (4 Oct. 1855), reproduced in Mamie Dickens and Georgina Hogarth (eds), *The Letters of Charles Dickens* (London, 1893), p. 379.

NOTE

1. [Ed.] As the first number of *Little Dorrit* did not appear until December 1855, this reference in October to 'No. 3' clearly indicates that, on this occasion, Dickens was well advanced in his pre-publication work for serialisation. It strengthens the impression we have of his especial seriousness of purpose in conceiving and writing *Little Dorrit*.

William Hepworth Dixon   (1857)

... 'Little Dorrit' – as a tale – a fragment of life, wrought up in the romancer's hand – is less complete than some of its author's works. During the year and a half of its existence as a proceeding fact in English literature, we have often heard that it was cloudy, diffuse, uninteresting – that it was false in Art, exaggerated as to character, and the like. We have not found these things true. We have had the fortune to peruse it all at once . . . and looking at the story as a contribution to literature – weighing it as we should weigh 'Tom Jones' or 'The Bride of Lammermoor', we have found it neither false nor weak. Some readers may honestly prefer other works by the same author to this work: we ourselves have our own preferences: but we know of no other author in our time who could have produced 'Little Dorrit'. The spirits are as fresh – the humours as droll – the pathos and tenderness as deep – as anything we know from the same hand. What an invention is the Circumlocution Office! What a marvel is Mrs Clennam! What a picture is that of the Marshalsea! Except in 'Amelia' where have we such another prison interior? We see in 'Little Dorrit' no decrease of power, no closing of eyes, no slackening of pulse. There is enough of genius in this book to have made a sensation for any other name. To say it is not worthy of Dickens, is to pay him an immense compliment.

'Little Dorrit' will meet with opposition from the Barnacles and the Merdles, and from all who are interested in the maintenance of humbug and circumlocution. Indeed we have seen Mr Dickens accused of running down England and the English, and of exalting all that is barbarous and outlandish, and tilted at accordingly in a grave way, which the knight of the rueful countenance would have bit his lip to see. But such has been the fortune of truth-tellers in all ages. We suppose the Author of 'Little Dorrit' was aware what would happen when he put on the prophet's cloak, – and prepared himself to hear it. Notwithstanding the mighty race of the Barnacles, we rejoice to hear from Mr Dickens that for his last tale he has enjoyed communication with a larger circle of readers than for any of his works. . . . [1]

SOURCE: extract from unsigned review in the *Athenaeum* (6 June 1857): no. 1545, pp. 722–4.

NOTE

1. [Ed.] W. H. Dixon's authorship of this anonymous review is identified by Philip Collins in *Dickens: the Critical Heritage* (London, 1971), p. 356.

Leader   (1857)

The completion of one of Mr Dickens's monthly number books is to
the critic what the termination of a year of great events is to the
politician, or the close of an epoch to the historian. The general reader
may pass from the perusal of the last chapter to the first chapter of
some new work without endeavouring to harmonise and arrange the
various impressions and emotions he has derived from the whole; but
it is the duty as well as the pleasure of the critic to turn the completed
globe round upon its axis, and trace the various lines as they converge
towards the final result. Even to him, however, the task is not easy.
There is such an affluence of life in all Mr Dickens's books – so vast a
range of character and observation of the world – so broad a canvas
crowded with so many shapes and incidents – that the effect on the
mind is not so much that of glancing over a finished story, as that of
looking at an epitome of life itself. If this involves some degree of
imperfection in the mere matter of story-telling, it also involves the
highest eulogy that can be pronounced on a novelist whose especial
calling is the portrayal of human nature and human action. Mr
Dickens is the most dramatic of the novelists. He reflects the whole
round of life, from the richest and most refined circles to the humblest
and roughest; and looks with a penetrating eye, and with the intuition
of intense sympathy, into all the depths of the human heart, all the
secret nooks of the affections, all the crooked subtleties of villainy, all
the tangled combinations of good and bad, which make us what we
are. We do not exaggerate when we say that his genius possesses some
points of resemblance to that of Shakspeare[1] – something of the very
thing which, more than anything else, makes Shakspeare the
greatest of dramatic poets. . . .

    As with his other works, so is it with *Little Dorrit*. The whole picture
is quick and warm with life. Passing from the hot southern flush and
glare of Marseilles, in the opening chapter, to the grim old twilight
house in London, with its haunting mysteries and uneasy secrets, in
which Mrs Clennam and Mr Flintwinch plot and counterplot –
changing from the dull prison rooms and yard, with their attendant
poverty, made glorious by the divine light and love of Little Dorrit, to
the stately palaces of Rome and Venice, glowing with the pomp of
wealth – everywhere and under all circumstances, the vitality of the
conceptions asserts itself with all the supremacy of genius. A complete
character will start before you within the compass of a few lines; as in
the case of the little Frenchwoman of whom Mr Dorrit purchases the

gifts for Mrs General, or that of the Swiss host whom Mr Dorrit
almost annihilates for a fancied slight, or in that of the landlady of the
Break of Day at Chalons. But these are the mere overflowings of the
cup. The main characters are those to which we must chiefly look.
And first of Mr Dorrit. What awful truth and solemn voice of warning
is there in that weak, selfish, pompous, insanely proud man! – proud
and vain in his poverty, while descending to depths of meanness;
flaunting his shabby family scutcheon in the face of the visitors of
whom he begs, and pretending to a gentlemanly independence while
his daughter toils for him, almost starves for him; equally, but not
more, proud and vain when he suddenly becomes wealthy, and
fancies himself compelled to resort to miserable shifts to conceal his
former state, which his daughter's devotion should have made noble
in his eyes; proud and vain to the last, though, when the over-
excitement of his changed life topples over his reason and his health,
he divulges in his mental wanderings the fact of his previous poverty,
and dies with the shadow of the Marshalsea upon him. Mr Dorrit is
the very type of flunkeyism; and our time stands in need of a lesson
against that sordid vice. But a manly detestation of servility is one of
the most prominent elements in this tale. We see it again in the
character of Mr Merdle, the swindling speculator. Mr Merdle, it is
well known, is a portrait from life; but it may be as well to recollect
that he is not merely a reflex of one individual. He is true to a very
large, and it is to be feared an increasing, class: a class of individuals
not merely corrupt in themselves, but the cause of corruption in
others. What matter that the Merdles of real life, like the Merdle of
Mr Dickens's fiction, are poor in heart and brain – mere rattling husks
of men, with nothing inside but a few dead conventional ideas and
phrases; what matter that they are dull in thought, embarrassed in
manner, constantly taking themselves into custody under their
coat-cuffs with that intuition of their own villainy noted by Mr
Dickens; what matter that they tremble before their butlers, and
move about their drawing-rooms like icebergs that have preserved all
their coldness and lost all their sparkle? They are rich, though by the
ruin of others; and Bar and Bishop, Horse-Guards[2] and Treasury,
Nobility and Commerce, bow down before them, till, as in the typical
instance here portrayed, 'the shining wonder, the new constellation,
to be followed by the wise men bringing gifts, stops over certain
carrion at the bottom of a bath, and disappears'. . . .

We must confess to some disappointment at the explanation,
towards the close of the book, of the mystery connected with Mrs
Clennam and the old house with its strange noises. It is deficient in
clearness, and does not fulfil the expectations of the reader, which

have been wound up to a high pitch. Indeed, the woof of the entire story does not hold together with sufficient closeness – a fault perhaps inseparable from the mode of publication. The writing, however, shows all Mr Dickens's singular union of close observation and rich fancy. A few instances suggest themselves as we write. Of Jeremiah Flintwinch (whose head is always on one side, so that the knotted ends of his cravat dangle under one ear, and who has 'a swollen and suffused look'), we are told that 'he had a weird appearance of having hanged himself at one time or another, and of having gone about ever since, halter and all, exactly as some timely hand had cut him down'. The watch worn by the same old man was deposited in a deep pocket, 'and had a tarnished copper key *moored above it, to show where it was sunk*'. The garret bedroom of the old house contains 'a lean set of fire irons like the skeleton of a set deceased', and 'a bedstead with four bare atomies of posts, each terminating in a spike, *as if for the dismal accommodation of lodgers who might prefer to impale themselves*'. Very poetical, also, is the identification of the pent-up fire in Mrs Clennam's sick-room with the invalid herself. 'The fire shone sullenly all day and sullenly all night. On rare occasions, it flashed up passionately as she did; but for the most part it was suppressed, like her, and preyed upon itself, evenly and slowly.' The light of this fire throws the shadows of Mrs Clennam, old Flintwinch, and his wife, Mistress Affery, on a gateway opposite, like figures from a magic lantern. 'As the room-ridden invalid settled for the night, these would gradually disappear: Mistress Affery's magnified shadow always flitting about, last, until it finally glided away into air, as though she were off upon a witch-excursion. Then the solitary light would burn unchangingly, until it burned pale before the dawn, and at last died under the breath of Mistress Affery, as her shadow descended on it from the witch-region of sleep.' This is true poetry; but there are a thousand such touches in the book, as in all Mr Dickens's books, which every reader of cultivated perceptions will perceive for himself. In *Little Dorrit*, Mr Dickens has made another imperishable addition to the literature of his country.

SOURCE: extracts from unsigned review in the *Leader* (26 June 1857), pp. 616–17.

NOTES

1. [Ed.] This spelling-form in the original is retained here.

2. [Ed.] 'Horse-Guards': a general allusion to the state's military establishment, the Horse-Guard's building at this date being the headquarters of the army's commander-in-chief.

E. B. Hamley   (1857)

. . . in these post-Pickwickian works the author aspires not only to be a humourist, but an artist and a moralist; and in his later productions . . . he aims at being, besides artist and moralist, politician, philosopher, and ultra-philanthropist. If we direct attention to his weakness in these latter characters, it is solely because he has for years past evinced more and more his tendency to abandon his strong point as humourist and comic-writer, and to base his pretensions on grounds which we consider utterly false and unstable. For as a humourist we prefer Dickens to all living men – as artist, moralist, politician, philosopher, and ultra-philanthropist, we prefer many living men, women, and children to Dickens. It is because we so cordially recognised, and so keenly enjoyed, his genius in his earlier works, that we now protest against the newer phase he chooses to appear in. . . .

The first broad general conclusions which we arrive at from reading this last book, so far as it has gone [Hamley is reviewing *Little Dorrit* before its monthly part-publication was completed – Ed.], is, that Dickens, with all his fertility of invention, has less constructiveness than falls to the lot of five novel-writers out of six, including all the worst. Even if, in the few remaining numbers, the joints of the story should be tightened up, and the different parts of the machinery made to work in something like harmony, yet that would not now retrieve the character of so aimless a work. A most cumbrous array of characters and scenes has been set in motion, and all for what?

Absolutely, the only event yet described which can be called a leading incident, is the deliverance of old Dorrit from the Marshalsea. And how is this brought about? Not by any cause with which any of the characters are even remotely connected, but by the extremely probable circumstance, accidentally discovered, that the old gentleman, after a captivity of twenty years or so, has been all the time the right heir of the great estates of the 'Dorrits of Dorsetshire', of which distinguished family we then hear for the first time. We would pardon this violent wrench in the story if the dislocution produced any interesting results, but the contrary is the case; for, whereas old Dorrit was, in his character of Father of the Marshalsea, the best-drawn personage and most interesting study (we might really say the only of any value) in the book, he becomes, on his accession to wealth, a prosy old driveller, whose inanities are paraded and circumstantially described in a long succession of twaddle, till the favourable impression made in his former phase is quite effaced before his decease, which happily took place in the last number, and which, to all appearances, might just as well have occurred a long time ago. There is positively no dramatic result whatever from the marvellous convulsion in the fortunes of the Dorrit family up to the old man's decease, except that one of his daughters is married to a Mr Sparkler, one of the amateur idiots of the book, who is the stepson of the great speculator, Mr Merdle, another of the amateur idiots of the book.

The fortunes of the Clennam family, occupying as they do a space nearly as large as that of the Dorrits, would, by an artistic writer, have been so interwoven that the opposing, or blending, interests should have elicited character and sustained curiosity; yet four-fifths of the book have elapsed without any connection being even hinted at. . . .

. . . There is some hint of some influence that some Clennam may have had formerly on the fate of old Dorrit, but so obscure and shadowy as to induce the reader to believe that the author had not made up his mind as to what it should turn out to be, and was, therefore, anxious not to commit himself – a blemish that might injure a much better work than this. . . .

With these facts before them, Mr Dickens's blindest admirers will scarcely pretend that this is a work of art. . . .

What can be weaker in itself, to say nothing of the total want of art in connecting it with the story, than the intended satire on the Circumlocution Office? We don't in the least wish to stand up for the Circumlocution Office – curse the Circumlocution Office, say we. We know well the amount of insolence and ignorance to be found among Government officials of all departments. But the attempt to show it up in *Little Dorrit* is as artificial as if he had cut half-a-dozen leading articles out of an Opposition newspaper, and stuck them in anyhow, anywhere. Besides, in all his attempts to embody political questions, Dickens has never shown a spark of original thought. . . . We don't blame him for not being a great politician. It would be almost miraculous if a man with such rare powers of individualising as he is endowed with, should possess also the power of habitually considering questions in their most comprehensive and abstract bearing. What we blame him for is, for leaving the circle where none dare walk but him, to elbow his way on a thoroughfare open to tagrag and bobtail. The next time Mr Dickens dines out, the gentlemen on each side of him will probably be just as much entitled to a hearing on a political question as he is. We don't want him to be a politician, of whom there are plenty; we want him to be a humourist, and painter of passion and life, where he stands almost without a peer. . . .[1]

SOURCE: extracts from unsigned article entitled 'Remonstrance with Dickens', *Blackwood's Magazine* (April 1857): LXXXI, pp. 490–503.

NOTE

1. [Ed.] For the attribution of this anonymous article to E. B. Hamley, see Collins, op. cit., p. 358. Its sharpest jibe against Dickens (not included in our excerpts here) was the mock-lament: 'In the wilderness of *Little Dorrit* we sit down and weep when we remember thee, O Pickwick!'

James Fitz James Stephen   (1857)

. . . 'Little Dorrit' is not one of the most pleasing or interesting of Mr Dickens's novels. The plot is singularly cumbrous and confused – the characters rather uninteresting – and the style often strained to excess. We are not however tempted, by the comparative inferiority of this production of a great novelist, to forget the indisputable merits of Mr Dickens. Even those who dislike a good deal of the society to which he introduces his readers, and who are not accustomed to the language of his personages, must readily acknowledge that he has described modern English low life with infinite humour and fidelity, but without coarseness. He has caught and reproduced that native wit which is heard to perfection in the repartees of an English crowd: and though his path has often lain through scenes of gloom, and poverty, and wretchedness, and guilt, he leaves behind him a spirit of tenderness and humanity which does honour to his heart. We wish he had dealt as fairly and kindly with the upper classes of society as he has with the lower; and that he had more liberally portrayed those manly, disinterested, and energetic qualities which make up the character of an English gentleman. Acute observer as he is, it is to be regretted that he should have mistaken a Lord Decimus for the type of an English statesman, or Mr Tite Barnacle for a fair specimen of a public servant. But in truth we cannot recall any single character of his novels, intended to belong to the higher ranks of English life, who is drawn with the slightest approach to truth or probability. His injustice to the institutions of English society is, however, even more flagrant than his animosity to particular classes in that society. The rich and the great are commonly held up to ridicule for their folly, or to hatred for their selfishness. But the institutions of the country, the laws, the administration, in a word the government under which we live, are regarded and described by Mr Dickens as all that is most odious and absurd in despotism or in oligarchy. In every new novel he selects one or two of the popular cries of the day, to serve as seasoning to the dish which he sets before his readers. It may be the Poor Laws, or Imprisonment for Debt, or the Court of Chancery, or the harshness of Mill-owners, or the stupidity of Parliament, or the inefficiency of the Government, or the insolence of District Visitors, or the observance of Sunday, or Mammon-worship, or whatever else you please. He is equally familiar with all these subjects. If there was a popular cry against the management of a hospital, he would no doubt write a novel on a month's warning about the ignorance and temerity with which surgical operations are performed. . . . Even the catastrophe in 'Little Dorrit' is evidently borrowed from the recent fall of houses in Tottenham Court Road, which happens to have appeared in the newspapers at a convenient moment. . . .

By examining the justice of Mr Dickens's general charges, . . . we shall endeavour to show how much injustice may be done, and how much unfounded discontent may be engendered, by these one-sided and superficial pictures of popular abuses.

It is not a little curious to consider what qualifications a man ought to possess before he could, with any kind of propriety, hold the language Mr Dickens sometimes holds about the various departments of social life. . . . The greatest of our statesmen, lawyers, and philosophers would shrink from delivering any trenchant and unqualified opinion upon so complicated and obscure a subject as the merits of the whole administrative Government of the empire. To Mr Dickens the question presents no such difficulty. He stumbles upon the happy phrase of 'the Circumlocution Office' as an impersonation of the Government; strikes out the brilliant thought, repeated just ten times in twenty-three lines, that whereas ordinary people want to know how to do their business, the whole art of Government lies in discovering 'how not to do it'; and with these somewhat unmeaning phrases he proceeds to describe, in a light and playful tone, the government of his country.

Everybody has read the following chapter of 'Little Dorrit;' but we are not equally sure that everybody has asked himself what it really means. It means, if it means anything, that the result of the British constitution, of our boasted freedom, of parliamentary representation, and of all we possess, is to give us the worst government on the face of the earth – the clatter of a mill grinding no corn, the stroke of an engine drawing no water. [Stephen quotes the first six paragraphs

of ch. 10 of Book I, 'Containing the whole science of Government' –
Ed.] . . .

This is no isolated ebullition. The Circumlocution Office forms one
of the standing decorations of the work in which it is depicted. The
cover of the book is adorned by a picture, representing, amongst other
things, Britannia in a Bath-chair, drawn by a set of effete idiots, an old
woman, a worn-out cripple in a military uniform, and a supercilious
young dandy, who buries the head of his cane in his moustaches. The
chair is pushed on behind by six men in foolscaps, who are followed by
a crowd of all ages and both sexes, intended, we presume, to represent
that universal system of jobbing and favouritism, which was introduced into the public service by Sir Charles Trevelyan and Sir
Stafford Northcote,[1] shortly before the time when Mr Dickens began
his novel. The spirit of the whole book is the same. The Circumlocution Office is constantly introduced as a splendid example of all that is
base and stupid. Messrs Tite Barnacle and Stiltstalking are uniformly
put forward as the representatives of the twenty or thirty permanent
under-secretaries and heads of departments, by whom so large a
portion of the public affairs is conducted, and every species of
meanness, folly, and vulgarity is laid to their charge.

It is difficult to extract the specific accusations which Mr Dickens
means to bring against the Government; but we take the principal
counts in his indictment to be, that the business of the country is done
very slowly and very ill; that inventors and projectors of improve-
ments are treated with insolent neglect; and that the Government is
conducted by, and for the interest of, a few aristocratic families, whose
whole public life is a constant career of personal jobs. Most men will
consider these rather serious charges. . . .

As to the personal corruption, and the neglect of talent, which Mr
Dickens charges against the Government of the country, we can only
say that any careful observer of his method might have predicted with
confidence that he would begin a novel on that subject within a very
few months after the establishment of a system of competitive
examinations for admission into the Civil Service. He seems, as a
general rule, to get his first notions of an abuse from the discussions
which accompany its removal, and begins to open his trenches and
mount his batteries as soon as the place to be attacked has
surrendered. This was his course with respect both to imprisonment
for debt and to Chancery reform; but in the present instance, he has
attacked an abuse which never existed to anything like the extent
which he describes. A large proportion of the higher permanent
offices of state have always been filled by men of great talent, whose
promotion was owing to their talent. . . . [To] take a single and

well-known example, how does he account for the career of Mr Rowland Hill?[2] A gentleman in a private and not very conspicuous position, writes a pamphlet recommending what amounted to a revolution in a most important department of the Government. Did the Circumlocution Office neglect him, traduce him, break his heart, and ruin his fortune? They adopted his scheme, and gave him the leading share in carrying it out, and yet this is the Government which Mr Dickens declares to be a sworn foe to talent, and a systematic enemy to ingenuity. . . .[3]

SOURCE: extracts from unsigned article entitled 'The License of Modern Novelists', *Edinburgh Review* (July 1857): CVI, pp. 124–56.

NOTES

1. [Ed.] Sir Charles Trevelyan and Sir Stafford Northcote (later Lord Iddesleigh) were jointly responsible for the report on the Civil Service which, in 1853, recommended that entry to the public service should be on merit, by competitive examination.

2. [Ed.] Rowland Hill was the originator of the penny-post and the great pioneer of Post Office reform. Although Chief Secretary of the Post Office from 1847 to 1864, his career was marked by frequent opposition to his views from the Establishment: a point which Dickens was to seize on in his reply to this attack on *Little Dorrit*: see next excerpt.

3. [Ed.] Stephen's authorship of this anonymous article is certain. (In it he also attacked Charles Reade's *It is Never Too Late to Mend* and, from a somewhat different viewpoint, Mrs Gaskell's *Life of Charlotte Brontë*.) Stephen's father was Under-Secretary to the Colonies, and the son took considerable offence at Dickens's satire on governmental bureaucracy, reviewing *Little Dorrit* several times in a hostile way.

Dickens   (1857)

A Rejoinder

The Edinburgh Review, in an article in the last number, on 'The License of Modern Novelists' [by J. F. Stephen: see above – Ed.], is angry with Mr Dickens and other modern novelists, for not confining themselves to the mere amusement of their readers, and for testifying in their works that they seriously feel the interest of true Englishmen

in the welfare and honor of their country. To them should be left the
making of easy occasional books for idle young gentlemen and ladies
to take up and lay down on sofas, drawing-room tables, and
window-seats; to the Edinburgh Review should be reserved the
settlement of all social and political questions, and the strangulation
of all complainers. . . .

The License of Modern Novelists is a taking title. But it suggests
another – the License of Modern Reviewers. Mr Dickens's libel on the
wonderfully exact and vigorous English government, which is always
ready for any emergency, and which, as everybody knows, has never
shown itself to be at all feeble at a pinch within the memory of men, is
License in a novelist! Will the Edinburgh Review forgive Mr Dickens
for taking the liberty to point out what is License in a Reviewer?

Even the catastrophe in 'Little Dorrit' is evidently borrowed from the recent
fall of houses in Tottenham Court Road, which happens to have appeared in
the newspapers at a convenient period.

Thus the Reviewer. The Novelist begs to ask him whether there is no
License in his writing those words and stating that assumption as a
truth, when any man accustomed to the critical examination of a book
cannot fail, attentively turning over the pages of 'Little Dorrit', to
observe that that catastrophe is carefully prepared for from the very
first presentation of the old house in the story; that when Rigaud, the
man who is crushed by the fall of the house, first enters it (hundreds of
pages before the end), he is beset by a mysterious fear and
shuddering; that the rotten and crazy state of the house is laboriously
kept before the reader, whenever the house is shown; that the way to
the demolition of the man and the house together, is paved all through
the book with a painful minuteness and reiterated care of presentation, the necessity of which (in order that the thread may be kept in
the reader's mind through nearly two years), is one of the adverse
incidents of that serial form of publication? It may be nothing to the
question that Mr Dickens now publicly declares, on his word and
honor, that the catastrophe was written, was engraven on steel, was
printed, had passed through the hands of compositors, readers for the
press, and pressmen, and was in type and in proof in the Printing
House of Messrs Bradbury and Evans, before the accident in
Tottenham Court Road ocurred. But, it is much to the question that
an honorable reviewer might have easily traced this out in the internal
evidence of the book itself, before he stated, for a fact, what is utterly
and entirely, in every particular and respect, untrue. More; if the
Editor of the Edinburgh Review (unbending from the severe official
duties of a blameless branch of the Circumlocution Office) had

happed to condescend to cast his eye on the passage, and had referred even its mechanical probabilities and improbabilities to his publishers, those experienced gentlemen must have warned him that he was getting into danger; must have told him that on a comparison of dates, and with a reference to the number printed of 'Little Dorrit', with that very incident illustrated, and to the date of the publication of the completed book in a volume, they hardly perceived how Mr Dickens *could* have waited, with such a desperate Micawberism, for a fall of houses in Tottenham Court Road, to get him out of his difficulties, and yet could have come up to time with the needful punctuality. . . .

The Novelist now proceeds to the Reviewer's curious misprint. The Reviewer, in his laudation of the great official departments, and in his indignant denial of there being any trace of a Circumlocution Office to be detected among them all, begs to know, 'what does Mr Dickens think of the whole organisation of the Post Office, and of the system of cheap Postage?' Taking St Martins-le-Grand in tow, the wrathful Circumlocution steamer, puffing at Mr Dickens to crush him with all the weight of that first-rate vessel, demands, 'to take a single and well-known example, how does he account for the career of Mr Rowland Hill? . . . [Dickens quotes the rest of the passage in Stephen's article, assigning credit to the governmental system for Hill's reforms – Ed.]

The curious misprint here is the name of Mr Rowland Hill. Some other and perfectly different name must have been sent to the printer. Mr Rowland Hill!! Why, if Mr Rowland Hill were not, in toughness, a man of a hundred thousand; if he had not had in the struggles of his career a stedfastness of purpose overriding all sensitiveness, and steadily staring grim despair out of countenance, the Circumlocution Office would have made a dead man of him long and long ago. Mr Dickens, among his other darings, dares to state, that the Circumlocution Office most heartily hated Mr Rowland Hill; that the Circumlocution Office most characteristically opposed him as long as opposition was in any way possible; that the Circumlocution Office would have been most devoutly glad if it could have harried Mr Rowland Hill's soul out of his body, and consigned him and his troublesome penny project to the grave together. . . .

Source: extracts from article entitled 'Curious Misprint in the Edinburgh Review', *Household Words* (1 Aug. 1857), pp. 97–100.

George Eliot ·   (1856)

. . . We have one great novelist who is gifted with the utmost power of
rendering the external traits of our town population; and if he could
give us their psychological character – their conceptions of life, and
their emotions – with the same truth as their idiom and manners, his
books would be the greatest contribution Art has ever made to the
awakening of social sympathies. But while he can copy Mrs Plornish's
colloquial style with the delicate accuracy of a sun-picture . . . he
scarcely ever passes from the humorous and external to the emotional
and tragic, without becoming as transcendent in his unreality as he
was a moment before in his artistic truthfulness. . . .

> SOURCE: extract from article entitled 'The Natural History of
> German Life', *Westminster Review* (July 1856): LXVI, pp. 51–79.

Thomas Carlyle   (1856)

. . . Long life to you dear F. and recommend me to Dickens; and thank
him a hundred times for 'the Circumlocution Office'; which is
priceless after its sort! We have laughed long and loud over it here;
and *laughter* is by no means the supreme result in it. Oh, Heavens! . . .

> SOURCE: extract from letter to John Forster, cited in D. A. Wilson,
> *Carlyle to Threescore and Ten* (London, 1929), p. 211.

David Masson   (1859)

. . . Mr Thackeray . . . is singularly acquiescent and conservative for a
man of such general strength of intellect. Mr Dickens, on the other
hand, is singularly aggressive and opinionative. There is scarcely a

social question on which he has not touched; and there are few of his novels in which he has not blended the functions of a social and political critic with those of the artist, to a degree detrimental, as many think, to his genius in the latter capacity. For Mr Dickens's wonderful powers of description are no guarantee for the correctness of his critical judgements in those particulars to which he may apply them . . . and yet how much we owe to Mr Dickens for this very opinionativeness! With his real shrewdness, his thoughtfulness, his courage, what noble hits he has made! The Administrative Reform Association might have worked for ten years without producing half of the effect which Mr Dickens has produced in the same direction, by flinging out the phrase, 'The Circumlocution Office'. He has thrown out a score of such phrases, equally efficacious for social reform; and it matters little that some of them might turn out on enquiry to be ludicrous exaggerations. . . .

SOURCE: extract from Masson's *British Novelists and Their Styles* (Cambridge and London, 1859), pp. 246–7.

John Forster   (1874)

The writing of the novel

. . . At Christmas 1855 came out the first number of *Little Dorrit*, and in April 1857 the last [a slip for June 1857 – Ed.].

The book took its origin from the notion he had of a leading man for a story who should bring about all the mischief in it, lay it all on Providence, and say at every fresh calamity, 'Well, it's a mercy, however, nobody was to blame you know!' The title first chosen, out of many suggested, was *Nobody's Fault*; and four numbers had been written, of which the first was on the eve of appearing, before this was changed. When about to fall to work he excused himself from an engagement he should have kept because 'the story is breaking out all round me, and I am going off down the railroad to humour it'. The humouring was a little difficult, however; and such indications of a droop in his invention as presented themselves in portions of *Bleak House*, were noticeable again. 'As to the story I am in the second number, and last night and this morning had half a mind to begin again, and work in what I have done, afterwards' (Aug. 19). It had occurred to him, that, by making the fellow-travellers at once known to each other, as the opening of the story stands, he had missed an effect. 'It struck me that it would be a new thing to show people coming together, in a chance way, as fellow-travellers, and being in the same place, ignorant of one another, as happens in life; and to connect them afterwards, and to make the waiting for that connection a part of the interest.' The change was not made; but the mention of it was one of several intimations to me of the altered conditions under which he was writing, and that the old, unstinted, irrepressible flow of fancy had received temporary check. In this view I have found it very interesting to compare the original notes, which as usual he prepared for each number of the tale, and which with the rest are in my possession, with those of *Chuzzlewit* or *Copperfield*; observing in the former the labour and pains, and in the latter the lightness and confidence of handling. 'I am just now getting to work on number three: sometimes enthusiastic, more often dull enough. There is an enormous outlay in the Father of the Marshalsea chapter, in the way of getting a great lot of matter into a small space. I am not quite resolved, but I have a great idea of overwhelming that family with wealth. Their condition would be very curious. I can make Dorrit very strong in the story, I hope' (Sept. 16). The Marshalsea part of the tale undoubtedly was excellent, and there was masterly treatment of character in the contrasts of the brothers Dorrit; but of the family generally it may be said that its least important members had most of his genius in them. The younger of the brothers, the scapegrace son, and 'Fanny dear', are perfectly real people in what makes them unattractive; but what is meant for attractiveness in the heroine becomes often tiresome by want of reality.

The first number appeared in December 1855, and on its sale there was an exultant note. '*Little Dorrit* has beaten even *Bleak House* out of the field. It is a most tremendous start, and I am overjoyed at it'; to which he added, writing from Paris on the 6th of the month following, 'You know that they had sold 35,000 of number two on new year's day.' He was still in Paris on the day of the appearance of that portion of the tale by which it will always be most vividly remembered, and thus wrote on the 30th of January 1856: 'I have a grim pleasure upon me to-night in thinking that the Circumlocution Office sees the light, and in wondering what effect it will make. But my head really stings with the visions of the book, and I am going, as we French say, to disembarrass it by plunging out into some of the strange places I glide into of nights in these latitudes.' The Circumlocution heroes led to the Society scenes, the Hampton-court dowager-sketches, and Mr

Gowan; all parts of one satire levelled against prevailing political and social vices. Aim had been taken, in the course of it, at some living originals, disguised sufficiently from recognition to enable him to make this thrust more sure; but there was one exception self-revealed. 'I had the general idea', he wrote while engaged on the sixth number, 'of the Society business before the Sadleir affair, but I shaped Mr Merdle himself out of that precious rascality. Society, the Circumlocution Office, and Mr Gowan, are of course three parts of one idea and design. Mr Merdle's complaint, which you will find in the end to be fraud and forgery, came into my mind as the last drop in the silver cream-jug on Hampstead Heath. I shall beg, when you have read the present number, to enquire whether you consider "Bar" an instance, in reference to K F, of a suggested likeness in not many touches?' The likeness no one could mistake; and, though that particular Bar has since been moved into a higher and happier sphere, Westminster-hall is in no danger of losing 'the insinuating Jury-droop, and persuasive double eye-glass', by which this keen observer could express a type of character in half a dozen words.

Of the other portions of the book that had a strong personal interest for him I have spoken on a former page . . . and I will now only add an allusion of his own. 'There are some things in Flora in number seven that seem to me to be extraordinarily droll, with something serious at the bottom of them after all. Ah, well! was there *not* something very serious in it once? I am glad to think of being in the country with the long summer mornings as I approach number ten, where I have finally resolved to make Dorrit rich. It should be a very fine point in the story. . . . Nothing in Flora made me laugh so much as the confusion of ideas between gout flying upwards, and its soaring with Mr F—— to another sphere' (April 7). He had himself no inconsiderable enjoyment also of Mr F.'s Aunt; and in the old rascal of a patriarch, the smooth-surfaced Casby, and other surroundings of poor Flora, there was fun enough to float an argosy of second-rates, assuming such to have formed the staple of the tale. It would be far from fair to say they did. The defect in the book was less the absence of excellent character or keen observation, than the want of ease and coherence among the figures of the story, and of a central interest in the plan of it. The agencies that bring about its catastrophe, too, are less agreeable even than in *Bleak House*; and, most unlike that well-constructed story, some of the most deeply-considered things that occur in it have really little to do with the tale itself. The surface-painting of both Miss Wade and Tattycoram, to take an instance, is anything but attractive, yet there is under it a rare force of likeness in the unlikeness between the two which has much subtlety of intention; and they must both have had, as well as Mr Gowan himself, a striking effect in the novel, if they had been made to contribute in a more essential way to its interest or development. The failure nevertheless had not been for want of care and study, as well of his own design as of models by masters in his art. . . .

. . . Dickens rightly judged his purpose also to have been, to supply a kind of connection between the episode and the story. 'I don't see the practicability of making the History of a Self-Tormentor, with which I took great pains, a written narrative. But I do see the possibility' (he saw the other practicability before the number was published) 'of making it a chapter by itself, which might enable me to dispense with the necessity of the turned commas. Do you think that would be better? . . . I have no doubt that a great part of Fielding's reason for the introduced story, and Smollett's also, was, that it is sometimes really impossible to present, in a full book, the idea it contains (which yet it may be on all accounts desirable to present), without supposing the reader to be possessed of almost as much romantic allowance as would put him on a level with the writer. In Miss Wade I had an idea, which I thought a new one, of making the introduced story so fit into surroundings impossible of separation from the main story, as to make the blood of the book circulate through both. But I can only suppose, from what you say, that I have not exactly succeeded in this.' . . .

. . . all it is necessary to add of the completed book will be, that, though in the humour and satire of its finer parts not unworthy of him, and though it had the clear design, worthy of him in an especial degree, of contrasting, both in private and in public life, and in poverty equally as in wealth, duty done and duty not done, it made no material addition to his reputation. His public, however, showed no falling-off in its enormous numbers. . . .

SOURCE: extracts from Forster's *The Life of Charles Dickens* (1872–74): ch. 1 of Book VIII.

2. CRITICAL APPRAISALS, 1887–1937

Frank T. Marzials   (1887)

'The Father of the Marshalsea'

. . . the 'Circumlocution Office', where the clerks sit lazily devising all day long 'how *not* to do' the business of the country, and devote their energies alternately to marmalade and general insolence, – the 'Circumlocution Office' occupies after all only a secondary position in the book. The main interest of it circles round the place that had at one time been almost a home to Dickens. Again he drew upon his earlier experiences. We are once more introduced into a debtors' prison. Little Dorrit is the child of the Marshalsea, born and bred within its walls, the sole living thing about the place on which its taint does not fall. Her worthless brother, her sister, her father – who is not only her father, but the 'father of the Marshalsea' – the prison blight is on all three. Her father especially is a piece of admirable character-drawing. Dickens has often been accused of only catching the surface peculiarities of his personages, their outward tricks, and obvious habits of speech and of mind. Such a study as Mr Dorrit would alone be sufficient to rebut the charge. No novelist specially famed for dissecting character to its innermost recesses could exhibit a finer piece of mental analysis. We follow the poor weak creature's deterioration from the time when the helpless muddle in his affairs brings him into durance. We note how his sneaking pride seems to feed even on the garbage of his degradation. We see how little inward change there is in the man himself when there comes a transformation scene in his fortunes, and he leaves the Marshalsea wealthy and prosperous. It is all thoroughly worked out, perfect, a piece of really great art. No wonder that Mr Clennam pities the child of such a father; indeed, considering what a really admirable woman she is, one only wonders that his pity does not sooner turn to love. . . .

SOURCE: extract from Marzial's *Life of Charles Dickens* (London, 1887), pp. 130–1.

George Gissing   (1898)

'Some of the best work Dickens ever did'

... Of *Little Dorrit* (1857), as of *Martin Chuzzlewit*, who can pretend to
bear the story in mind? There is again a moral theme; the evils of
greed and vulgar ambition. As a rule, we find this book dismissed
rather contemptuously; it is held to be tedious, and unlike Dickens in
its prevalent air of gloom. For all that, I believe it to contain some of
his finest work, some passages in which he attains an artistic finish
hardly found elsewhere; and to these I shall return. There were
reasons why the book should be lacking in the old vivacity – never
indeed to be recovered, in so far as it had belonged to the golden years
of youth; it was written in a time of domestic unhappiness and of
much unsettlement, the natural result of which appeared three years
later, when Dickens left the study for the platform. As a narrative,
Little Dorrit is far from successful; it is cumbered with mysteries which
prove futile, and has no proportion in its contrasting parts. Here and
there the hand of the master is plainly weary. . . .

★

... I have heard it very truly remarked that, in our day, people for the
most part criticise Dickens from a recollection of their reading in
childhood; they do not come fresh to him with mature mind; in
general, they never read him at all after childish years. This is an
obvious source of much injustice. Dickens is good reading for all times
of life, as are all the great imaginative writers. Let him be read by
children together with Don Quixote. But who can speak with
authority of Cervantes who knows him only from an acquaintance
made at ten years old? To the mind of a child Dickens is, or ought to be
fascinating – (alas for the whole subject of children's reading
nowadays!) – and most of the fascination is due to that romantic
treatment of common life which is part, indeed, of Dickens's merit,
but has smaller value and interest to the older mind. Much of his
finest humour is lost upon children; much of his perfect description;
and all his highest achievement in characterisation. Taking Dickens
'as read', people inflict a loss upon themselves and do a wrong to the
author. Who, in childhood, ever cared much for *Little Dorrit*? The
reason is plain; in this book Dickens has comparatively little of his
wonted buoyancy; throughout, it is in a graver key. True, a house falls
down in a most exciting way, and this the reader will remember; all

else is to him a waste. We hear, accordingly, that nothing good can be said for *Little Dorrit*. Whereas, a competent judge, taking up the book as he would any other, will find in it some of the best work Dickens ever did; and especially in this matter of characterisation; pictures so wholly admirable, so marvellously observed and so exquisitely presented, that he is tempted to call *Little Dorrit* the best book of all. . . .

★

. . . Among the finest examples of characterisation (I postpone a review of the figures which belong more distinctly to satire) must be mentioned the Father of the Marshalsea. Should ever proof be demanded – as often it has been – that Dickens is capable of high comedy, let it be sought in the 31st chapter of book I of *Little Dorrit*. There will be seen the old Marshalsea prisoner, the bankrupt of half a lifetime, entertaining and patronising his workhouse pensioner, old Mr Nandy. For delicacy of treatment, for fineness of observation, this scene, I am inclined to think, is unequalled in all the novels. Of exaggeration there is no trace; nothing raises a laugh; at most one smiles, and may very likely be kept grave by profound interest and a certain emotion of wonder. We are in a debtors' prison, among vulgar folk; yet the exquisite finish of this study of human nature forbids one to judge it by any but the highest standards. The Dorrit brothers are both well drawn; they are characterisations in the best sense of the word; and in this scene we have the culmination of the author's genius. That it reveals itself so quietly is but the final assurance of consummate power. . . .

★

. . . But read, I beg, that passage of *Little Dorrit* where Amy herself and her idiot friend Maggy, wandering about the streets at night, are addressed by a woman of the town (book I, ch. 14); read that passage and wonder that the same man who penned this shocking rubbish could have written in the same volume pages of a truthfulness beyond all eulogy. . . .

★

. . . Narrative, of course, includes description; but in description by itself and in elaborate picturing, as distinguished from the hints which so often serve his purpose, Dickens is very strong. Before speaking of the familiar instances let me mention that chapter at the beginning of *Little Dorrit*, which opens with a picture of London as seen on a gloomy Sunday – if the phrase be not tautological. It is very curious reading.

For once we have Dickens quite divested of his humour, and beholding the great city in something like a splenetic mood. As conveying an impression, the passage could not be better; it makes us feel precisely what one has felt times innumerable amid the black lifeless houses, under a sky that crushes the spirit. But seldom indeed can Dickens have seen and felt thus. Compare with it his picture of the fog – Mr Guppy's 'London particular' – at the opening of *Bleak House*. This darkness visible makes one rather cheerful than otherwise, for we are spectators in the company of a man who allows nothing to balk his enjoyment of life, and who can jest unaffectedly even in such circumstances. Those few pages of *Little Dorrit*, admirable as art, suggest the kind of novels Dickens might have written without his humour. But in that case he would not have written them all. . . .

SOURCE: extracts from Gissing's *Charles Dickens: A Critical Study* (London, 1898), pp. 58–9; 85–6; 98–9; 159; 190–1.

Edwin Pugh   (1908)

'The Circumlocution Office'

. . . It is just that invention – which was no invention – of the Circumlocution Office which constitutes the real triumph of *Little Dorrit*. The book would have been well worth writing, if only for that sake. Nothing better has been done in English literature, in the way of bold and just satire, than this immortal exposure of the methods of Red Tape and Place-Making, and of the policy, not merely of Letting Things Be, but of Hindering Things From Being Better, which has always stood in the way of British advancement. 'If I might offer any apology', says Dickens in his Preface, 'for so exaggerated a fiction as the Barnacles and the Circumlocution Office, I would seek it in the common experience of an Englishman, without presuming to mention the unimportant fact of my having done that violence to good manners, in the days of a Russian war, and of a Court of Enquiry at Chelsea.' Well, we have had a South African War and a Pall Mall Enquiry,[1] since then.

'So exaggerated a fiction as the Barnacles' – one thinks of the Hungry Hamiltons and the Hotel Cecil![2] – 'and the Circumlocution Office', says Dickens . . . of course, ironically. For the sole aim and purpose of the Circumlocution Office, which was to obstruct justice and to thwart the claims of equity, not to speak of common honesty and irrefutable right, are sustained today with almost unabated vigour by our Government officials, our heads of departments – the overpaid heirs of privilege and usurpation – our legal luminaries, and all the rest of our ordained public administrators, whatever their grade or rank. Even now, as these words are written, a case (in which, curiously enough, Dickens's name has frequently cropped up) is engaging the Courts, in its preliminary stages, which has already wasted years and years of time, and thousands and thousands of pounds – all to no effect – and which a couple of ordinary labourers, armed with a few simple implements, could settle in a quarter of an hour, if plain reason ruled over the counsels of the State instead of crass unreason. And it would be amazing if it were not English, that so little should have been done to improve off the face of the earth the evils which Dickens so searchingly and caustically laid bare, by means of types and nicknames that are among the many utterances of his genius which have since passed into the language. One would imagine that our national sense of humour alone would have availed, long ago, to sweep away these costly absurdities and slow cumbrous survivals of a dead-and-gone, hole-and-corner medievalism, if one could credit the English people with such a sense. One wonders that these anachronisms were not laughed out of existence fifty years ago, instead of enduring even unto this day, as they do. For what Dickens wrote in 1856 is as true, at the opening of the twentieth century, of our modern anarchic lack of method and system, and our clogging superfluity of machinery and process, in dealing with most matters of public policy as ever it was.

    And circling about the Circumlocution Office, in their various eccentric orbits, we are shown a host of ugly giddy satellites, held precariously in their places by that centrifugal force and only very occasionally eclipsing one another, when they are immediately replaced by others as ugly and destructive; such feeble constellations as the Tite Barnacles and the Stiltstalkings, and such solitary planets as the Merdles, the Edmund Sparklers, the Mrs Generals, ay, and even the good perverse Mr Meagleses.

SOURCE: extract from Pugh's *Charles Dickens: The Apostle of the People* (London, 1908), pp. 208–10.

NOTE

1. [Ed.] 'Pall Mall Enquiry': the Butler Report on military efficiency, prompted by the South African campaign. The War Office at that time was in Pall Mall, not Whitehall.

2. [Ed.] 'Hungry Hamiltons and the Hotel Cecil': satirical allusion to family connections in government circles in the late Victorian period.

A. C. Swinburne   (1913)

'The fusion of humour and horror'

... The conception of *Little Dorrit* was far happier and more promising than that of *Dombey and Son*; which indeed is not much to say for it. Mr Dombey is a doll; Mr Dorrit is an everlasting figure of comedy in its most tragic aspect and tragedy in its most comic phase. Little Dorrit herself might be less untruly than unkindly described as Little Nell grown big, or, in Milton's phrase, 'writ large'. But on that very account she is a more credible and therefore a more really and rationally pathetic figure. The incomparable incoherence of the parts which pretend in vain to compose the incomposite story may be gauged by the collapse of some of them and the vehement hurry of cramped and halting invention which huddles up the close of it without an attempt at the rational and natural evolution of others. It is like a child's dissected map with some of the counties or kingdoms missing. Much, though certainly not all, of the humour is of the poorest kind possible to Dickens; and the reiterated repetition of comic catchwords and tragic illustrations of character is such as to affect the nerves no less than the intelligence of the reader with irrepressible irritation. But this, if he be wise, will be got over and kept under by his sense of admiration and of gratitude for the unsurpassable excellence of the finest passages and chapters. The day after the death of Mr Merdle is one of the most memorable dates in all the record of creative history – or, to use one word in place of two, in all the record of fiction. The fusion of humour and horror in the marvellous chapter which describes it is comparable only with the kindred works of such creators as the authors of *Les Misérables* and *King Lear*. And nothing in the work of Balzac is newer and truer and more terrible than the relentless yet not unmerciful evolution of the central figure in the story. The Father of the Marshalsea is so pitiably worthy of pity as well as of scorn that it would have seemed impossible to heighten or to deepen the contempt or the compassion of the reader; but when he falls from adversity to prosperity he succeeds in soaring down and sinking up to a more tragicomic ignominy of more aspiring degradation. And his end is magnificent. . . .

SOURCE: extract from Swinburne's posthumously published study *Charles Dickens* (London, 1913), pp. 44–7.

W. Walter Crotch   (1916)

'Mrs Clennam: Dickens's greatest achievement in female portraiture'

. . . If it were only for . . . two great achievements: for Sydney Carton and Richard Carstone, we must, I think, agree that Dickens more than justified his departure from the old rambling method that gave us *Pickwick* and *Copperfield* – admittedly his masterpieces. But, in point of fact, though superior people are found to deride alike his plots and his psychology, as he developed them in his later novels, both were consummate. Let us take one novel only as an example of his genius for blending both – *Little Dorrit*, which Mr Bernard Shaw described as one of the greatest in any language. The character of Mrs Clennam; the presentation of her parched and withered soul; supported by an iron resolution and with unbending fortitude; the process of self-deception which poisoned the strength of her really robust nature; that, and the method of her final delivery, when the paralysed woman leaves the house, which, unknown to all, has been cracking and tottering for decades, and that falls at last crushing her tormentor, [Rigaud] Blandois, to death; the picture here, as it seems to me, is one of the most convincing and remorseless descriptions of feminine psychology in all literature. Though the personality that it dissects has passed largely unnoticed while thousands of commentators have prosed about Little Em'ly and Agnes Wickfield, few have touched on this, Dickens's greatest achievement in female portraiture. Yet I do not think that it can be matched anywhere. The image of Mrs Clennam, seated in the doomed house and by sheer strength of will and resolution conducting its business affairs, might have been drawn by Albert Dürer, or rendered in music by Beethoven. Its

symbolism is worthy of that greatest of all symbolists, Ibsen, whose
fundamental outlook on life partook so much of Dickens's own. If, in
his myriad characters, it has escaped attention, it is because that
sense of the tragic to which I have referred is one that has dwindled in
our time, so that even the touch of a master does not always revive it.

For us it has, perhaps, a peculiar interest. We, who have followed
Dickens in all the windings of his genius, and all the varied efforts of
his life, would like to form for ourselves some concrete embodiment,
perchance a crude one, but still easily recognisable, of the soul of the
man himself. It may be that Mrs Clennam can help us to that
visualisation, for nearly everything that made her memorable we can
oppose to some element of Dickens; and nearly all her characteristics
were fought by him with all the fire of the intense conviction that
burnt in the man, and all the wit and genius that flowed from him.

The England of his time sat like Mrs Clennam, a frigid prisoner,
ice-bound by a false pride, with great reserves of energy and great
strength of purpose, but with the cracks almost showing in the walls of
her house, and with her own high nature vitiated by a gloomy pride
and an insane insularity; by suspicions that made her charity odious
and left her philanthropy a byword. What was Dickens's part –
Dickens, who marched into the choking atmosphere of this Mid-
Victorian stiffness with the blithe jollity of Pickwick and the high
spirits of David Copperfield? Perhaps it is best expressed in that scene
from Ibsen's *Pillars of Society* when the emancipated but human
heroine, Lona, finds the choking workroom full of feminine austerities
who are making 'garments for the lapsed and the lost'.

'Allow me, Miss Hessel, to ask what *you* will do in our Society?' And
she, having thrown wide the windows and door, replies: 'I will let in
fresh air, Pastor.'

SOURCE: extract from Crotch's *The Soul of Dickens* (London, 1916),
pp. 159–61

T. A. Jackson   (1937)

'The revolutionary implication of *Little Dorrit*'

... The plot-mechanism of *Little Dorrit* has to be set out at fairly full
length, because it is of prime significance in a critical evaluation of
Dickens's last-period novels to note that the whole of this complexity

of tragic and melodramatic themes and incidents forms in fact merely the incidental background to – (so to speak, the purely phenomenal obverse side of) – the *real* substance of the novel.

The real villain of *Little Dorrit* is neither the scoundrel [Rigaud] Blandois, nor the treacherous Flintwich, nor the ineffable Casby, nor the forger Merdle, nor the heartless Henry Gowan, nor the self-tormenting Miss Wade, nor is it those rival egoists and social-climbers, Mrs Merdle and Fanny Dorrit; nor the drifting waster, Amy's brother. Nor is it the tragically wilful Mrs Clennam. Nor all of these put together. Behind all of these human phenomena, using them as its instruments, is a vaster and more impalpable Evil, of whose true being we get indications in the shadow of the Marshalsea walls, in the heart-breaking immobility of the Circumlocution Office, and in the terrifying gloom of Mrs Clennam's theology.

Little Dorrit is, in fact, an allegory – of whose true purport its author was only partly conscious. In its first Part, to which the author gives the title 'Poverty', we live constrained within the Marshalsea walls. Yet for all their abiding shadow, and the ever-present consciousness of imprisonment, there are within those walls, compassion, courage and kindliness, unconquerable even amid the heart-break and the despair. In the second Part, which the author entitles 'Riches', the prisoners of the Marshalsea escape into Good Society. There, despite wealth, means of enjoyment, travel, Italian skies, luxury and deference, they meet with heartlessness, callous self-seeking, treachery, malice, envy, greed, cowardice, petulance – everything in short which is mean, contemptible, hateful and soul-destroying. The degeneration of poverty into mendicancy within the Marshalsea walls – its squalor thrown into sharper relief by the pitifully hollow gaiety of the club room – is pathetic to the limit of pathos. But in contrast with the world of wealth and fashion the Marshalsea and its society of imprisoned debtors stands out as light to darkness, or as heaven to hell. The released prisoners – the Father and the Child of the Marshalsea – find, each in a different way, that they have only changed one prison for a worse. And there is Mrs Clennam and her victim, Arthur, to prove to them that worse, even, than the Hell of Riches, is the hellishness of orthodox theology, which turns the universe itself into one huge, inescapable Marshalsea, whose jailer is a fiendishly vengeful God; who holds all men prisoners for eternity with as little reason, and as little compunction, as the Circumlocution Office held the Father of the Marshalsea a prisoner for a full quarter of a century.

Only when the riches have been annihilated and the theology has crashed into ruin, are the long-tormented prisoners set free to make

138   T. A. JACKSON   (1937)

what they can of what is left of their lives, and of such slender
resources as have been left to them.

Tried by Betsy Trotwood's test – 'never be mean, never be false,
never be cruel'[1] – the two categories of the author's own contrasting,
Poverty and Riches, show all these vices flourishing luxuriantly in the
latter category, and the corresponding virtues coming to their fullest
flower in the former.

This is most clearly apparent if we try to sort out the actors in *Little
Dorrit* in terms of the conventional classification of Hero and Villain.

Little Dorrit herself is, of course, clearly on the side of Virtue – and
is also, as the central figure, the heroine. But her virtue is that of
Andromeda chained to the rock (of Poverty and Humiliation), the
virtue of undeserved slights and sufferings patiently endured; of
humble duty done, for meagre rewards, or none at all. And Perseus
comes to her rescue, not in the blazing glory of a demi-god, borne on
the sweeping wings of a glittering Pegasus, but in the lowly guise of
Arthur Clennam (himself only half-escaped from the clutches of that
Giant Despair, which is his mother's god), and his supporters, the
grubby but indefatigable Panks, the artificer-inventor Doyce, and
the kind-hearted, sorrowing, but businesslike plebeian Meagles.

Observe: all of them are victims to the Dragon in one form or
another. Arthur, to the religion-infuriated Mrs Clennam; Panks to
the greedy impostor Casby; Doyce to the Circumlocution Office;
Meagles – through his affection for his daughter – to the Tite-
Barnacles and Stiltstalkings as embodied in their kinsman Henry
Gowan; and all, except Meagles, to the thief and forger, Merdle.
Moreover, this aggregative Perseus has but a blunt sword, with no
Gorgon's head, and no Pegasus. Hence the Dragon is not slain – he is
only for the time being beaten off. Andromeda is released from the
rock, and that, so far, is victory. But for her there are no royal palaces.
And even though her rescuer is not a glittering demi-god who will
desert her as soon as the flush of victory has cooled, her prospect holds
no promise brighter than the purely negative blessing of release into a
grey, toil-weary world; a world in which the kindest hearts are found
suffering privations and unemployment in Bleeding Heart Yard, or
eating their hearts out in a debtor's prison.

Every character in *Little Dorrit* who counts on the side of Virtue and
Heroism is, it will be seen, made to suffer, and that acutely. Arthur
Clennam, his dead parents, his partner Doyce, his friends the
Meagles, his assistant Panks, the amiable (though adipose) and
romantic Flora, the kindly proletarians the Plornishes, the whole
population of Bleeding Heart Yard, the cheerful Cavaletto, the
lugubriously infatuated, but noble-hearted son of Chivery the jailer –

even Henry Gowan's dog – the only admirable thing connected with him – all suffer each in their degree as do the Dorrit family. In fact, beyond the crashing frustration and disaster which overtakes them, the vicious and villainous characters – Blandois, Flintwich, Henry Gowan, Miss Wade, the Merdles, Mrs General, Mrs Clennam, etc. – all suffer considerably less, so far as we can see, than do the admirable characters. And the wickedest villains of all, the Circumlocution Office (with its swarms of Tite-Barnacles and Stiltstalkings) and with it Mrs Clennam's torturing theology, not only do not suffer at all, but show no sign of being capable of suffering or of overthrow.

That the general outlook implicit in *Little Dorrit* is therefore heavily pessimist – and that more so than either *Bleak House* or *Hard Times* – must be admitted. For all its gloom *Bleak House* is redeemed from despair, not so much by the somewhat whimsical goodness of John Jarndyce (to say nothing of Esther and her husband) as by the tragic (even if melodramatic) splendour of Lady Dedlock, by the unsuspected vein of real nobility in Sir Leicester, and by the sturdy, self-reliant competence of Mrs Bagnet and her 'children' (which includes both her husband and his friend George). *Hard Times* shows a break in the gloom both by means of the repentance of Gradgrind, by the unspoiled sympathy and kindliness of Sissy, and by the courageous humanity and buoyancy of her circus friends.

In *Little Dorrit*, while there is a wider and deeper sense of the masses – and a far closer approximation to the proletarian standpoint – there is, in the foreground of the action, little foothold for optimism. Yet, at the same time, too, there is a dawning suggestion of an imminent Doom. In the physical crash of the Clennam mansion – so long the spiritual prison of the young and ardent – so long the stronghold of Wrong inflicted under the guise of Righteousness – one cannot help but sense a prophecy of a like fate awaiting the Circumlocution Office and all that it implies. It would be definitely wrong to say that *Little Dorrit* is revolutionary in the conscious or overt sense. But it would be no less wrong to deny that in the negative or potential sense – in that it shows, by the totality of its implications, what things would be if Fate were just – it is near to being the most revolutionary novel that Dickens ever wrote.

Source: extract from *Charles Dickens: The Progress of a Radical* (London, 1937), pp. 164–9.

NOTE

1. [Ed.] Cf. ch. 15 of *David Copperfield*.

George Bernard Shaw   (1937)

'A more seditious book than *Das Kapital*'

... The difference between Marx and Dickens was that Marx knew that he was a revolutionist whilst Dickens had not the faintest suspicion of that part of his calling. Compare the young Dickens looking for a job in a lawyer's office and teaching himself shorthand to escape from his office stool to the reporters' gallery, with the young Trotsky, the young Lenin, quite deliberately facing disreputable poverty and adopting revolution as their profession with every alternative of bourgeois security and respectability much more fully open to them than to Dickens. . . .

Yet *Little Dorrit* is a more seditious book than *Das Kapital*. All over Europe men and women are in prison for pamphlets and speeches which are to *Little Dorrit* as red pepper to dynamite. Fortunately for social evolution Governments never know where to strike. Barnacle and Stiltstalking were far too conceited to recognize their own portraits. Parliament, wearying its leaders out in a few years in the ceaseless drudgery of finding out how not to do it, and smothering it in talk, could not conceive that its heartbreaking industry could have any relation to the ridiculous fiction of the Coodle-Doodle discussions in Sir Leicester Dedlock's drawingroom. As to the Circumlocution Office, well, perhaps the staffs, owing their posts to patronage and regarding them as sinecures, were a bit too insolent to the public, and would be none the worse for a little chaff from a funny fellow like Dickens; but their inefficiency as a public service was actually a good thing, as it provided a standing object lesson in the superiority of private enterprise. Mr Sparkler was not offended: he stuck to his job and never read anything. *Little Dorrit* and *Das Kapital* were all the same to him: they never entered his world; and to him that world was the whole world.

The mass of Dickens readers, finding all these people too funny to be credible, continued to idolize Coodle and Doodle as great statesmen, and made no distinction between John Stuart Mill at the India Office and Mr Sparkler. In fact the picture was not only too funny to be credible: it was too truthful to be credible. But the fun was no fun to Dickens: the truth was too bitter. When you laugh at Jack Bunsby, or at The Orfling when the handle of her corkscrew came off and smote her on the chin, you have no doubt that Dickens is laughing with you like a street boy, despite Bunsby's tragic end. But whilst you laugh at Sparkler or young Barnacle, Dickens is in deadly earnest: he means that both of them must go into the dustbin if England is to survive. . . .

SOURCE: extract from Shaw's Foreword to a limited edition of *Great Expectations* (Edinburgh, 1937); reprinted in 'The Novel Library' (London, 1947), pp. *ix, xii*.

3. CRITICAL STUDIES SINCE 1940

Edmund Wilson   'The Symbol of the Prison'
(1940)

. . . Dickens now tackles the Marshalsea again, but on a larger scale
and in a more serious way. It is as if he were determined once for all to
get the prison out of his system. The figure of his father hitherto has
always haunted Dickens's novels, but he has never known quite how
to handle it. In Micawber, he made him comic and lovable; in
Skimpole, he made him comic and unpleasant – for, after all, the
vagaries of Micawber always left somebody out of pocket, and there is
another aspect of Micawber – the Skimpole aspect he presented to his
creditors. But what kind of person, really, had John Dickens been in
himself? How had the father of Charles Dickens come to be what he
was? Even after it had become possible for Charles to provide for his
father, the old man continued to be a problem up to his death in 1851.
He got himself arrested again, as the result of running up a wine bill;
and he would try to get money out of his son's publishers without the
knowledge of Charles. Yet Dickens said to Forster, after his father's
death: 'The longer I live, the better man I think him'; and *Little Dorrit*
is something in the nature of a justification of John.

Mr Dorrit is 'a very amiable and very helpless middle-aged
gentleman . . . a shy, retiring man, well-looking, though in an
effeminate style, with a mild voice, curling hair, and irresolute hands
– rings upon the fingers in those days – which nervously wandered to
his trembling lip a hundred times in the first half-hour of his
acquaintance with the jail' [Bk i, ch. 6]. The arrival of the Dorrit
family in prison and their gradual habituation to it are done with a
restraint and sobriety never displayed by Dickens up to now. The
incident in which Mr Dorrit, after getting used to accepting tips in his
rôle of the Father of the Marshalsea, suddenly becomes insulted when
he is offered copper halfpence by a workman, has a delicacy which
makes up in these later books for the ebb of Dickens's bursting
exuberance. If it is complained that the comic characters in these
novels, the specifically 'Dickens characters', are sometimes mechanical and boring, this is partly, perhaps, for the reason that they stick

out in an unnatural relief from a surface that is more quietly realistic. And there are moments when one feels that Dickens might be willing to abandon the 'Dickens character' altogether if it were not what the public expected of him. In any case, the story of Dorrit is a closer and more thoughtful study than any that has gone before of what bad institutions make of men.

But there is also in *Little Dorrit* something different from social criticism. Dickens is no longer satisfied to anatomise the organism of society. The main symbol here is the prison (in this connection, Mr Jackson's chapter[1] is the best thing that has been written on *Little Dorrit*); but this symbol is developed in a way that takes it beyond the satirical application of the symbol of the fog in *Bleak House* and gives it a significance more subjective. In the opening chapter, we are introduced, not to the debtors' prison, but to an ordinary jail for criminals, which, in the case of Rigaud and Cavalletto, will not make the bad man any better or the good man any worse. A little later, we are shown an English businessman who has come back from many years in China and who finds himself in a London – the shut-up London of Sunday evening – more frightening, because more oppressive, than the thieves' London of *Oliver Twist*. ' "Heaven forgive me", said he, "and those who trained me. How I have hated this day!" There was the dreary Sunday of his childhood, when he sat with his hands before him, scared out of his senses by a horrible tract which commenced business with the poor child by asking him, in its title, why he was going to Perdition?' [Bk I, ch. 3]. At last he gets himself to the point of going to see his mother, whom he finds as lacking in affection and as gloomy as he could have expected. She lives in a dark and funereal house with the old offices on the bottom floor, one of the strongholds of that harsh Calvinism plus hard business which made one of the mainstays of the Victorian Age; she lies paralysed on 'a black bier-like sofa', punishing herself and everyone else for some guilt of which he cannot discover the nature. The Clennam house is a jail, and they are in prison, too. So are the people in Bleeding Heart Yard, small tenement-dwelling shopkeepers and artisans, rack-rented by the patriarchal Casby; so is Merdle, the great swindler-financier, imprisoned, like Kreuger or Insull, in the vast scaffolding of fraud he has contrived, who wanders about in his expensive house – itself, for all its crimson and gold, as suffocating and dark as the Clennams' – afraid of his servants, unloved by his wife, almost unknown by his guests, till on the eve of the collapse of the edifice he quietly opens his veins in his bath.

At last, after twenty-five years of jail, Mr Dorrit inherits a fortune and is able to get out of the Marshalsea. He is rich enough to go into

Society; but all the Dorrits, with the exception of the youngest, known as 'Little Dorrit', who has been born in the Marshalsea itself and has never made any pretensions, have been demoralised or distorted by the effort to remain genteel while tied to the ignominy of the prison. They cannot behave like the people outside. And yet that outside world is itself insecure. It is dominated by Mr Merdle, who comes, as the story goes on, to be universally believed and admired – is taken up by the governing class, sent to Parliament, courted by lords. The Dorrits, accepted by Society, still find themselves in prison. The moral is driven home when old Dorrit, at a fashionable dinner, loses control of his wits and slips back into his character at the Marshalsea: ' "Born here", he repeated, shedding tears. "Bred here. Ladies and gentlemen, my daughter. Child of an unfortunate father, but – ha – always a gentleman. Poor, no doubt, but – hum – proud" ' [Bk ii, ch. 19]. He asks the company for 'Testimonials', which had been what he had used to call his tips. (Dr Manette, in *A Tale of Two Cities*, repeats this pattern with his amnesic relapses into the shoemaking he has learned in prison.) Arthur Clennam, ruined by the failure of Merdle, finally goes to the Marshalsea himself; and there at last he and Little Dorrit arrive at an understanding. The implication is that, prison for prison, a simple incarceration is an excellent school of character compared to the dungeons of Puritan theology, of modern business, of money-ruled Society, or of the poor people of Bleeding Heart Yard who are swindled and bled by all of these.

The whole book is much gloomier than *Bleak House*, where the fog is external to the characters and represents something removable, the obfuscatory elements of the past. The murk of *Little Dorrit* permeates the souls of the people, and we see more of their souls than in *Bleak House*. Arthur Clennam, with his broodings on his unloving mother, who turns out to be his real mother (a poor doomed child of natural impulse, like Lady Dedlock's lover), is both more real and more depressing than Lady Dedlock. Old Dorrit has been spoiled beyond repair: he can never be rehabilitated like Micawber. There is not even a villain like Tulkinghorn to throw the odium on a predatory class: the official villain [Rigaud] Blandois has no organic connection with the story save as a caricature of social pretence. (Though the illustrations suggest that he may have been intended as a sort of cartoon of Napoleon iii, whose régime Dickens loathed – in which case the tie-up between Blandois and the Clennams may figure a close relationship between the shady financial interests disguised by the flashy façade of the Second Empire and the respectable business interests of British merchants, so inhuman behind their mask of morality. Blandois is crushed in the end by the collapse of the Clennam's house, as people were already predicting that Napoleon would be by that of his own.) The rôle of the Court of Chancery is more or less played by the Circumlocution Office and the governing-class family of Barnacles – perhaps the most brilliant thing of its kind in Dickens: that great satire on all aristocratic bureaucracies, and indeed on all bureaucracies, with its repertoire of the variations possible within the bureaucratic type and its desolating picture of the emotions of a man being passed on from one door to another. But the Circumlocution Office, after all, only influences the action in a negative way.

The important thing to note in *Little Dorrit* – which was originally to have been called *Nobody's Fault* – is that the fable is here presented from the point of view of imprisoning states of mind as much as from that of oppressive institutions. This is illustrated in a startling way by *The History of a Self-Tormentor*, which we find toward the end of the book [Bk II, ch. 21]. Here Dickens, with a remarkable pre-Freudian insight, gives a sort of case history of a woman imprisoned in a neurosis which has condemned her to the delusion that she can never be loved. There is still, to be sure, the social implication that her orphaned childhood and her sense of being slighted have been imposed on her by the Victorian attitude toward her illegitimate birth. But her handicap is now simply a thought-pattern, and from that thought-pattern she is never to be liberated. . . .

SOURCE: extract from Wilson's essay (1940), included in *The Wound and the Bow* (London, 1941; paperback edn, 1961), pp. 46–51.

[Ed.] Edmund Wilson's essay has a complicated publishing history. It originated in lectures given in 1939 at the University of Chicago. These were published during the following year in the *New Republic* and the *Atlantic Monthly*, before appearing in an enlarged and revised form under the title 'Dickens: The Two Scrooges' in *The Wound and the Bow* (1941): a collection of the writer's essays. This volume appeared in a revised edition in 1952, and in a paperback edition – from which our extract here is taken – in 1961.

NOTE

1. [Ed.] Wilson here alludes to T. A. Jackson's study, *Charles Dickens: The Progress of a Radical* (London, 1937), excerpted above, in section 2, Part Two of this Casebook.

Lionel Trilling   'Society and the Individual
Human Will'   (1953)

Little Dorrit is one of the three great novels of Dickens's great last period, but of the three it is perhaps the least established with modern readers. When it first appeared – in monthly parts from December 1855 to June 1857 – its success was even more decisive than that of *Bleak House*, but the suffrage of later audiences has gone the other way, and of all Dickens's later works it is *Bleak House* that has come to be the best known. As for *Our Mutual Friend*, after having for some time met with adverse critical opinion among the enlightened – one recalls that the youthful Henry James attacked it for standing in the way of art and truth – it has of recent years been regarded with ever-growing admiration. But *Little Dorrit* seems to have retired to the background and shadow of our consciousness of Dickens.

This does not make an occasion for concern or indignation. With a body of work as large and as enduring as that of Dickens, taste and opinion will never be done. They will shift and veer as they have shifted and veered with the canon of Shakespeare, and each generation will have its special favourites and make its surprised discoveries. *Little Dorrit*, one of the most profound of Dickens's novels and one of the most significant works of the nineteenth century, will not fail to be thought of as speaking with a peculiar and passionate intimacy to our own time.

Little Dorrit is about society, which certainly does not distinguish it from the rest of Dickens's novels unless we go on to say, as we must, that it is *more* about society than any other of the novels, that it is about society in its very essence. This essential quality of the book has become apparent as many of the particular social conditions to which it refers have passed into history. Some of these conditions were already of the past when Dickens wrote, for although imprisonment for debt was indeed not wholly given up until 1869, yet imprisonment for small debts was done away with in 1844, the prison of the Marshalsea was abolished in 1842 and the Court of the Marshalsea in 1849. Bernard Shaw said of *Little Dorrit* that it converted him to socialism; it is not likely that any contemporary English reader would feel it appropriate to respond to its social message in the same way. The dead hand of outworn tradition no longer supports special privilege in England; for good or bad, in scarcely any country in the world can the whole art of government be said to be How Not To Do It. Mrs General cannot impose the genteel discipline of Prunes and

Prisms, and no prestige whatever attaches to 'the truly refined mind' of her definition – 'one that will seem to be ignorant of the existence of anything that is not perfectly proper, placid, and pleasant'. At no point, perhaps, do the particular abuses and absurdities upon which Dickens directed his terrible cold anger represent the problems of social life as we must now conceive them.

Yet this makes *Little Dorrit* not less but more relevant to our sense of things. As the particulars seem less immediate to our case, the general force of the novel becomes greater, and *Little Dorrit* is seen to be about a problem which does not yield easily to time. It is about society in relation to the individual human will. This is certainly a matter general enough – general to the point of tautology, were it not for the bitterness with which the tautology is articulated, were it not for the specificity, and the subtlety, and the boldness with which the human will is anatomised.

The subject of *Little Dorrit* is borne in upon us by the informing symbol, or emblem, of the book, which is the prison. The story opens in a prison in Marseilles. It goes on to the Marshalsea, which in effect it never leaves. The second of the two parts of the novel begins in what we are urged to think of as a sort of prison, the monastery of the Great St Bernard. The Circumlocution Office is the prison of the creative mind of England. Mr Merdle is shown habitually holding himself by the wrist, taking himself into custody, and in a score of ways the theme of incarceration is carried out, persons and classes being imprisoned by their notions of predestined fate or of religious duty, or by their occupations, their life-schemes, their ideas of themselves, their very habits of language.

Symbolic or emblematic devices are used by Dickens to one degree or another in several of the novels of his late period, but nowhere to such good effect as in *Little Dorrit*. The fog of *Bleak House*, the dust-heap and the river of *Our Mutual Friend* are very striking, but they scarcely equal in force the prison image which dominates *Little Dorrit*. This is because the prison is an actuality before it is ever a symbol; its connection with the will is real, it is the practical instrument for the negation of man's will which the will of society has contrived. As such, the prison haunted the mind of the nineteenth century, which may be said to have had its birth at the fall of the Bastille. The genius of the age, conceiving itself as creative will, naturally thought of the prisons from which it must be freed, and the trumpet call of the *Leonore* overture sounds through the century, the signal for the opening of the gates, for a general deliverance, although it grows fainter as men come to think of the prison not as a political instrument merely, but as the ineluctable condition of life in society. 'Most men in a brazen prison live' – the line in which Matthew Arnold echoes Wordsworth's 'shades of the prison-house begin to close Upon the growing boy', might have served as the epigraph of *Little Dorrit*. In the mind of Dickens himself the idea of the prison was obsessive, not merely because of his own boyhood experience of prison life through his father's three months in the Marshalsea (although this must be given great weight in our understanding of his intense preoccupation with the theme), but because of his own consciousness of the force and scope of his will.

If we speak of the place which the image of the prison occupied in the mind of the nineteenth century, we ought to recollect a certain German picture of the time, inconsiderable in itself but made significant by its use in a famous work of the early twentieth century. It represents a man lying in a medieval dungeon; he is asleep, his head pillowed on straw, and we know that he dreams of freedom because the bars of his window are shown being sawed by gnomes. This picture serves as the frontispiece to Freud's *Introductory Lectures on Psychoanalysis* – Freud uses it to make plain one of the more elementary ideas of his psychology, the idea of the fulfilment in dream or fantasy of impulses of the will that cannot be fulfilled in actuality. His choice of this particular picture is not fortuitous; other graphic representations of wish-fulfilment exist which might have served equally well his immediate didactic purpose, but Freud's general conception of the mind does indeed make the prison-image peculiarly appropriate. And Freud is in point here because in a passage of *Little Dorrit* Dickens anticipates one of Freud's ideas, and not one of the simplest but nothing less bold and inclusive than the essential theory of the neurosis; and the quality of mind that makes this striking anticipation is at work everywhere in *Little Dorrit*.

The brief passage to which I make reference occurs in the course of Arthur Clennam's pursuit of the obsessive notion that his family is in some way guilty, that its fortune, although now greatly diminished, has been built on injury done to someone. And he conjectures that the injured person is William Dorrit, who has been confined for debt in the Marshalsea for twenty years. Clennam is not wholly wrong in his supposition – there is indeed guilt in the family, incurred by Arthur's mother, and it consists in part of an injury done to a member of the Dorrit family. But he is not wholly right, for Mr Dorrit has not been imprisoned through the wish or agency of Mrs Clennam. The reasoning by which Arthur reaches his partly mistaken conclusion is of the greatest interest. It is based upon the fact that his mother, although mentally very vigorous, has lived as an invalid for many years. She has been imprisoned in a single room of her house, confined to her chair, which she leaves only for her bed. And her son conjectures that her imprisoning illness is the price she pays for the guilty gratification of keeping William Dorrit in his prison. In order to have the right to injure another, she must injure herself in an equivalent way. 'A swift thought shot into [Arthur Clennam's] mind. In that long imprisonment here [i.e. Mr Dorrit's] and in her long confinement to her room, did his mother find a balance to be struck? I admit that I was accessory to that man's captivity. I have suffered it in kind. He has decayed in his prison; I in mine. I have paid the penalty.'

I have dwelt on this detail because it suggests, even more than the naked fact of the prison itself, the nature of the vision of society of *Little Dorrit*. One way of describing Freud's conception of the mind is to say that it is based upon the primacy of the will, and that the organisation of the internal life is in the form, often fantastically parodic, of a criminal process in which the mind is at once the criminal, the victim, the police, the judge and the executioner. And this is a fair description of Dickens's own view of the mind, as, having received the social impress, it becomes in turn the matrix of society.

In emphasising the psychological aspects of the representation of society of *Little Dorrit* I do not wish to slight those more immediate institutional aspects of which earlier readers of the novel were chiefly aware. These are of as great importance now as they ever were in Dickens's career. Dickens is far from having lost his sense of the cruelty and stupidity of institutions and functionaries, his sense of the general rightness of the people as a whole and of the general wrongness of those who are put in authority over them. He certainly has not moved to that specious position in which all injustice is laid at the door of the original old Adam in each of us, not to be done away with until we shall all, at the same moment, become the new Adam. The Circumlocution Office is a constraint upon the life of England which nothing can justify. Mr Dorrit's suffering and the injustice done to him are not denied or mitigated by his passionate commitment to some of the worst aspects of the society which deals with him so badly.

Yet the emphasis on the internal life and on personal responsibility is very strong in *Little Dorrit*. Thus, to take but one example, in the matter of the Circumlocution Office Dickens is at pains to remind us that the responsibility for its existence lies even with so good a man as Mr Meagles. In his alliance with Daniel Doyce against the torpor of the Office, Mr Meagles has been undeviatingly faithful. Yet Clennam finds occasion to wonder whether there might not be 'in the breast of his honest, affectionate, and cordial Mr Meagles, any microscopic portion of the mustard-seed that had sprung up into the great tree of the Circumlocution Office'. He is led to this speculation by his awareness that Mr Meagles feels 'a general superiority to Daniel Doyce, which seemed to be founded, not so much on anything in Doyce's personal character, as on the mere fact of [Doyce's] being an originator and a man out of the beaten track of other men'.

Perhaps the single best index of the degree of complexity with which Dickens views society in *Little Dorrit* is afforded by the character of [Rigaud] Blandois and his place in the novel. Blandois is wholly wicked, the embodiment of evil; he is, indeed, a devil. One of the effects of his presence in *Little Dorrit* is to complicate our response to the theme of the prison, to deprive us of the comfortable, philanthropic thought that prisons are nothing but instruments of injustice. Because Blandois exists, prisons are necessary. The genera-tion of readers that preceded our own was inclined, I think, to withhold credence from Blandois – they did not believe in his aesthetic actuality because they did not believe in his moral actuality, the less so because they could not account for his existence in specific terms of social causation. But we have been forced to believe that there really are people who seem entirely wicked, and almost unaccountably so; the social causes of their badness lie so far back that they can scarcely be reached, and causation pales into irrele-vance before the effects of their action; our 'understanding' becomes a mere form of thought.

In this novel about the will and society, the devilish nature of Blandois is confirmed by his maniac insistence upon his gentility, his mad reiteration that it is the right and necessity of his existence to be served by others. He is the exemplification of the line in *Lear*: 'The prince of darkness is a gentleman.' The influence of Dickens upon Dostoievski is perhaps nowhere exhibited in a more detailed way than in the similarities between Blandois and the shabby-genteel devil of *The Brothers Karamazov* and also Smerdyakov of the same novel. It is of consequence to Dickens as to Dostoievski that the evil of the unmitigated social will should own no country, yet that the flavour of its cosmopolitanism should be 'French' – that is, rationalistic and subversive of the very assumption of society. Blandois enfolds himself in the soiled tatters of the revolutionary pathos. So long as he can play the game in his chosen style, he is nature's gentleman dispossessed of his rightful place, he is the natural genius against whom the philistine world closes its dull ranks. And when the disguise, which deceives no one, is off, he makes use of the classic social rationalisation: Society has made him what he is; he does in his own person only what society does in its corporate form and with its corporate self-justification. 'Society sells itself and sells me: and I sell society.'

Around Blandois are grouped certain characters of the novel of whose manner of life he is the pure principle. In these people the social will, the will to status, is the ruling faculty. To be recognised, deferred to, and served – this is their master passion. Money is of course of great consequence in the exercise of this passion, yet in *Little Dorrit* the desire for money is subordinated to the desire for deference. The Midas figure of Mr Merdle must not mislead us on this point – should, indeed, guide us aright, for Mr Merdle, despite his destructive power, is an innocent and passive man among those who live by the social will. It is to be noted of all these people that they justify their insensate demand for status by some version of Blandois's pathos; they are confirmed in their lives by self-pity, they rely on the great modern strategy of being the insulted and injured. Mr Dorrit is too soft a man for his gentility-mania ever to be quite diabolical, but his younger daughter Fanny sells herself to the devil, damns herself entirely in order to torture the woman who once questioned her social position. Henry Gowan, the cynical, incompetent gentleman-artist who associates himself with Blandois in order to *épater* society, is very nearly as diabolical as his companion. From his mother – who must dismiss once for all any lingering doubt of Dickens's ability to portray what Chesterton calls the delicate or deadly in human character – he has learned to base his attack on society upon the unquestionable rightness of wronged gentility. Miss Wade lives a life of tortured self-commiseration which gives her licence to turn her hatred and her hand against everyone, and she imposes her principle of judgement and conduct upon Tattycoram.

In short, it is part of the complexity of this novel which deals so bitterly with society that those of its characters who share its social bitterness are by that very fact condemned. And yet – so much further does the complexity extend – the subversive pathos of self-pity is by no means wholly dismissed, the devil has not wholly lied. No reader of *Little Dorrit* can possibly conclude that the rage of envy which Tattycoram feels is not justified in some degree, or that Miss Wade is wholly wrong in pointing out to her the insupportable ambiguity of her position as the daughter-servant of Mr and Mrs Meagles and the sister-servant of Pet Meagles. Nor is it possible to read Miss Wade's account of her life, 'The History of a Self Tormentor', without an understanding that amounts to sympathy. We feel this the more – Dickens meant us to feel it the more – because the two young women have been orphaned from infancy, and illegitimate. Their bitterness is seen to be the perversion of the desire for love. The self-torture of Miss Wade – who becomes the more interesting if we think of her as the exact inversion of Esther Summerson of *Bleak House* – is the classic manoeuvre of the child who is unloved, or believes herself to be unloved – she refuses to be lovable, she elects to be hateful. The sense of injustice precedes the sense of justice by many years. It haunts the infancy of all of us, and even the most dearly loved of children may conceive themselves to be oppressed. Such is the nature of the human will, so perplexed is it by the disparity between what it desires and what it is allowed to have. With Dickens as with Blake, the perfect image of injustice is the unhappy child, and, like the historian Burckhardt, he connects the fate of nations with the treatment of children. It is a commonplace of the biography and criticism of Dickens that this reflects his own sense of having been unjustly treated by his parents, specifically in ways which injured his own sense of social status, his own gentility; the general force of Dickens's social feelings derives from their being rooted in childhood experience, and something of the special force of *Little Dorrit* derives from Dickens having discovered its matter in the depths of his own social will.

At this point we become aware of the remarkable number of false and inadequate parents in *Little Dorrit*. To what pains Dickens goes to represent delinquent parenthood, with what an elaboration of irony he sets it forth! The Father of the Marshalsea – this is the style borne by Mr Dorrit, who, preoccupied by the gratification of being the First Gentleman of a prison, is unable to exercise the simplest paternal function; who corrupts two of his children by his dream of gentility; who will accept any sacrifice from his saintly daughter Amy, Little Dorrit, to whom he is the beloved child to be cherished and forgiven. The Patriarch – this is the title bestowed upon Mr Casby, who stands as a parody of all Dickens's benevolent old gentlemen from Mr Pickwick through the Cheerybles to John Jarndyce, an astounding unreality of a man who, living only to grip and grind, has convinced the world by the iconography of his dress and mien that he is the repository of all benevolence. The primitive appropriateness of the strange, the unEnglish, punishment which Mr Pancks metes out to this hollow paternity, the cutting off of his long hair and the broad brim of his hat, will be understood by any reader with the least tincture of psychoanalytical knowledge. Then the Meagles, however solicitous of their own daughter, are, as we have seen, but indifferent parents to Tattycoram. Mrs Gowan's rearing of her son is the root of his corruption. It is Fanny Dorrit's complaint of her enemy, Mrs Merdle, that she refuses to surrender the appearance of youth, as a mother should. And at the very centre of the novel is Mrs Clennam, a false mother in more ways than one; she does not deny love but she perverts and prevents it by denying all that love feeds on – liberty, demonstrative tenderness, joy, and, what for Dickens is the guardian of love in society, art. It is her harsh rearing of her son that has given him cause to say in his fortieth year, 'I have no will'.

Some grace – it is, of course, the secret of his birth, of his being really a child of love and art – has kept Arthur Clennam from responding to the will of his mother with a bitter, clenched will of his own. The alternative he has chosen has not, contrary to his declaration, left him no will at all. He has by no means been robbed of his ethical will, he can exert ᴗnergy to help others, and for the sake of Mr Dorrit or Daniel Doyce's invention he can haunt the Circumlocution Office with his mild, stubborn 'I want to know –'. But the very accent of that phrase seems to forecast the terrible 'I prefer not to' of Bartleby the Scrivener in Melville's great story of the will in its ultimate fatigue.

It is impossible, I think, not to find in Arthur Clennam the evidence of Dickens's deep personal involvement in *Little Dorrit*. If we ask what Charles Dickens has to do with poor Clennam, what The Inimitable has to do with this sad depleted failure, the answer must be – Nothing, save what is implied by Clennam's consciousness that he has passed the summit of life and that the path henceforward leads down, by his belief that the pleasures of love are not for him, by his 'I want to know –', by his wish to negate the will in death. Arthur Clennam is that mode of Dickens's existence at the time of *Little Dorrit* which makes it possible for him to write to his friend Macready: 'However strange it is never to be at rest, and never satisfied, and ever trying after something that is never reached, and to be always laden with plot and plan and care and worry, how clear it is that it must be, and that one is driven by an irresistible might until the journey is worked out.' And somewhat earlier and with a yet more poignant relevance: 'Why is it, that as with poor David, a sense always comes crushing upon me now, when I fall into low spirits, as of one happiness I have missed in life, and one friend and companion I have never made?'

If we become aware of an autobiographical element in *Little Dorrit*, we must of course take notice of the fact that the novel was conceived after the famous incident of Maria Beadnell, who, poor woman, was the original of Arthur Clennam's Flora Finching. She was the first love of Dickens's proud, unfledged youth; she had married what Dickens has taught us to call Another, and now, after twenty years, she had chosen to come back into his life. Familiarity with the story cannot diminish our amazement at it – Dickens was a subtle and worldly man, but his sophistication was not proof against his passionate sentimentality, and he fully expected the past to come back to him, borne in the little hands of the adorable Maria. The

actuality had a quite extreme effect upon him, and Flora, fat and
foolish, is his monument to the discovered discontinuity between
youth and middle age, she is the nonsensical spirit of the anti-climax
of the years. And if she is in some degree forgiven, being represented
as the kindest of foolish women, yet it is not without meaning that she
is everywhere attended by Mr F's Aunt, one of Dickens's most
astonishing ideas, the embodiment of senile rage and spite, flinging to
the world the crusts of her buttered toast. 'He has proud stomach, this
chap', she cries when poor Arthur h_itates over her dreadful gift.
'Give him a meal of chaff!' It is the voice of one of the Parcae.

It did not, of course, need the sad comedy of Maria Beadnell for
Dickens to conceive that something in his life had come to an end. It
did not even need his growing certainty that, after so many years and
so many children, his relations with his wife were insupportable – this
realisation was as much a consequence as it was a cause of the sense of
termination. He was forty-three years old and at the pinnacle of a
success unique in the history of letters. The wildest ambitions of his
youth could not have comprehended the actuality of his fame. But the
last infirmity of noble mind may lead to the first infirmity of noble
will. Dickens, to be sure, never lost his love of fame, or of whatever of
life's goods his miraculous powers might bring him, but there came a
moment when the old primitive motive could no longer serve, when
the joy of impressing his powers on the world no longer seemed
delightful in itself, and when the first, simple, honest, vulgar energy of
desire no longer seemed appropriate to his idea of himself.

We may say of Dickens that at the time of *Little Dorrit* he was at a
crisis of the will which is expressed in the characters and forces of the
novel, in the extremity of its bitterness against the social will, in its
vision of peace and selflessness. This moral crisis is most immediately
represented by the condition of Arthur Clennam's will, by his sense of
guilt, by his belief that he is unloved and unlovable, by his retirement
to the Marshalsea as by an act of choice, by his sickness unto death.
We have here the analogy to the familiar elements of a religious crisis.
This is not the place to raise the question of Dickens's relation to the
Christian religion, which was a complicated one. But we cannot speak
of *Little Dorrit* without taking notice of its reference to Christian
feeling, if only because this is of considerable importance in its effect
upon the aesthetic of the novel.

It has been observed of *Little Dorrit* that certain of Dickens's
characteristic delights are not present in their usual force. Something
of his gusto is diminished in at least one of its aspects. We do not have
the amazing thickness of fact and incident that marks, say, *Bleak House*
or *Our Mutual Friend* – not that we do not have sufficient thickness, but

we do not have what Dickens usually gives us. We do not have the great population of characters from whom shines the freshness of their autonomous life. Mr Pancks and Mrs Plornish and Flora Finching and Flintwich are interesting and amusing, but they seem to be the fruit of conscious intention rather than of free creation. This is sometimes explained by saying that Dickens was fatigued. Perhaps so, but if we are aware that Dickens is here expending less of one kind of creative energy, we must at the same time be aware that he is expending more than ever before of another kind. The imagination of *Little Dorrit* is marked not so much by its powers of particularisation as by its powers of generalisation and abstraction. It is an imagination under the domination of a great articulated idea, a moral idea which tends to find its full development in a religious experience. It is an imagination akin to that which created *Piers Plowman* and *The Pilgrim's Progress*. And, indeed, it is akin to the imagination of *The Divine Comedy*. Never before has Dickens made so full, so Dantean, a claim for the virtue of the artist, and there is a Dantean pride and a Dantean reason in what he says of Daniel Doyce, who, although an engineer, stands for the creative mind in general and for its appropriate virtue: 'His dismissal of himself [was] remarkable. He never said, I discovered this adaptation or invented that combination; but showed the whole thing as if the Divine artificer had made it, and he had happened to find it. So modest was he about it, such a pleasant touch of respect was mingled with his quiet admiration of it, and so calmly convinced was he that it was established on irrefragable laws.' Like much else that might be pointed to, this confirms us in the sense that the whole energy of the imagination of *Little Dorrit* is directed to finding the non-personal will in which shall be our peace.

We must accept – and we easily do accept, if we do not permit critical cliché to interfere – the aesthetic of such an imagination, which will inevitably tend to a certain formality of pattern and to the generalisation and the abstraction we have remarked. In a novel in which a house falls physically to ruins from the moral collapse of its inhabitants, in which the heavens open over London to show a crown of thorns, in which there are characters named nothing else than Bar, Bishop, Physician, we are quite content to accept the existence of a devil. And we do not reject, for all our inevitable first impulse to do so, the character of Little Dorrit herself. Her untinctured goodness does not appal us or make us misdoubt her, as we expect it to do. This novel at its best is only incidentally realistic, its finest power of imagination appears in the great general images whose abstractness is their actuality, like Mr Merdle's dinner parties, or the Circumlocution Office itself, and in such a context we understand Little Dorrit to be the Beatrice of the Comedy, the Paraclete in female form. Even the physical littleness of this grown woman, an attribute which is insisted on and which seems so likely to repel us, does not do so, for we perceive it to be the sign that she not only is the Child of the Marshalsea, as she is called, but also the Child of the Parable, the negation of the social will.

SOURCE: Trilling's 'Introduction' to the Oxford Illustrated Edition of *Little Dorrit* (London, 1953), pp. *v–xvi*.

J. Hillis Miller   'Dickens's Darkest Novel'
(1958)

... *Little Dorrit* is without doubt Dickens's darkest novel. No other of his novels has such a sombre unity of tone. Though we move from house to house and from one extremity of society to the other, we never lose for more than a moment the sense of shadowed, suffocating enclosure which oppresses us from the beginning. Mrs Clennam's gloomy house in London, the Marshalsea prison, Casby's stuffy, silent house – '. . . one might have fancied it to have been stifled by Mutes in the Eastern manner' [Bk I, ch. 13] – Miss Wade's dreary apartment in Calais, the fashionable homes of the Merdles, Barnacles or Sparklers, all 'stuffed and close' and smelly [Bk II, ch. 24]: all these milieux simply repeat with variations the interior of the 'villainous prison' in Marseilles to which we are introduced in the opening pages of the novel.

But one does not need to be within doors to experience this feeling of suffocating enclosure. The entire city of London is itself a prison, and keeps off the freedom and purity of the country air as completely as do the walls of the Marshalsea. We are introduced to the real scene of the novel in the description of Arthur Clennam's return to London after a twenty-year absence. It is a passage whose powerful picture of the gloom of the city and the despair of people within it is Baudelairean in its intensity (and indeed parallels many of the key images of Baudelaire's dark city scenes):

It was a Sunday evening in London, gloomy, close and stale. Maddening church bells of all degrees of dissonance, sharp and flat, cracked and clear, fast and slow, made the brick-and-mortar echoes hideous. Melancholy streets in a penitential garb of soot, steeped the souls of the people who were condemned to look at them out of windows, in dire despondency. In every thoroughfare, up almost every alley, and down almost every turning, some doleful bell was throbbing, jerking, tolling, as if the Plague were in the city and the dead-carts were going round. Everything was bolted and barred that could by possibility furnish relief to an overworked people. . . . Nothing to see but streets, streets, streets. Nothing to breathe but streets, streets, streets. Nothing to change the brooding mind, or raise it up. . . .

. . . Ten thousand responsible houses surrounded [Arthur Clennam], frowning . . . heavily on the streets they composed . . . . Fifty thousand lairs surrounded him where people lived so unwholesomely, that fair water put into their crowded rooms on Saturday night, would be corrupt on Sunday morning . . . . Miles of close wells and pits of houses, where the inhabitants gasped for air, stretched far away towards every point of the compass. Through the heart of the town a deadly sewer ebbed and flowed, in the place of a fine fresh river. . . .

He sat in the same place as the day died, looking at the dull houses opposite, and thinking, if the disembodied spirits of former inhabitants were ever conscious of them, how they must pity themselves for their old places of imprisonment. Sometimes a face would appear behind the dingy glass of a window, and would fade away into the gloom as if it had seen enough of life and had vanished out of it. Presently the rain began to fall in slanting lines between him and those houses, and people began to collect under cover of the public passage opposite, and to look out hopelessly at the sky as the rain dropped thicker and faster.   [Bk I, ch. 3]

Dickens, then, has found for his novel a profound symbol for the universal condition of life in the world of his imagination: imprisonment. The enclosure, the narrowness, the blindness, of the lives of most of the characters in all Dickens's novels receive here their most dramatic expression. And, lest we should imagine that this condition is really peculiar to one time or place or kind of civilisation, Dickens in one passage explicitly defines human life in any place or time as imprisonment: 'aslant across the city, over its jumbled roofs, and through the open tracery of its church towers, struck the long bright rays [of the early morning sun], bars of the prison of this lower world' [Bk II, ch. 30]. All the world's a prison, and even the bright sunshine itself is only a barrier cutting this lower world off from heaven. Imprisonment has, we can see, a religious or metaphysical meaning for Dickens as well as a psychological or social one. To be in this world at all, whether one is good or bad, rich or poor, a lord of the Circumlocution Office or a debtor in the Marshalsea, is to be in prison, and this condition will apparently persist as long as life itself.

But, even in its psychological or social context, imprisonment is in *Little Dorrit* not simply a powerful symbol of enclosure or limitation imposed from without by an indifferent or unjust society administering impersonally its absurd or wicked laws. As Edmund Wilson has observed, *Little Dorrit* advances beyond Dickens's earlier novels in the way it shows so persuasively that imprisonment is a state of mind. The word 'shadow' is Dickens's key term linking physical imprisonment and imprisoning states of soul. Like the word 'gentleman' and the word 'secret', the word 'shadow' recurs again and again in *Little Dorrit* in the most diverse contexts. These words tie together the lives of all the various characters we meet and remind us that they are all like one another. Each use of the key words reflects on all the others, and eventually these words take on a subtly ironic meaning contracting in a single node all the complex themes of the novel. So the ambiguities of 'Society' are defined by the interaction of various uses of the word 'gentleman'; 'Gentleman' is the word the diabolically villainous Blandois uses to describe himself; the Circumlocution Office is a 'school for gentlemen' [Bk i, ch. 26]; old Dorrit's progressive degradation in the Marshalsea is marked by his increasing insistence on his 'forlorn gentility' [Bk i, ch. 7]; and after Merdle's suicide the clairvoyant Chief Butler says: 'Sir, Mr Merdle never was the gentleman, and no ungentlemanly act on Mr Merdle's part would surprise me' [Bk ii, ch. 25]. And so the word 'secret' is used again and again to express the isolation of the characters from one another either in their inturned selfishness or in their self-effacing goodness. But 'shadow' is the most frequently recurring of these key words. It is used most obviously to express the literal shadow of the Marshalsea, but it appears, often metaphorically, in connection with almost all the characters and eventually we understand that the real shadow here is 'a deeper shadow than the shadow of the Marshalsea Wall' [Bk ii, ch. 9], and that to be 'shadowed' by some sadness or blindness or delusion or deliberate choice of the worse rather than the better course is the universal condition of all the dwellers in this prison of a lower world. The 'shadow', then, is spiritual rather than physical. It is only by recognising this crucial extension of imprisonment from physical to spiritual incarceration that we can understand, for example, that Mrs Clennam is as effectively imprisoned within the walls of her false interpretation of Christianity as Little Dorrit's father is imprisoned by the walls of the Marshalsea. It is just as true to say that Mr Dorrit's literal imprisonment is only the physical correlative of his imprisonment within the labyrinth of his own weakness, vacillation, and selfishness as it is to say that Mrs Clennam's physical paralysis and enclosure in her dark house are the expression and result of her mental condition.

Indeed, all the many forms of imprisonment in this novel are primarily spiritual rather than physical: Miss Wade's imprisonment within the narrow circle of her sadism toward others and masochism toward herself; Merdle's suicidal anxiety, evident in his way of oozing 'sluggishly and muddily' [Bk II, ch. 12] around the rooms of his luxurious mansion and in his unconsciously symbolic habit of taking himself in custody as if he were a criminal – which he is; Flora Casby's imprisonment within the mad sequences of her own involuntary mental associations and within the perpetual reenactment of her lost past; Blandois's wicked imprisonment in his idea of himself as a gentleman 'by right and by nature' [Bk I, ch. 30]; John Chivery's constant anticipation of his own death, comically expressed in his habit of composing epitaphs for his own tombstone; Pancks's slavery to his master, Casby, always conjugating in the present tense, imperative mood, the verb 'to keep at it'; Mrs Merdle's servitude to society; the sprightly Ferdinand Barnacle's willing acquiescence in the sham of the Circumlocution Office; Little Dorrit's brother's corruption by the prison atmosphere, so that '[w]herever he went, this foredoomed Tip appeared to take the prison walls with him, and to set them up in such trade or calling; and to prowl about within their narrow limits in the old slip-shod, purposeless, down-at-heel way . . .' [Bk I, ch. 7].

But the central event of *Little Dorrit* is itself an explicit dramatisation of this discovery that imprisonment is not accidental and exterior, but inner and permanent. Little Dorrit's father, after his imprisonment for debt, 'languidly [slips] into [a] smooth descent, and never more [takes] one step upward' [Bk I, ch. 6], until finally he reaches a complete state of degradation, 'now boasting, now despairing, in either fit a captive with the jail-rot upon him, and the impurity of his prison worn into the grain of his soul' [Bk I, ch. 19]. Then suddenly, and just as unpredictably as he was first imprisoned, Dorrit is discovered to be the inheritor of a great fortune, and becomes a free and wealthy man. But his story is not merely another expression of Dickens's notion that life in the city is commanded by incomprehensible forces. Its real significance is defined by Little Dorrit's 'sorrowful' acknowledgment 'that no space in the life of man could overcome that quarter of a century behind the prison bars' [Bk II, ch. 5]. And there is no more poignant or effective expression of the theme of *Little Dorrit* than old Dorrit's dying speech. He suffers a stroke at a fashionable dinner party, and, imagining himself back in the Marshalsea, welcomes the dinner guests to what is symbolically their true abode: 'Ladies and gentlemen, the duty – ha – devolves upon me of – hum – welcoming you to the Marshalsea. Welcome to the Marshalsea! The space is – ha – limited – limited – the parade might be wider; but you will find it apparently grow larger after a time – a time, ladies and gentlemen – and the air is, all things considered, very good' [Bk II, ch. 19].

Old Dorrit, then, does not escape from the Marshalsea when he leaves its walls, and like all the characters in the novel is doomed to carry his prison with him wherever he goes. But the image of static enclosure, the prison cell, is interwoven with two other images which are almost as important as definitions of life in the world of *Little Dorrit*: the image of a labyrinth and the image of life as a journey.

The image of a labyrinth suggests that life is not immobile enclosure but is endless wandering within a maze whose beginning, ending, or pattern cannot be perceived. Since all places within the maze are the same, its prisoner moves freely but without getting anywhere, and without coming any closer to an understanding of his place in the world or of the forces determining his life. So Little Dorrit's Uncle Frederick, who is, people say, 'dead without being aware of it' [Bk I, ch. 20], accepts without comprehension 'every incident of the labyrinthian world in which he [has] got lost' [Bk I, ch. 19]; Miss Wade lives in a 'labyrinth' of little stately-melancholy streets near Park Lane [Bk I, ch. 27]; and Dickens speaks of 'the multiplicity of paths in the labyrinth trodden by the sons of Adam' [Bk II, ch. 12].[1] The image of the labyrinth is Dickens's way of expressing the idea that the human world is an incomprehensible tangle. People find it even more impossible there than in *Bleak House* to understand how things got the way they are or what is the meaning of the present situation. *Little Dorrit* was originally to be called *Nobody's Fault*, which is another way of saying it is everybody's fault, that the sad state of this world is the result of a collective human crime of selfishness, hypocrisy, weakness of will or sham. No specific cause or explanation of any individual's suffering can be found. Thus Mr Dorrit has no idea how much money he owes to whom or what he might do to get out of prison, and Mr Plornish's perplexed monologue on the life of the poor and unemployed inhabitants of Bleeding Heart Yard ends with another version of the image of a labyrinth: 'As to who was to blame for it, Mr Plornish didn't know who was to blame for it. He could tell you who suffered, but he couldn't tell you whose fault it was. It wasn't *this* place to find out, and who'd mind what he said, if he did find out? He only know'd that it wasn't put right by them what undertook that line of business, and that it didn't come right of itself. And in brief his illogical opinion was, that if you couldn't do nothing for him, you had better take nothing from him for doing of it; so far as he could make out, that was about what it come to. Thus, in a prolix, gently growling, foolish way, did Plornish turn the tangled skein of his estate about and about, like a blind man who was trying to find some beginning or end to it . . .' [Bk I, ch. 12].

Little Dorrit creates a disquieting sense of the selfish indifference diffused everywhere in things and people. By making certain characters vessels for the concentration of this guilt, it allays our terror and gives us something concrete to hate and fear. Mrs Clennam, Merdle, Blandois and Casby are materialisations of this undefined evil, but in *Little Dorrit*, nevertheless, evil exceeds any particularisation of it, and we are left at the end with an undefined and unpurged sense of menace. The image of the labyrinth is one of Dickens's chief ways of expressing the mystery of evil. The most striking appearance in *Little Dorrit* of the symbolic labyrinth is the Circumlocution Office, with its inextricably tangled halls, offices, passageways and levels of authority through which Arthur Clennam and Daniel Doyce meander hopelessly, filling out reams of forms and making appeal after appeal without coming any closer to a satisfactory answer to their question: 'Numbers of people were lost in the Circumlocution Office. . . . [T]hey melted away. In short, all the business of the country went throught the Circumlocution Office, except the business that never came out of it; and *its* name was Legion' [Bk i, ch. 10]. As in the stories of Kafka, though without quite Kafka's deliberate universalisation of the labyrinth as a symbol of the metaphysical alienation of man, the individual's relation in *Little Dorrit* to any sort of tangible earthly authority is expressed as an impossible appeal for judgement on his case, an appeal addressed to an infinitely complex bureaucracy dedicated to the science of 'how not to do it'. Like one of Kafka's heroes, Daniel Doyce is made to feel like a criminal as soon as he becomes related to the Circumlocution Office, though he is not conscious of having done wrong, and Arthur Clennam's appeal to the Circumlocution Office on behalf of his friend never receives any definite response at all. In *Bleak House* the case of Jarndyce and Jarndyce at least finally came to an end, though only because all the money was consumed in costs, but Clennam's search for an answer from the Circumlocution Office remains at the end of *Little Dorrit* like a loose thread of the plot dangling unresolved. The Circumlocution Office is the labyrinthine prison transformed into an institution of government. Produced by the irresponsibility and greed of the upper class, with its legion of parasitical 'Barnacles', the Circumlocution Office can imprison a man in its endless corridors and miles of red tape as securely as any Marshalsea or as any moral flaw. The ominous portrait of the Circumlocution Office is one of those elements of *Little Dorrit* which have led Marxist critics to find Marxism in Dickens and which led G. B. Shaw to say that *Little Dorrit* made him a socialist. Dickens was neither socialist nor Marxist, but his judgement of the Circumlocution Office is as near as he ever gets to asserting the radical instability of the present social order: 'As they went along, certainly one of the party, and probably more than one, thought that Bleeding Heart Yard was no inappropriate destination for a man who had been in official correspondence with my lords and the Barnacles – and perhaps had a misgiving also that Britannia herself might come to look for lodgings in Bleeding Heart Yard, some ugly day or other, if she over-did the Circumlocution Office' [Bk I, ch. 10].

If the symbol of imprisonment expresses Dickens's sense of human life as enclosed and limited, whether by physical or spiritual walls, and if the image of life as a labyrinth expresses his sense that human beings are all lost inextricably in a maze without beginning, end, or pattern, the recurrent image of 'travellers on the pilgrimage of life' expresses the idea that people are fatefully intertwined in one another's lives, often without knowing it or intending it. It also expresses Dickens's sense that a human life is not motionless but is perpetually flowing on with the river of time toward its destined adventures and toward the ultimate ocean of death: 'And thus ever, by day and night, under the sun and under the stars, climbing the dusty hills and toiling along the weary plains, journeying by land and journeying by sea, coming and going so strangely, to meet and to act and react on one another, move all we restless travellers through the pilgrimage of life' [Bk I, ch. 2]. The image of life as a long arduous journey, like images of prisons and labyrinths, recurs again and again in *Little Dorrit*. It reinforces the others by suggesting that this world is a lonely place where man is a stranger passing continually on in search of a haven which is to be found anywhere in the 'prison of this lower world'. Taken all together, these three images, the basic symbolic metaphors of the novel, present a terrifyingly bleak picture of human life.

But what is perhaps darkest of all here is Dickens's new way of showing many of his characters altogether aware of their spiritual states and even deliberately choosing them. There is a great increase here over the earlier novels in the self-consciousness and articulateness of suffering or malice, an increase of which the extraordinary chapter of 'The History of a Self Tormentor' is only the most striking example [Bk II, ch. 21]. Of this chapter Dickens wrote to the uncomprehending Forster, who found it 'the least interesting part of *Little Dorrit*': 'In Miss Wade I had an idea, which I thought a new one, of making the introduced story so fit into surroundings impossible of separation from the main story, as to make the blood of the book circulate through both.'[2] We can indeed see that the lifeblood of *Little Dorrit* flows through Miss Wade's interpolated story when we recognise how frequently her coldly lucid justification of a life of self-destructive selfishness is echoed in various ways in other characters: in Merdle and Mrs Merdle, in Henry Gowan and Ferdinand Barnacle, in Mrs Clennam's justification of her distorted Christianity, and in Casby's deliberate cultivation of a hypocritical surface of benignity. Of all Dickens's novels it is true to say that many of the characters exist in a nightmare of unreality, committed to lives of self-seeking, sham or vacillation. But the novelty of *Little Dorrit* lies in the fact that many characters are perfectly aware of this, and therefore live in a condition of continual restlessness or anxiety, even of despair or paralysis of will, incapable, like Arthur Clennam, of deciding what to do with their lives, or incapable, like old Dorrit, of making the least motion of spiritual ascent.

There seems, then, no escape from shadow in the world of *Little Dorrit*. Whether the characters are literally imprisoned or not, they are condemned to an endless wandering in a narrow dark labyrinth whose stations repeat one another as Calais and Italy repeat the Marshalsea [Bk II, chs 20 & 7]. Little Dorrit will never really 'see' her father in her life [Bk I, ch. 19]; whether he is in jail or out he will always be 'a captive with the jail-rot upon him'. . . .

Little Dorrit, like *A Tale of Two Cities*, has at its center a recognition of the inalienable secrecy and otherness of every human being. Here Dickens makes explicit his repudiation of the idea that another person can be a kind of transparent alter ego whom I can know and possess without the intervention of any shadow of mystery or strangeness. . . .

Little Dorrit centers on the secrecy, the otherness, of Little Dorrit herself. Whereas Esther Summerson [in *Bleak House*] got her strength to order the world around her through intermittent contact with the divine transcendence, Little Dorrit is the mystery of incarnate goodness. She does not need to be shown receiving strength from God's grace, because goodness is permanently immanent in her life, though Dickens does tell us that she is something different from everyone and everything about her only because she has been 'inspired . . . to be that something, different and laborious, for the sake of the rest' [Bk I, ch. 7]. Her grace to remain good, Dickens says, is exactly like 'the inspiration of a poet or a priest' [*ibid.*]. Little Dorrit is Esther Summerson presented, as it were, through the eyes of Allan Woodcourt. Arthur Clennam, the Woodcourt of *Little Dorrit*, functions as one of the chief protagonists and the central point of view of his novel. At first, when he returns to London after twenty years absence in China, Clennam's will is paralysed; he cannot make the least motion of voluntary and directed action; he cannot plan what to do with his life: 'I am such a waif and stray everywhere, that I am

liable to be drifted where any current may set. . . . I have no will. That
is to say, . . . next to none that I can put in action now. Trained by
main force; broken, not bent; heavily ironed with an object on which I
was never consulted and which was never mine; . . . always grinding
in a mill I always hated; what is to be expected from *me* in middle life?
Will, purpose, hope? All those lights were extinguished before I could
sound the words' [Bk i, ch. 2]. Indeed, as we have seen, the novel is
full of people whose wills are paralysed, who are, like Miss Wade,
'self-tormentors', but the central dramatic action is Arthur's own
search for some means by which his will may be reconstituted. He
tests various modes of relation to society. They all fail, and he finally
discovers that the pivot of his world, the center to which all roads lead,
is 'the least, the quietest, and weakest of Heaven's creatures' [Bk i,
ch. 9], Little Dorrit:

> To review his life, was like descending a green tree in fruit and flower, and
> seeing all the branches wither and drop off one by one, as he came down
> towards them.
> 'From the unhappy suppression of my youngest days, through the rigid and
> unloving home that followed them, through my departure, my long exile, my
> return, my mother's welcome, my intercourse with her since, down to the
> afternoon of this day with poor Flora', said Arthur Clennam, 'what have I
> found!'
> His door was softly opened, and these spoken words startled him, and came
> as if they were an answer:
> 'Little Dorrit.'   [Bk i, ch. 13]

> Looking back upon his own poor story, she was its vanishing-point. Every
> thing in its perspective led to her innocent figure. He had travelled thousands
> of miles towards it; previous unquiet hopes and doubts had worked
> themselves out before it; it was the centre of the interest of his life; it was the
> termination of everything that was good and pleasant in it; beyond there was
> nothing but mere waste and darkened sky.   [Bk ii, ch. 27]

Without Little Dorrit, Clennam would be, like so many other people
in the novel, lost in a patternless maze. Only Little Dorrit gives form
to his world and an orientation to his life. She is their center, just as
God himself is the hidden radiant center of the larger world.

Clennam's relation to Little Dorrit is a direct relation to the area of
mystery in another person. She keeps the secret of his family's guilt
toward her. She is the center which is absent, the abnegation of
perfect charity. By being the absence of self-assertion, total unselfish-
ness, the voluntary refusal to will, she succeeds in dominating the
world, or at least a small area of it, whereas total failure results from
all the direct selfish attempts either to spread outward and dominate

all (like Merdle or [Rigaud] Blandois or Pancks), or to create or accept voluntarily a private imprisoning circle protected from the world, an enclosure where one will be safe and in complete control of one's surroundings (Mrs Clennam, Miss Wade, old Dorrit). Little Dorrit sustains Clennam when everything else collapses beneath him. Indeed, she is really a human incarnation of divine goodness. The latter is present in the novel, but unavailable; it is seen in recurrent glimpses of nature beyond or above the imprisoning city streets. Clennam's relation to Little Dorrit is a relation to the unattainable divine through her mediation. It is only through Little Dorrit that Clennam can escape from the spiritual (and literal) imprisonment and deathlike stagnation to which his life finally comes:

> Changeless and barren, looking ignorantly at all the seasons with its fixed, pinched face of poverty and care, the prison had not a touch of any . . . beauties on it. Blossom what would, its bricks and bars bore uniformly the same dead crop. Yet Clennam, listening to the voice as it read to him, heard in it all that great Nature was doing, heard in it all the soothing songs she sings to man. At no Mother's knee but hers, had he ever dwelt in his youth on hopeful promises, on playful fancies, on the harvests of tenderness and humility that lie hidden in the early-fostered seeds of the imagination; . . . But, in the tones of the voice that read to him, there were memories of an old feeling of such things, and echoes of every merciful and loving whisper that had ever stolen to him in his life. [Bk II, ch. 34, & see II, ch. 29]

But if Clennam can escape from the valley of the shadow only through the miraculous goodness of Little Dorrit, she herself can escape from her isolation only through Clennam's return of her love, and because he too has kept intact a kernel of his childhood innocence and belief in good. The novel, then, ends happily with the usual Dickensian scene of reciprocal love, as Arthur Clennam and Little Dorrit leave the Marshalsea for the last time to be married. But here there is even less emphasis than usual on the completeness of the lovers' escape from the shadow, and there is a firm assertion that their happiness is limited to themselves alone and leaves the selfish, restless and deluded multitudes still locked in the prison of the world: 'They went quietly down into the roaring streets, inseparable and blessed; and as they passed along in sunshine and shade, the noisy and the eager, and the arrogant and the forward and the vain, fretted, and chafed, and made their usual uproar' [Bk II, ch. 34].

SOURCE: extracts from Miller's *Charles Dickens: The World of His Novels* (Cambridge, Mass., 1958), pp. 227–36, 243–7.

NOTES

1. Elsewhere we read of 'this labyrinth of a world' [Bk I, ch. 2], of 'The gloomy labyrinth of [Mrs Clennam's] thoughts' [Bk I, ch. 5], of 'a maze of shabby streets which went about and about' [Bk I, ch. 12], of a labyrinth of bare passages and pillaried galleries' [Bk II, ch. 3], and at Pet Meagles's ill-fated marriage we meet Lord Decimus Tite Barnacle 'trotting, with the complacency of an idiotic elephant, among howling labyrinths of sentences, which he seemed to take for high roads, and never so much as wanted to get out of' [Bk I, ch. 34].

2. Forster, *Life of Dickens*, ch. 1 of book VIII. [See the excerpt concluding section 1 of Part Two of this Casebook, above – Ed.]

F. R. Leavis 'An Inquest into Contemporary Civilisation' (1970)

. . . He was intensely an artist, unlike as he was either to Flaubert or to Henry James, and as he develops he becomes more and more describable as a dedicated one. *Dombey and Son* . . . solved only partially Dickens's problem: that of achieving the wholly significant work of art as a successful serial-writer, writing always against time and for the popular market. *Bleak House* again, rich and diverse as it is in the creative felicities of a great novelist and poet, doesn't altogether solve that problem. But in *Little Dorrit* the thing is done. There are no large qualifications to be urged, and the whole working of the plot, down to the melodramatic dénouement, is significant – that is, serves the essential communications felicitously. When the secret of Arthur Clennam's birth is revealed, it completes the presented significance of Mrs Clennam and the Clennam house:

'. . . Satan entered into that Frederick Dorrit, and counselled him that he was a man of innocent and laudable tastes who did kind actions, and that here was a poor girl with a voice for singing music with. Then he is to have her taught. Then Arthur's father, who has all along been secretly pining, in the ways of virtuous ruggedness, for those accursed snares which are called the Arts, becomes acquainted with her. And so a graceless orphan, training to be a singing girl, carries it, by that Frederick Dorrit's agency, against me, and I am humbled and deceived. . . .'   [Bk II, ch. 30]

This emphasis on art at the moment of confession – Mrs Clennam's characteristic kind of confession – has nothing gratuitous about it.

What Dickens hated in the Calvinistic commercialism of the early and middle Victorian age – the repressiveness towards children, the hard righteousness, the fear of love, the armed rigour in the face of life – he sums up now in its hatred of art. That he should do so is eloquent of the place he gave to art in human life and of the conception of art that informs his practice (it seems to be essentially Blake's). He conveyed his criticism of Victorian civilisation in a creative master-piece, a great work of art, which it would be fatuous to suppose he achieved accidentally and unconsciously, without meaning it and without knowing it. What, at a religious depth, Dickens hated about the ethos figured by the Clennam house was the offence against life, the spontaneous, the real, the creative, and, at this moment preceding the collapse of the symbolic house, he represents the creative spirit of life by art.

For Arthur Clennam the ethos is that which oppressed his childhood, glowering on spontaneity, spirit and happiness and inculcating guilt, and which, in its institutional manifestation, appals him as the English Sunday, wrapping London in a pall of gloom on his first morning back, he being bound towards the old childhood home to see his 'mother' again after twenty years of exile. It is the beginning of the sustained criticism of English life that the book enacts. For Clennam himself it is the beginning of an urgently personal criticism of life in Arnold's sense – that entailed in the inescapable and unrelenting questions: 'What shall I do? What *can* I do? What are the possibilities of life – for me, and, more generally, in the very nature of life? What are the conditions of happiness? What is life for?' Despondent, muted, earnest, with an earnestness derived from the upbringing the anti-life ethos of which he intensely rejects, he can't but find himself with such a criticism of life as his insistent preoccupation.

> So here I am, in the middle way, having had twenty years—
> Twenty years largely wasted . . .

The resonance as of a religious concern with basic criteria and ultimate issues carried by this from its context in *Four Quartets* and from the opening of the *Divina Commedia* doesn't make it inappropriate here – for the usual easy and confident denial of any profundity of thought to Dickens is absurd and shameful.

The inquest into contemporary civilisation that he undertook in *Little Dorrit* might equally be called a study of the criteria implicit in an evaluative study of life. What it commits him to is an enterprise of thought; thought that it is in our time of the greatest moment to get recognised, consciously and clearly, *as* thought – an affair (that is) of the thinking intelligence directed to a grasp of the real. Dickens's capacity for effective thought about life is indistinguishable from his genius as a novelist. A great novelist is addicted to contemplating and pondering life with an intensity of interest that entails – that *is* the thought that asks questions, seeks answers and defines. And (whatever that last verb might seem to imply) he doesn't need to be told that he must take a firm hold on the truth that life, for a mind truly intent on the real, is life in the concrete; that life is concretely 'there' only in individual lives; and that individual lives can't be aggregated, generalised or averaged.

On the other hand, he knows that the serious and developed study of the individual life can't but be a study of lives in relation, and of social conditions, conventions, pressures as they affect essential life. The really great novelist can't but find himself making an evaluative inquiry into the civilisation in which he finds himself – which he more and more finds himself in and of.

I might have added a couple of sentences ago that he doesn't need to be reminded – or to remind himself – that 'life' is a necessary word and that the impossibility of arriving at any abstract definition acceptable to him is far from being evidence of an unreality about what the word portends: it is the opposite.

Dickens in the nature of his creative undertaking aims at communicating generally valid truths about what can't be defined. I point here to the importance of getting it recognised that his genius as a novelist is a capacity for profound and subtle thought. His method, with all its subtleties and complexities, is a method of tackling what is in one aspect an intellectual problem: he tackles it, beyond any doubt, consciously and calculatingly.

I have already noted how Clennam, returned after twenty years of exile, dejected and without momentum or aim, opens, out of a particular history, the critique of Victorian civilisation. The questioning, so largely for him a matter of self-interrogation that implicitly bears on the criteria for judgement and value-perception, starts in that reverse of theoretical way, but – or so – with great felicity. The answer implicit in *Little Dorrit* is given creatively by the book, and it is not one that could have been given by Clennam himself. Not only is it something that can't be stated; the Clennam evoked for us is obviously not adequate to its depth and range and fulness, his deficiency being among the characteristics that qualify him for his part in the process by which the inclusive communication of the book is generated. Each of the other characters also plays a contributory part, inviting us to make notes on his or her instinctive 'value' in relation to the whole.

Nevertheless, about Dickens's art there is nothing of the rigidly or insistently schematic. We find ourselves bringing together for significant association characters as unlike, for instance, as Miss Wade, Henry Gowan, William Dorrit and Mrs Clennam, or seeing a rightness that is other than one of piquant or pleasing complementarity in the mutual attraction that manifests itself (a fact of the narrative) between Doyce, Clennam, Pancks and Cavalletto. And when we have got as far as that we are aware of already having made a note that Gowan (for instance) associates in significant relationship with characters who form a quite different grouping from that in which I have just placed him, so that, if in our diagrammatic notation we have been representing groupings by lines linking names, the lines run across one another in an untidy and undiagrammatic mess. The diagrammatic suggestion is soon transcended as the growing complexity of lines thickens; we arrive at telling ourselves explicitly what we have been implicitly realising in immediate perception and response: 'This, brought before us for pondering contemplation, is life – life as it manifests itself variously in this, that and the other focusing individual (the only way in which it can).'

In the striking power with which the book achieves the effect I point to here Clennam plays an important part, one that entails the unique status he has among the characters. That he is very important doesn't mean that he competes for inclusion among the 'Dickens characters', for he isn't a character in that sense, though he decidedly exists for us – is felt (that is) as a real personal presence. He has in this respect a clear affinity with Pip of *Great Expectations*, who, though so centrally important in that book, is not described at all, or endowed with describable, or at any rate very distinctive, characteristics. What is required of Pip is that he shall be felt unquestionably to exist as a centre of sentience, an identity, and Dickens's art ensures that he shall, for it ensures that the reader shall implicitly identify himself with Pip and *be* his sentience – while remaining, nevertheless, as the reader, another person. . . .

Little Dorrit, the equally astonishing and very different masterpiece, is very differently organised; Clennam is not 'I' in it, and not the ubiquitous immediate consciousness that registers and presents. Yet he too is felt as a pervasive presence, or something approaching it. He has been very early, with a subtlety of purpose and touch Dickens isn't as a rule credited with, established as that – established as the presence of what one may very well find oneself referring to as plain unassertive normality. And what that means is that we tend to *be* Clennam, as we obviously don't William Dorrit, Mr Meagles, Daniel Doyce, Henry Gowan, Pancks – or any other character in the book.

He is for us a person, *the* decently ordinary person among the *dramatis personae* ('ordinary' here not being used in a placing or pejorative way, but reassuringly), and he has at the same time a special status, unavowed but essential to his importance; it is implicit in his being, not a queer or unpleasant case, but the immediate focal presence of representative human sentience – ours (for ours, being our own, *is* that; it is the immediate concrete 'presence of life').

Clennam's consciousness of deprivation and disablement, avowed by him directly at the outset, in his exchange with Mr Meagles [Bk I, ch. 2],[1] where the quarantine-freed travellers prepare to disperse, isn't at all a contradiction that has to be reconciled with this special status, or with the suggestions of the word 'normality'; without having suffered his childhood, we accept with ready sympathy the sense of the world represented by this earnest, intelligent and pre-eminently civilised man: we respect him as we respect ourselves. The way in which Clennam serves the effect that the intellectual-imaginative purpose of *Little Dorrit* requires has nothing of the diagrammatic or the logical about it; it works by imaginatively prompting suggestion, so that the reader sees and takes in immediate perception what logic, analysis and statement can't convey. The effect is to make us realise explicitly why we are right to pick on *Little Dorrit* as a supreme illustration of the general truth about great creative writers, that their creative genius is a potency of *thought*. We tell ourselves that in presenting the large cast of diverse characters and the interplay between them Dickens is conducting a sustained, highly conscious and subtly methodical study of the human psyche; that he is concerned to arrive at and convey certain general validities of perception and judgment about life – enforcing implicitly in the process the truth that 'life' is a necessary word; that it is not a mere word, or a word that portends nothing more than an abstraction.

It won't, perhaps, be out of place to clinch this critical insistence with a comparative reference to Blake. Blake too was a creative writer whose genius was a penetrating insight into human nature and the human condition, and whose creativity was a potency of thought. The mythical works, with the complexities, ambiguities and shifting 'symbolic' values that defy the diagrammatising interpreter, give us Blake's method of grappling with the problem ('lives' and 'life') that Dickens tackles with the innovating resources of an inspired and marvellously original novelist in *Little Dorrit*.

SOURCE: extract from 'Dickens and Blake: *Little Dorrit* ', in F. R. and Q. D. Leavis, *Dickens the Novelist* (London, 1970), pp. 215–20.

NOTE

1. Viz. [Bk I, ch. 2]:

'... And now, Mr Clennam, perhaps I may ask you, whether you have come to a decision where to go next?'

'Indeed no, I am such a waif and stray everywhere, that I am liable to be drifted where any current may set.'

'It's extraordinary to me – if you'll excuse my freedom in saying so – that you don't go straight to London', said Mr Meagles, in the same tone of a confidential adviser.

'Perhaps I shall.'

'Ay! But I mean with a will.'

'I have no will. That is to say', he coloured a little, 'next to none that I can put in action now. . . .'

John Carey   'Two Aspects: Comic Method, and Symbolic Writing'   (1973)

I   Comic Method in Little Dorrit

... The irony and facetiousness which Dickens developed so that he could face the cruelty of Oliver Twist's workhouse or Squeers' Yorkshire school has eventually produced Eugene Wrayburn [in *Our Mutual Friend*]. Being cool and detached, it has inevitably turned vicious in the long run. It still leaves Dickens with no comic method that can express sympathy for the object of his humour, and yet see its humour. The sympathy has to be pronounced by the sad, lofty voice which occasionally breaks in on the facetious one. But in *Little Dorrit* the depiction of Mr Dorrit does – and it is a unique achievement – demonstrate a comic method where humour and depth of sympathy combine. Dorrit, in some sense a portrait of Dickens's father, who was also imprisoned in the Marshalsea, never gets detached from his creator enough to be treated with disdain. His great scenes – like that at the grand banquet in Rome where he forgets where he is and addresses the guests as if they were newcomers to the Marshalsea – are both funny and painful. The occasion is not sentimentalised. Dorrit's speech is presented with acute comic accuracy. But we wince with embarrassment, and also, as Amy Dorrit does, with pity at her father's breakdown [Bk II, ch. 19]:

Ladies and gentlemen, the duty – ha – devolves upon me of – hum –
welcoming you to the Marshalsea! The space is – ha – limited – limited – the
parade might be wider; but you will find it apparently grow larger after a time
– a time, ladies and gentlemen – and the air is, all things considered, very
good. It blows over the – ha – Surrey hills. Blows over the Surrey hills. This is
the Snuggery. Hum. Supported by a small subscription of the – ha –
Collegiate body.

Dorrit letting out his guilty secret would naturally move Dickens,
since he harboured one himself. He had never been able to tell even
his own wife and children of the months he spent working in Warren's
Blacking warehouse as a boy or of his father's confinement in the
Marshalsea. But the identification of Dorrit with himself as well as his
father might easily have led to a sentimentalised figure, like Oliver in
Fagin's den. Instead Dorrit's vanities and his baseness are scrupulously observed: the pathetic pride, for instance, with which, when in
the Marshalsea, he treats Old Nandy from the workhouse to tea;
patronising him; commenting sadly and with evident relish on the old
man's infirmities; arranging for Nandy to consume his shrimps and
bread and butter at a little distance from himself and his family [Bk i,
ch. 31]:

'If Maggy will spread that newspaper on the window-sill, my dear', remarked
the Father complacently and in a half whisper to Little Dorrit, 'my old
pensioner can have his tea there, while we are having ours.'

When it is time for Nandy to depart, he is dismissed with a final burst
of patronage from Dorrit: 'We don't call this a shilling, Nandy, you
know', he said, putting one in his hand. 'We call it tobacco.' But the
finest of Dorrit's scenes, and also Dickens's greatest piece of comic
writing, occurs earlier in the novel when Amy Dorrit has just
discouraged the attentions of John Chivery, son of the Marshalsea
gate-keeper, with the result that her father finds old Chivery treating
him with less indulgence than usual. Dorrit is too ashamed to ask
Amy to encourage John so that her father will get better treatment.
He is almost, but not quite, too ashamed to broach the subject at all.
He pretends to feel unwell, to gain Amy's sympathy, and begins to
fabricate a devious story about a man called Jackson who used to be
turnkey at the prison [Bk i, ch. 19]:

and – hem! – and he had a – brother, and this – young brother paid his
addresses to – at least, did not go so far as to pay his addresses to – but
admired – respectfully admired – the – not the daughter, the sister – of one of
us; a rather distinguished Collegian; I may say, very much so. His name was
Captain Martin.

Dorrit rambles on about the fictitious Captain Martin – 'highly respected in the army' – who opined that his sister might well tolerate the young man's advances 'on her father's – I should say, brother's – account'. But at last even he grows ashamed of the shabby pretence, and dwindles into silence.

His voice died away, as if she could not bear the pain of hearing him, and her hand had gradually crept to his lips. For a while, there was a dead silence and stillness; and he remained shrunk in his chair.

The silence continues. He starts eating his dinner. Father and daughter avoid each other's eyes.

By little and little he began; laying down his knife and fork with a noise, taking things up sharply, biting at his bread as if he were offended with it, and in other similar ways showing that he was out of sorts.

This is a prelude to a pettish outburst; he calls himself a 'squalid, disgraced wretch', and eventually bursts into tears of self-pity. Weeping he tells his daughter how proud she would have been of him had she known him before he lost his fortune:

and how (at which he cried again) she should . . . have ridden at his fatherly side on her own horse, and how the crowd (by which he meant in effect the people who had given him the twelve shillings he then had in his pocket) should have trudged the dusty roads respectfully.

That last sardonic parenthesis retrieves the scene from mawkishness just as it was about to slip out of the sharp comic perspective. Of course, it is a very different brand of comedy from that of Squeers' school or Mrs Gamp. There is no touch of facetiousness and no touch of condescension. Dickens had too much respect for his victim to suggest that he can be smilingly indulged, as Mrs Gamp can. The respect is shown in the unerring attention that is paid to the shifts of Dorrit's mood, his exact psychological lineaments.

As if Dorrit himself were not a remarkable enough attainment for one novel, the book contains, we should notice, a second comic figure whose presentation is also cleansed of that genial humour which Dickens exudes over the Gamps and the Pecksniffs. This is Merdle, the mighty financier. The portrait consists of a few bare but masterly strokes. We see little of Merdle, and know almost nothing of what goes on in his head. He is an intriguing blank. He feels nervous of his own butler, and when he sticks his finger into his parrot's cage to assert the fact that he is master of the house, the parrot bites it. Eventually he pays a desultory call on his son's wife, and asks to borrow a penknife. She offers him a mother of pearl one [Bk ii, ch. 24]:

'Thank you', said Mr Merdle; 'but if you have got one with a darker handle, I think I should prefer one with a darker handle.'
   'Tortoise-shell?'
   'Thank you', said Mr Merdle; 'Yes. I think I should prefer tortoise-shell.'

Merdle's drab phrasing (carefully drab: both manuscript and proof corrections show Dickens angling here for the flat note), conceals, we later discover, a curious aestheticism. For Mr Merdle wishes to borrow the penknife in order to cut his throat. When he is found dead that night in a bath full of blood and water, we recall the scene at the end of the previous chapter when his daughter-in-law, who had been bored to tears by his visit, saw him and her penknife off:

Waters of vexation filled her eyes; and they had the effect of making the famous Mr Merdle, in going down the street, appear to leap, and waltz, and gyrate, as if he were possessed by several Devils.

This bland aside, which seems to look forward to the Conrad of *The Secret Agent*, is all we have to suggest any internal tumult in the doomed man. Merdle's mind is closed to us, and this distinguishes him from Mr Dorrit. But they are alike in the respect Dickens shows them. Not moral respect, of course. Morally he despises both. But he respects them as creations. Neither is subjected to the jovial condescension with which he regards comic characters in other novels. With Dorrit Dickens's respect takes the form of acute scrutiny; with Merdle, of reticence. When Merdle's butler hears of the suicide, he is not surprised: 'erect and calm', says Dickens, he greets the news with 'these memorable words. "Sir, Mr Merdle never was the gentleman, and no ungentlemanly act on Mr Merdle's part would surprise me." ' That we deprecate this comment, and are at once inclined to take Merdle's side, is a testimony to the respect with which Dickens has treated him. . . .

II   Limitations of Dickens's 'Symbolic Writing'

. . . Dickens's symbolic writing is best . . . when it sticks closest to physical objects and doesn't break out into abstract – and especially religious – annotation. *Little Dorrit* is a novel which describes for its readers several instances of physical imprisonment. Opening in the prison at Marseilles, where [Rigaud] Blandois and John Baptist are incarcerated, and on a quarantine island where Mr Meagles refers to his fellow-travellers as 'jail-birds', it moves to the Marshalsea prison in which most of it is set. When the Dorrits escape from there, we first see them imprisoned by darkness and weather in the convent of the

Great St Bernard. Figurative examples of imprisonment are multiplied relentlessly. Mrs Clennam announces herself 'in prison' in her room; her Bible is bound with a 'chain'; Arthur recalls being marched to chapel 'morally handcuffed' to another boy; even his bed has spikes like the Marshalsea wall; Miss Wade sits behind the 'bars' of a lattice, avoided by the rest of the company; on the London Sunday all amusements are 'bolted and barred'; Mr Merdle is said to have a nervous habit of taking 'himself into custody by the wrists . . . as if he were his own Police Officer'; the Barnacle house off Grosvenor Square is called a 'coop' and a 'hutch'. The landscape, too, is made to conform to a strict segregation, as of a prison wall. The water in Marseilles harbour, we are told at the start, is foul; the sea outside, beautiful. 'The line of demarcation between the two colours, black and blue, showed the point which the pure sea would not pass.' Likewise at the beginning of the second part, it is vintage time on the Swiss side of the Alps, and the warm air is full of the scent of gathered grapes, while snow and ice cover the mountain, and the only vegetation is scrubby moss 'freezing in the chinks of rock'. This theme of segregation, to which so much of the novel's figurative language contributes, is evidently meant to lend 'significance' to otherwise innocuous details, like the fact that Clennam and Little Dorrit have their first private meeting on a bridge. 'Will you go by the Iron Bridge?' asks Clennam. And later, we learn, 'they emerged upon the Iron Bridge, which was as quiet after the roaring streets, as though it had been open country'.

The proliferation of so-called 'prison-images' in *Little Dorrit* is often much admired. We're told that the repetition unifies the novel, and that it reveals a deeper meaning. This deep meaning is represented by maxims like 'Society is a prison' or 'All the world's a prison', which you will find people seriously prepared to accept as the lesson the novel is intended to convey. A little thought, however, will tell us that if the novel is really designed to pass on such messages it fails in a very remarkable way. The scenes in the Marshalsea demonstrate with great imaginative conviction how being in prison corrodes the personality of a prisoner. We are shown in numerous scenes how the taint of prison has entered Dorrit's soul. We observe his desperate selfishness, the erosion of his self-respect, his pathetic attempts to keep up appearances. The prisoner becomes, by long incarceration, a separate species of human being. Even the ragged messengers who run errands for the prisoners are, we're told, a race apart [Bk i, ch. 9]:

Their walk was the walk of a race apart. They had a peculiar way of doggedly slinking round the corner, as if they were eternally going to the pawnbroker's. When they coughed, they coughed like people accustomed to be forgotten on door-steps and in draughty passages, waiting for answers to letters in faded ink, which gave the recipients of those manuscripts great mental disturbance and no satisfaction.

A special walk. Even a special way of coughing. But if the prison produces a 'race apart', there can be very little meaning in such assertions as 'Society is a prison' or 'All the world's a prison'. These can be using the word 'prison', we realise, only in some enfeebled figurative sense – a sense which no one who had ever really been in prison would condone. If society is a prison, then there's no great difference between being in prison and out of it. Dorrit would have been much the same had he never been in prison. Such suppositions run counter to everything the novel has shown us. However, it is not the critics who are to be blamed for introducing these trite formulations about the world and society, and brandishing them as the 'meaning' of *Little Dorrit*. Dickens, when he abandons his firm imaginative task of presenting what it's like inside the Marshalsea, can be found endorsing similar trite formulations himself. Apart from all the figurative language in the novel which, as we've seen, insinuates that being outside the prison is really like being in it, there are some quite blatant assertions of the idea. Little Dorrit, who has not the slightest appreciation of the cultural riches of Italy, and who, we are given to understand, is somehow the better for this obtuseness, is struck by a similarity between the devotees of culture in Venice and the Marshalsea prisoners [Bk II, ch. 7]:

It appeared on the whole, to Little Dorrit herself, that this same society in which they lived, greatly resembled a superior sort of Marshalsea. Numbers of people seemed to come abroad, pretty much as people had come into the prison; through debt, through idleness, relationship, curiosity, and general unfitness for getting on at home. They were brought into these foreign towns in the custody of couriers and local followers, just as the debtors had been brought into the prison. They prowled around the churches and picture galleries, much in the old, dreary, prison-yard, manner. . . . They had precisely the same incapacity for settling down to anything, as the prisoners used to have; they rather deteriorated one another, as the prisoners used to do; and they wore untidy dresses, and fell into a slouching way of life: still always like the people in the Marshalsea.

The vague phrases with which the analogy is recommended – 'on the whole', 'pretty much as' – warn us that we have drifted into a looser part of the book. In the Marshalsea scenes we were not told 'on the whole' but precisely and distinctly what it was like to be in prison. But there's no hint that we're meant to think less of Amy Dorrit for her dull-witted philistine fancy. On the contrary, the deeply-entrenched middle-class antagonism with which she watches people in picture galleries – bored herself, and convinced that everyone else's enthusiasm must be affected – is precisely Dickens's own. Visitors to picture galleries are an untidy, pretentious lot who ought to be doing a job of work. We may recall his complaint on visiting the untidy Thompsons at Nervi, a year or so before he began *Little Dorrit*, that they were allowing music and oil-painting to take precedence over 'household affairs'. These are the assumptions we encounter when the book leaves off its dark figurative intimations and actually spells out why it considers society is like a prison.

Similarly, while the sight of Miss Wade sitting behind the 'bars' of a lattice seems a firm imaginative moment, routine phrases like 'the prison of the self' with which critics gloss it, have a hollow sound. And here too the critics are not solely to blame. Dickens himself presents Miss Wade arguing with Meagles about imprisonment, and claiming that she knows by experience that a prisoner never forgives his prison. The figurative prison which Miss Wade is in is further explained by the clumsy artifice of her manuscript autobiography which she hands over to Clennam, and which is supposed to show her cut off from her fellow human beings by arrogance and hypersensitivity. In fact Miss Wade's fiery defiance bears no relation to the state which, as we know from Mr Dorrit, real prisons reduce their inmates to. Her experience of prison, like that of the visitors to the picture gallery, is a mere figure of speech.

As the novel approaches its climax, a further extension of the prison 'symbol' is attempted. 'The last day of the appointed week touched the bars of the Marshalsea' Dickens writes [Bk II, ch. 30]:

Black, all night, since the gate had clashed upon Little Dorrit, its iron stripes were turned by the early-glowing sun into stripes of gold. Far aslant across the city, over its jumbled roofs, and through the open tracery of its church towers, struck the long bright rays, bars of the prison of this lower world.

Now, it appears, not just society or the self but the whole world is a prison. Not that Dickens supports his hackneyed whim with any documentation. The presentation of the Marshalsea prison was dense with detail and actuality. Here the writing is just slipshod. A portion of religious verbiage is hopefully dropped into the narrative, along with a mention of church towers. The sense that a physical object – a prison – which was scrupulously investigated earlier in the novel is now being allowed to float out of focus in the interests of religion, is similar to the feeling one had on seeing Captain Cuttle's ocean becoming a sign of eternal love, or on watching the sunlight glorifying Jarndyce's hair.

It is habitual in *Little Dorrit* to refer to prisoners as birds. The Marseilles gaoler tells his daughter 'Look at the birds, my pretty' when indicating his charges. Clennam takes leave of Little Dorrit outside the Marshalsea: 'The cage door opened, and when the small bird, reared in captivity, had tamely fluttered in, he saw it shut again.' The Marshalsea veterans are called 'seasoned birds', and when Dorrit, after his breakdown, forgets everything but the Marshalsea, his spirit, we're told, remembered only 'the place where it had broken its wings'. John Chivery offers Clennam watercress in the Marshalsea, like someone putting food 'into the cage of a dull imprisoned bird'. The metaphor is made to cover other types of inmate too. Mr Plornish's father, inmate of the workhouse, is 'a poor little reedy piping old gentleman, like a worn-out bird'. Prisoners in the hypothetical prison of society are also birds. At Mr Merdle's party Lord Decimus Tite Barnacle urges 'his noble pinions' and soars up to the drawing-room, and the 'smaller birds . . . flutter up-stairs' after him. The bird metaphor, like the prison images, tends to confuse the issue. Why should our sympathy be specially canvassed for Little Dorrit, a 'small bird, reared in captivity', if in fact everyone is reared in captivity, whether in the Marshalsea or the grand houses of the upper middle class? . . .

SOURCE: extracts from Carey's *The Violent Effigy: A Study of Dickens's Imagination* (London, 1973; paperback edn, 1979): I, pp. 76–9; II, pp. 113–17.

SELECT BIBLIOGRAPHY

TEXTS

Both novels are available in the Clarendon Edition of Dickens's works: *Dombey and Son*, edited by Alan Horsman (Oxford, 1974); *Little Dorrit*, edited by Harvey Peter Sucksmith (Oxford, 1979). The Clarendon texts have been reprinted in the World's Classics paperback collection of the novels, with Introductions by the respective editors.

The Penguin English Library texts are also in paperback: *Dombey and Son*, with an Introduction by Raymond Williams (Harmondsworth, 1970); *Little Dorrit*, with an Introduction by John Holloway (Harmondsworth, 1967).

BIOGRAPHY, LETTERS AND BIBLIOGRAPHY

Of the many biographies of Dickens published, those by John Forster (1872–74) and Edgar Johnson – *Charles Dickens: His Tragedy and Triumph* (Boston, Mass., and London, 1952) – take precedence.

Dickens's letters – with volumes 1–5 published so far – are appearing in the Pilgrim Edition (Clarendon Press, Oxford), under the general editorship of Madeline House, Graham Storey and Kathleen Tillotson. The fullest earlier collection is that edited by Walter Dexter for the Nonesuch Press in 3 volumes (London, 1938).

Philip Collins gives a very useful bibliography of texts and criticism in his entry on Dickens to the *New Cambridge Bibliography of English Literature*: vol. III, *1800–1900* (Cambridge, 1969). This may be supplemented by R. C. Churchill, *A Bibliography of Dickensian Criticism, 1836–1975* (London, 1975).

CRITICAL STUDIES

Amongst books and articles not represented by extracts in this Casebook, the following are recommended.

(a) General
Philip Collins (ed.), *Dickens: The Critical Heritage* (London, 1971).
K. J. Fielding, *Dickens: A Critical Introduction* (London, 1958).
George Ford, *Dickens and His Readers* (Princeton, N.J., 1955).
John Lucas, *The Melancholy Man* (London, 1970).
Alexander Welsh, *The City of Dickens* (Oxford, 1971).
Angus Wilson, *The World of Charles Dickens* (London, 1970).

(b) On *Dombey and Son*
Peter Coveney, *The Image of Childhood* (London, 1967); originally published as *Poor Monkey* (London, 1957).
Susan Horton, *Interpreting Interpreting* (Baltimore and London, 1979).
Steven Marcus, *Dickens: From Pickwick to Dombey* (London, 1965).
Julian Moynahan, '*Dealings with the Firm of Dombey and Son:* Firmness *versus* Wetness', in J. Gross and G. Pearson (eds), *Dickens and the Twentieth Century* (London, 1962).

(c) On *Little Dorrit*
Monroe Engel, *The Maturity of Dickens* (London, 1959).
Robert Garis, *The Dickens Theatre* (Oxford, 1965).
D. W. Jefferson, 'The Moral Centre of *Little Dorrit*', *Essays in Criticism* (Oct. 1976), pp. 300–17.
Lionel Stevenson, 'Dickens's Dark Novels, 1851–57', *Sewanee Review*, 51 (1943), pp. 398–409.
D. Walder, *Dickens and Religion* (London, 1981).

NOTES ON CONTRIBUTORS

NINA AUERBACH: Associate Professor of the University of Pennsylvania; her publications include *Communities of Women* (1978) and articles on various aspects of nineteenth-century fiction.

JOHN CAREY: Merton Professor of English Literature in the University of Oxford; his critical books (in addition to that on Dickens) include *Thackeray: Prodigal Genius* (1977) and *John Donne: His Mind and Art* (1981).

THOMAS CARLYLE (1795–1881): essayist, moralist and historian.

G. K. CHESTERTON (1874–1936): essayist, poet, novelist and polemicist; his critical work includes *Charles Dickens* (1906) and a series of Introductions to 'Everyman' editions of Dickens's novels, later published together as *Appreciations and Criticisms of the Works of Charles Dickens* (1911).

W. WALTER CROTCH (1874–1947): with a varied career as parliamentary secretary, journalist and war correspondent, he also published a number of books on Dickens, on Thomas Hardy, on social questions and on wine. A founder-member of the Dickens Fellowship, he was its President, 1915–20.

WILLIAM HEPWORTH DIXON (1821–79): historian, journalist and critic, his literary career included the editorship of *The Athenaeum* from 1853 to 1869.

GEORGE ELIOT – Mary Ann Cross, *née* Evans (1819–80): novelist and critic, she is one of the supreme artists in English prose fiction.

EDWARD FITZGERALD (1809–83): English poet and translator, best-known for his version of *The Rubáiyát* of Omar Khayyám (1859), and for his letters to literary and other friends.

JOHN FORSTER (1812–76): friend and adviser to Dickens, critic and journal editor; in addition to his chief work, *The Life of Charles Dickens*, he wrote biographies of Swift, Goldsmith and Landor.

GEORGE GISSING (1857–1903): English novelist and critic who, though a proponent of realism, was much influenced by Dickens. His critical work includes his outstanding study of Dickens (1898), various literary essays and an abridgment of Forster's biography of Dickens (1903).

E. B. HAMLEY (1824–93): Soldier and man of letters; he had a varied military career, serving in the Crimea, in the Balkans and in Egypt, and was for a time

Professor of military history at Sandhurst. He contributed essays, reviews and stories to *Blackwood's Magazine*, and was a novelist in his own right.

HUMPHRY HOUSE (1908–55): Oxford scholar whose work, in addition to that on Dickens, includes studies of Aristotle (1956) and of Coleridge (1953), and the edited volume of *Notebooks and Papers of Gerard Manley Hopkins* (1937).

T. A. JACKSON (1879–1955): Marxist critic and political thinker; as well as his study of Dickens's radicalism, he wrote various works of political theory, including *Dialectics: The Logic of Marxism* (1936).

FRANCIS JEFFREY (1773–1850): Scottish man of letters and lawyer; a strong supporter of the Whig reform movement, he was a co-founder of the *Edinburgh Review* and eventually elevated to the Scottish judicial bench as Lord Jeffrey.

EDGAR JOHNSON: biographer and critic, his academic appointments have included the professorship of English at the City College of New York. His biographies include that on Dickens (1952) – the most comprehensive modern life of the novelist – and *Sir Walter Scott: The Great Unknown* (1970).

CHARLES KENT (1823–1902): author and journalist, acquainted with many Victorian literary figures, including Dickens (whose last letter, of 8 June 1870, was written to Kent). His many publications include his *Poems* (1870) and editor-commentator collections of the works of notable writers (e.g., Charles Lamb).

STEPHEN LEACOCK (1869–1944): Canadian scholar, critic and humorist. For many years (1903–36) professor of Economics and Political Science in McGill University, he was also prolific in writing books and essays spanning a wide gamut of interests, from studies on Dickens and Mark Twain, through humorous belles-lettres and parodies, to *Elements of Political Science* (1906) and *Our British Empire* (1940).

F. R. LEAVIS (1895–1978): famous teacher and critic. His work at Cambridge and the editorship of *Scrutiny* – together with *Revaluation* (1936), *The Great Tradition* (1948) and *D. H. Lawrence: Novelist* (1955) – form the basis of his reputation as one of the most influential literary critics of this century.

THOMAS BABINGTON MACAULAY – Lord Macaulay (1800–59): historian, Liberal politician, poet and essayist; in political and literary interests he was closely associated with the circle of the *Edinburgh Review*.

FRANK T. MARZIALS (1840–1912): civil servant, essayist and biographer; in addition to his life of Dickens, he wrote biographies of Victor Hugo, Browning and Molière.

DAVID MASSON (1822–1907): biographer and editor, and professor of English Literature in University College, London (1853–65), and of Rhetoric and

English Literature, University of Edinburgh (1865–95). His many publications include critical editions and biographies of major writers, and volumes of reminiscences of his life in London and Edinburgh. He was the founding-editor of *Macmillan's Magazine* (1859–1967).

J. HILLIS MILLER: Professor of English at Yale; among his numerous publications on nineteenth- and twentieth-century literature are to be noted his study of Dickens (1958), *The Disappearance of God* (1963) and *Thomas Hardy: Distance and Desire* (1971).

IAN MILNER: he has taught literature at Charles University, Prague; author of *The Structure of Values in George Eliot* (1968), he has also translated into English the work of the Czechoslovakian poet, Miroslav Holub.

EDWIN PUGH (1874–1930): novelist, essayist and idealist socialist; his realist novels of London life reflect his political enthusiasm.

GEORGE BERNARD SHAW (1856–1950): Irish playwright and critic of literature, music and the arts.

JAMES FITZJAMES STEPHEN (1829–94): barrister, literary journalist and writer of works on legal and political theory; among the latter is his *Liberty, Equality and Fraternity* (1873), a criticism of Liberal Utilitarianism. In his legal career he spent many years in India as a judge.

ALGERNON CHARLES SWINBURNE (1837–1909): poet and critic; his literary criticism includes *Essays and Studies* (1875), *Miscellanies* (1886), monographs on Shakespeare and other dramatists, and his volume on Dickens (1913) – published posthumously.

HIPPOLYTE A. TAINE (1828–93): French historian and literary critic, professor of Aesthetics at the Ecole des Beaux Arts.

WILLIAM MAKEPEACE THACKERAY (1811–63): novelist and essayist; his *English Humourists of the Eighteenth Century* is a keynote work of Victorian literary criticism.

KATHLEEN TILLOTSON: Hildred Carlile Professor of English Literature at Bedford College, London (1958–71); General Editor of the 'Clarendon' Dickens (for which she edited *Oliver Twist*) and Associate Editor of the Pilgrim Edition of Dickens's letters. Her publications include *Novels of the 1840s* (1954) and, with John Butt, *Dickens at Work* (1957).

LIONEL TRILLING (1905–75): American scholar and critic; among his academic appointments he was Charles Eliot Norton Professor of Poetry at Harvard (1965–70). His publications include *Matthew Arnold* (1939), *The Liberal Imagination* (1950), *The Opposing Self* (1955) and *Beyond Culture* (1965).

A. W. WARD (1837–1924): historian and literary scholar, and first professor of English at Owen's College (later the University of Manchester). Among his numerous works in both History and English Literature are studies on Chaucer and on Dickens for the 'English Men of Letters' series, and the 'Knutsford' edition of the works of Elizabeth Gaskell.

EDMUND WILSON (1895–1972): literary critic and historian of twentieth-century intellectual movements. His most celebrated books are *Axel's Castle* (1931), *To the Finland Station* (1940) and *The Wound and the Bow* (1941). He also wrote novels and short stories – *I Thought of Daisy* (1929, revised 1967), *Memoirs of Hecate County* (1946) and *Galahad* (1967).

ACKNOWLEDGEMENTS

The editor and publishers wish to thank the following, who have given permission for the use of copyright material: Nina Auerbach, extract from essay 'Dickens and Dombey: A Daughter After All' in *Dickens Studies Annual*, 5 (1976) by permission of AMS Press Inc.; John Carey, extracts from *The Violent Effigy* (1973), by permission of Faber and Faber Ltd; G. K. Chesterton, extracts from 'Introduction' in *Appreciation and Criticisms of Charles Dickens' Works* (1911), by permission of A. P. Watt Ltd on behalf of Miss D. E. Collins and J. M. Dent & Sons Ltd; W. Walter Crotch, extract from *The Soul of Dickens* (1916), by permission of Chapman & Hall Ltd; Humphrey House, extracts from *The Dickens World* (1941), by permission of Oxford University Press; T. A. Jackson, extract from *Charles Dickens: The Progress of a Radical* (1937), by permission of Lawrence & Wishart Ltd; Edgar Johnson, extract from *Charles Dickens – His Tragedy and Triumph* (1953), by permission of Laurence Pollinger Ltd on behalf of the estate of Edgar Johnson; Stephen Leacock, extract from *Charles Dickens His Life and Work* (1933), by permission of Doubleday & Company Inc.; F. R. Leavis, extracts from essay 'Dickens and Blake: Little Dorrit' in *Dickens the Novelist* (1970) by F. R. and Q. D. Leavis, by permission of Chatto and Windus Ltd on behalf of the Authors' Literary Estate; J. Hillis Miller, extracts from *Charles Dickens: The World of His Novel* (1958), by permission of Harvard University Press – Copyright © 1958 by the President and Fellows of Harvard College; Ian Milner, essay 'The Dickens Drama: Mr Dombey' in *Dickens Centennial Essays* (1971), by permission of the University of California Press, copyright © 1970 by the Regents of the University of California; Bernard Shaw, extract from Foreword to *The Novel Library* edition of *Great Expectations* (1974), by permission of The Society of Authors on behalf of the Bernard Shaw Estate; Kathleen Tillotson, extracts from *Novels of the 1840s* (1954), by permission of Oxford University Press; Lionel Trilling, Introduction to the New Oxford Illustrated Dickens edition (1953) of *Little Dorrit*; Edmund Wilson, extract from 'Dickens: The Two Scrooges' in *The Wound and the Bow* (1940), by permission of Farrar, Straus, and Giroux Inc.

INDEX

Page numbers in **bold** type relate to essays or excerpts in this Casebook.
Entries in SMALL CAPS denote literary characters.